Creation:
A Guide for the
Perplexed

BLOOMSBURY GUIDES FOR THE PERPLEXED

Bloomsbury's Guides for the Perplexed are clear, concise and accessible introductions to thinkers, writers and subjects that students and readers can find especially challenging. Concentrating specifically on what it is that makes the subject difficult to grasp, these books explain and explore key themes and ideas, guiding the reader towards a thorough understanding of demanding material.

GUIDES FOR THE PERPLEXED AVAILABLE FROM BLOOMSBURY INCLUDE:

Atonement: A Guide for the Perplexed, Adam Johnson

Balthasar: A Guide for the Perplexed, Rodney Howsare

Benedict XVI: A Guide for the Perplexed, Tracey Rowland

Bonhoeffer: A Guide for the Perplexed, Joel Lawrence

Calvin: A Guide for the Perplexed, Paul Helm

De Lubac: A Guide for the Perplexed, David Grummett

Luther: A Guide for the Perplexed, David M. Whitford

Pannenberg: A Guide for the Perplexed, Timothy Bradshaw

Pneumatology: A Guide for the Perplexed, Daniel Castelo

Political Theology: A Guide for the Perplexed, Elizabeth Philips

Postliberal Theology: A Guide for the Perplexed,
Ronald T. Michener

Schleiermacher: A Guide for the Perplexed, Theodore Vial

Scripture: A Guide for the Perplexed, William Lamb

Tillich: A Guide for the Perplexed, Andrew O' Neil

Wesley: A Guide for the Perplexed, Jason A. Vickers

Žižek: A Guide for the Perplexed, Sean Sheehan

FORTHCOMING GUIDES FOR THE PERPLEXED AVAILABLE FROM BLOOMSBURY INCLUDE:

Creation

A Guide for the Perplexed

Simon Oliver

Bloomsbury T&T Clark
An imprint of Bloomsbury Publishing Plc

B L O O M S B U R Y
LONDON · OXFORD · NEW YORK · NEW DELHI · SYDNEY

Bloomsbury T&T Clark

An imprint of Bloomsbury Publishing Plc

Imprint previously known as T&T Clark

50 Bedford Square	1385 Broadway
London	New York
WC1B 3DP	NY 10018
UK	USA

www.bloomsbury.com

BLOOMSBURY, T&T CLARK and the Diana logo are trademarks of Bloomsbury Publishing Plc

First published 2017

British Library Cataloguing-in-Publication Data
A catalogue record for this book is available from the British Library.

ISBN: HB: 978-0-5676-5609-4
PB: 978-0-5676-5608-7
ePDF: 978-0-5676-5610-0
ePub: 978-0-5676-5611-7

Library of Congress Cataloging-in-Publication Data
A catalog record for this book is available from the Library of Congress

Cover image © Yuri Afanasiev/Alamy Stock Photo

Typeset by Deanta Global Publishing Services, Chennai, India

For

Samuel James Francis
who once told me that God created
because he wants friends.

CONTENTS

ACKNOWLEDGEMENTS

A few words of thanks should accompany the completion of any book, even a modest one. I owe a particular debt to students of the University of Nottingham and Durham University with whom I have had the privilege of discussing the doctrine of creation in recent years. I am very grateful to Nathan Barczi, Edward Epsen, Ainsley Griffiths, Lara Harris, Aaron Jeffrey, Angus Reid, Verena Suchhart and Bruno Zazo for their questions and conversation.

A number of people have generously read and offered comments on drafts of this book. It has been greatly improved by their generosity and critical eye. Particular thanks are due to Carly Crouch, Peter Heath and Stephen Oliver. I am grateful to David Merrill for his assistance with research materials and references.

I have learnt so much from the work and conversation of friends. As well as all my colleagues past and present at Nottingham and Durham, I would like to thank Michael Hanby and Johannes Hoff. A very good friend and mentor, John Webster, died suddenly as this work was in progress. John was a source of ceaseless encouragement to his students and colleagues and a Christian theologian to his core. Some of his last published works are exemplary expositions of the doctrine of creation and major influences on this book.

Thanks are also due to the people of Durham Cathedral and my friends and colleagues on the Cathedral Chapter – Andrew, David, Rosalind, Ian, Ivor, Cathy, Harvey, Sophie (*seniores priores*), and our Chapter Clerk, Philip – who provide such a prayerful and supportive community within a uniquely beautiful shrine church. Praying every day between St. Cuthbert and St. Bede must surely be one of the greatest privileges imaginable.

I am very grateful to Anna Turton, Miriam Cantwell and their colleagues at Bloomsbury. I can only apologize profusely for giving them far too many opportunities to practise the virtue of patience.

Finally, my greatest thanks are reserved for Jayne, Benedict and Samuel. Without their gracious love, patience, encouragement and the increasingly exasperated exclamations over my left shoulder while I tapped away at a keyboard – 'Have you *still* not finished your homework, dad?' – this book would have been immeasurably poorer.

PREFACE

One formidable theologian figures prominently in this book: Thomas Aquinas. His work is a junction at which converge three roads: Greek philosophy in its Aristotelian and Neoplatonic guises; patristic theology of West and East; and, most importantly, scripture. He is often recognized as the great Christian theologian of creation. Subsequent theologies of creation, both Catholic and Protestant, are frequently interpretations, reformulations or rejections of Aquinas's position. I have therefore focused on Aquinas's work as the Christian tradition's most influential account of the doctrine of creation.

Some readers will be new to Aquinas. Negotiating a work by a thirteenth-century theologian, particularly one of Aquinas's philosophical and theological sophistication, can be daunting. There are many excellent introductions to Aquinas, but for the uninitiated who are required or encouraged to read Aquinas for themselves, I have included a brief appendix that describes how his most important work, the *Summa Theologiae*, is structured and referenced.

The footnotes in this book provide doorways to further reading; pass through them if you will. Occasionally, I have explained odd terminology or difficult and technical concepts at some length in a footnote, particularly in Chapter 3. I hope readers find this helpful. At the risk of stating the obvious, I should comment on the frequent use of the word 'creature'. This is used in its broadest possible sense to mean anything created, from rocks to angels, whether animate or inanimate.

Wherever possible, I have used readily available translations of ancient and medieval texts. The translation of Aquinas's *Summa Theologiae* used in this book (with occasional amendments) is that of the Fathers of the English Dominican Province (1920–1922).[1] It is a clear and literal translation that remains readily available. The more recent Blackfriars translation under the general editorship of

Thomas Gilby, O.P., which includes the Leonine Latin text on the facing page as well as helpful appendices in each volume, is also a fine resource.

All scriptural quotations are from the New Revised Standard Version (Anglicized Edition).

Introduction

What does it mean to say that the universe is 'created'? Is there a purpose or meaning to our existence? What explains the fact that there is something rather than nothing? Or is existence just a brute fact? Such persistent and fundamental questions prompt the human imagination to look for clues within the universe for a more essential source of existence that is not part of the universe. We tell dramatic stories about our origins, about what, if anything, might be the source of our existence, why it is as it is and what its purpose might be. Those stories include ancient myths, Greek philosophies of nature, the biblical saga of Genesis, creation *ex nihilo* (out of nothing), the evolution of life and the Big Bang. Amid such rich human enquiry, many religious traditions also discern an address or a word emerging *through* creation that is nevertheless not *from* creation: a 'revelation' of meaning and purpose from a source that transcends creation.

This book is about the Christian theological and philosophical tradition of exploration into the origins, nature and purpose of existence. It focuses on a crucial claim: that we are created. The view that we are created is the key characteristic that distinguishes a religious and theological approach to existence from the atheist claim that the universe is simply a brute fact with no universal purpose. How are we to understand the claim that we are part of 'creation'? Creation has been understood as good and yet fallen, but also the result of a catastrophic descent from a spiritual to a material condition. Creation has been understood as an emanation from a mysterious divine source, as the product of a seven-day process or a fourteen-billion-year evolution, as coming *ex nihilo*, as designed and as everlasting and yet in some way dependent on a source lying beyond time and change. It is sometimes thought that modern science, particularly since the nineteenth century, has debunked the idea that the universe is created because purely natural explanations of phenomena have reached to the beginning of time (Big Bang cosmology) and the fundamentals of life (evolutionary science). We will see that there are good reasons for thinking that this is not the case, and that science can only be one aspect of our exploration of creation; a different kind of philosophical and theological enquiry into our origins and purposes is also required if we are to have an intelligible and persuasive account of creation.

Appropriately enough, we will begin this exploration of creation 'in the beginning' with the opening chapters of Genesis, the first book of scripture. This drama is perhaps our best known, most influential and most controversial account of creation. What does this two-and-half-thousand-year-old book tell us about creation? How has it been interpreted and what does it mean for us today? Is Genesis necessarily in conflict with Darwin's legacy and the modern account of evolution? We will see that Genesis contains important ethical teachings concerning humanity's relationship with God. Genesis teaches that creation is good. The liturgical cycle of worship is part of the created order. This implies that the fundamental orientation of creation is towards the praise of God through a share in his life.

Having examined the key scriptural account of creation's origins and nature, we will examine the doctrine of creation as it emerged in early Christian theology. A remarkable consensus arises between Jewish and Christian thinkers (a view later to be shared by Islamic theologians), namely that if we are to talk about creation we must speak of it as *ex nihilo* (out of nothing). This is a curious teaching for two reasons. First, although many scholars debate apparent references to creation *ex nihilo* in Genesis, 2 Maccabees, Romans 4, Colossians 1 and Hebrews 11, such a view is not articulated in metaphysical or narrative detail within scripture. Indeed, many argue that Genesis describes God creating out of a pre-existent material chaos rather than 'from nothing'. Secondly, the notion of creation *ex nihilo* is not found in ancient Greek philosophy because, according to Parmenides' writing in the early fifth century BC, *ex nihilo nihil fit* ('from nothing, nothing comes'). Nevertheless, the theologians of early Christianity came to the view that creation *ex nihilo* is theologically fundamental and biblically founded. Why, and what are the implications of this teaching? We will see that the implications are radical: creation, in itself, is nothing and yet is the totally free and utterly gratuitous expression of God's love.

A rich combination of Christian teaching and ancient Greek philosophy allowed the thirteenth-century theologian Thomas Aquinas (c. 1225–1274) to articulate one of the most influential accounts of creation and divine providence in the Christian tradition. This will be the focus of Chapter 3, as we examine crucial questions concerning creation's relation to God, the purpose or 'teleology' of creation, and divine and creaturely action. We will see that Aquinas articulates in a particularly important way a certain view of creation's relation to the creator that has its origins in Neoplatonic and patristic theology: creation 'participates' in God at every moment and, as such, only exists in relation to God. This leads to the famous *analogia entis* – the analogy of being – in which creation exists 'analogically' in relation to God. We will examine the crucial implications of this approach for the doctrine of creation, particularly the distinction between primary and secondary causation. For Aquinas, when God creates, there is not one thing – God – and then suddenly two things – God plus creation. There is only ever one focus of existence – God – and everything else exists in a relation of participation in God.

In antiquity and the medieval period, the theology of creation was always articulated within, and influenced by, a wider intellectual and cultural context. At the birth of modernity, around 1500 (although the roots lie deeper, in the late Middle Ages), the cultural and intellectual context began to change significantly. This will be the subject of Chapter 4 as we enter a more historical mode. The Reformation brought changes in the interpretation of scripture that impacted on the interpretation of God's other great book, the book of nature. No longer was nature understood as a symbolic order with spiritual meaning; now it came to be seen as a resource for human beings' physical and economic needs. For the historian of science Peter Harrison, this theological shift paved the way for a very different kind of investigation of nature. Unlike the natural philosophy of ancient and medieval thinkers, the early modern approach used experimentation and mathematics. The first natural philosophers included Nicolaus Copernicus (1473–1543), Galileo Galilei (1564–1642), Johannes Kepler (1571–1630) and Isaac Newton (1642–1727). The discipline of natural philosophy, which today we would recognize as broadly akin to natural science, was closely allied to natural theology, namely the attempt to discern God from nature by means of reason rather than through revelation.

This gave rise to the discipline of physico-theology and the idea that, in the experimental investigation of God's creation, the early modern natural philosophers or 'scientists' (a term coined in the nineteenth century) were also engaged in a theological enterprise. At this time, God came to be understood as the designer of an intricate mechanical universe. How did this alter the traditional doctrine of creation? We will see that significant changes occurred to the doctrine of God and the understanding of the relationship of creation to creator. Theology had to contend with a very different account of the natural world in the form of modern science. Could the doctrine of creation's intelligibility be preserved in this environment?

The late twentieth century witnessed a growing concern with humanity's relationship with nature and the possibility of catastrophic damage to the environment by our technological and economic activity. In this debate, science and religion have been seen as both culprit and potential saviour. Chapter 5 will be concerned with the specific contribution of the theology of creation to this debate, notably through the category of gift. This will draw together numerous strands from earlier chapters, particularly the idea that creation at every moment receives its existence as a gift from God. We will also reflect on the meaning of God's most basic gift in creation (Gen. 1.29): food. Does the knowledge that creation's being, and therefore nature's existence, is a gift have any bearing on our self-understanding as creatures and our understanding of our relationship with the natural order? In short, can we delineate a theological ethics of the environment using the resources of the doctrine of creation?

It goes without saying that the theology of creation is a huge and fundamental topic. Preparing this book has required great selectivity. There are, however, two related questions which appear throughout the discussion and which were fundamental for the theologians of early Christianity: how are we to distinguish between God and creation, and how does creation relate to God? On the one hand, there is a danger of not making a sufficiently fundamental distinction between God and creation. This results in God becoming part of the created order – a big cause among other causes, one more item in the list of things that exist. We cease to speak the language of creation and lapse into unintelligible idolatry – speaking about God as if he were a big person in the sky who is *part* of creation, not its source.

On the other hand, one might describe the difference between God and creation in a way that makes God an occasional intervener in the created order or introduces God as an object of superstition to fill the gaps in the scientific explanation of natural phenomena. There is, therefore, a need to articulate, with theological and philosophical care and rigour, the God–creation relation. Although this question receives its most sustained treatment in Chapter 3 through the so-called 'analogy of being' and Aquinas's understanding of creation's participation in God, it animates every aspect of this book.

This book deals with issues of fundamental theology and philosophy – particularly creation's relation to God – and the intellectual context in which the doctrine of creation has been discussed. The theologians of early Christianity had a clear sense that, unless we are clear before all else about exactly how creation is distinguished from God and yet relates to God, the edifice of Christian theology will quickly crumble into confusion and superstition. I believe they were right. There is ample evidence in modern systematic theology of the unfortunate consequences of a rush to link different areas of Christian doctrine without first clarifying the fundamental doctrines of God and creation. This book is a brief attempt to draw attention to those fundamentals and hint at the consequences of not doing so.

1

Genesis: In the Beginning

Our best-known story of creation is found in Genesis, the first book of the Bible.[1] We read that 'in the beginning when God created the heavens and the earth, the earth was a formless void and darkness covered the face of the deep, while a wind from God swept over the face of the waters'. The first three chapters of Genesis chart the creation of the heavens and the earth over six days (1.1–1.24), the formation of male and female on the sixth day (1.26–1.31), a seventh day when God completes the work of creation and rests (2.1–2.4), a second account of the formation of human beings and their life in the Garden of Eden (2.5–2.25) and the tragic and inexplicable sin of the first man and woman, leading to what has become known as 'the Fall' – the expulsion from Eden (Chapter 3). The twentieth-century theologian Karl Barth referred to Genesis as the great 'saga' of creation; it is a cosmic drama that is one of the most influential and controversial narratives in our intellectual and cultural history.

Today we live in a culture that has, for the most part, come to understand that the universe and the earth's abundant life were not the outcome of a seven-day process of creation but of billions of years of cosmic development and millions of years of evolution. The latest accounts of the origins of the universe from the sciences of cosmology, geology and evolutionary biology paint a completely different picture to the one that we find in the Bible. Our science-dominated culture significantly affects the way that we approach an ancient text such as Genesis, and we often make demands on the text that are alien to its original setting and to the tradition of theological interpretation through which we receive the text. For example, we ask whether Genesis measures up to Darwin's *On the Origin of Species* as a piece of natural history. We might also ask whether

Genesis can offer any significant cosmological insights, given the power of modern theoretical physics. After all, today's science uses extraordinary mathematics to trace the origins of the universe to the tiniest fraction of a second after a cataclysmic 'big bang'.

In this chapter we will see that Genesis cannot be approached with a set of priorities and questions that belong to twenty-first-century science. That would be a little like asking whether Shakespeare's *Romeo and Juliet* tells us anything about the neurophysiology of human love. Of course it does not. But *Romeo and Juliet* teaches us a great deal about human emotion and relationships – through drama, poetry and human character. It seeks truth, but not the prosaic biological facts of human love and conflict. Likewise, Genesis teaches us a great deal about creation. It seeks truth, but not in the same way as modern cosmology or evolutionary biology. In fact, we will see that Genesis addresses questions which are far more profound, perplexing and interesting. It is a text that is not especially concerned with the factual details of how God did or did not assemble the universe.

Instead, Genesis asks about the *meaning* of creation. It begins with the same realization upon which the edifice of science is built: the idea that the cosmos is ordered and rational in such a way that we can make sense of it, not from some external objective standpoint but from within the cosmos itself. We will see that Genesis adds another crucial claim, which is more alien to our scientific culture: creation is rational precisely because it is good.

So what are we to make of Genesis, a book whose history probably extends back over 2,500 years to a foreign and ancient culture? How have theologians interpreted the saga of creation? Can it be read literally or must we approach it figuratively? Is Genesis merely a fanciful myth? Does Genesis have any claim on our attention in the twenty-first century? These are the questions we will be addressing in this first chapter.

The ancient Near Eastern background to Genesis

The drama of Genesis is just one of myriad creation myths which circulated in the culture of the ancient Near East from around 2000 BC. The scriptural account seems to be influenced, positively and negatively, by Canaanite, Egyptian and Mesopotamian stories of the formation of the cosmos. The region of Mesopotamia, roughly equivalent to the area between the rivers Tigris and Euphrates covered by modern-day Kuwait, Iraq and northeast Syria, is particularly important for the development of Hebrew culture and theology. These ancient creation myths share some common themes: the overcoming of conflict and chaos, giving rise to a harmonious order; reflection on the sheer contingency of existence; and life's fragility and the constant struggle against dissolution and death. Of particular concern is the place of human beings within the created order, their relationship with the gods, and human mortality. Nevertheless, the question of ultimate cosmic origins that dominates our modern scientific perspective does not seem to be an overriding concern in the ancient Near East. Stories of the formation of an ordered cosmos from a situation of conflict or chaos via the actions of frequently quarrelling deities are used to explore, through myth, a more prevalent concern with national politics, tribal status and the continual search for political order and peace. In other words, when we read about battling deities and the ordering of chaos in these ancient creation stories, we are reading cosmic allegories of the conflicts between peoples and nations, and the chaotic contingencies of the natural world that make human existence so precarious. These accounts are not primarily concerned with providing a kind of philosophical or scientific view of how the natural world came into existence; they are concerned with tribal or national identity, peoples' struggle for political stability or dominance and their relationship to cosmic divine powers.

A number of ancient creation myths seem to have influenced the writing of Genesis. A good example is the Babylonian epic known as *Atrahasis*, which dates from the eighteenth century BC.[2] The title, which means 'exceedingly wise', is the name of the story's central character. It was written on tablets in Akkadian cuneiform, the language of ancient Babylon, and elaborates a theme that was to become common in later myths, namely the idea that humans were created as workers for the gods. According to *Atrahasis*, the world is divided into three realms: the upper realm ruled by the god Anu; Middle Earth (our realm) ruled by the god Enlil; and the underworld ruled by the god Enki. The ruler of Middle Earth, Enlil, commanded the lesser gods, known as the Igigi, to labour in the digging of trenches for the irrigation of the land. These lesser gods decided they had a rough deal and went on strike, destroying their tools and rebelling against Enlil. In need of support, Enlil approached

Anu and Enki who, being sympathetic to the Igigi, enlisted the help of the mother goddess Mami to make creatures of a lower kind who could labour on behalf of the Igigi. Mami and the wise god of the underworld, Enki, mixed the blood of a rebellious minor god, Ilawela, with the clay of the earth to create seven male and seven female figures. According to the narrative of *Atrahasis*, humans are formed from the earth and have a divine element in the form of Ilawela's blood, yet they also inherit Ilawela's tendency to rebel. As the population of the earth grew, the tumultuous noise of the labouring humans disturbed Enlil's peace so he began to send famine and plague to reduce the population, every 1,200 years. Because Enki kept intervening to assuage the effects of Enlil's plagues and famines, Enlil then sent a huge flood to wipe out the creatures of Middle Earth. Stories of deluge are common in ancient myths. *Atrahasis* is one of three Babylonian creation myths that include a flood from which select humans and animals escape by means of a boat, in this case the pious Atrahasis, his family and a selection of animals.[3] The similarities with the story of Noah in Genesis chapters 6–9 are clear.[4]

A second ancient Near Eastern creation story worth noting is *Enuma Elish* (often given the English title *The Epic of Creation*), a dramatic cosmogony that has been dated as early as *Atrahasis*. Unlike many other ancient creation stories, the *Epic* does not begin with a pantheon of gods, but only with undifferentiated and chaotic waters. These are brought into order at creation, rather like the opening verses of Genesis. The gods are formed from the male Apsû, representing subterranean fresh water, and the female Tiāmat (a kind of bovine sea creature), representing the salt water of the oceans.

> When the heavens above did not exist,
> And earth below had not come into being –
> There was Apsû, the first in order, their begetter,
> And demiurge Tiāmat, who gave birth to them all;
> They had mingled their waters together
> Before meadow-land had coalesced and reed-bed was to be found –
> When not one of the gods had been formed
> Or had come into being, when no destinies had been decreed,
> The gods were created within them ...[5]

Enuma Elish tells of the violent and chaotic origins of the gods, culminating in a battle between Tiāmat and Marduk, who is made king of the gods as a reward for having established good order and peace. He then creates sky and earth from Tiāmat's body. To take on the labour of the higher gods, Marduk creates human beings from the earth's clay mixed with the blood of Kingu, Tiāmat's malicious ally. When *Enuma Elish* was written, Marduk was the national god of Babylon. In establishing his prominence, *Enuma Elish* is as much concerned with politics and Babylon's dominance over other regional cultures, particularly the southern city-states of the old Sumerian region, as it is with cosmogony. Later, when the Assyrians came to dominate the ancient Near East, including Babylonia, they adapted the *Enuma Elish* and substituted the Babylonian god Marduk for their own national god, Ashur.[6] The purpose of these ancient myths is as much about politics as it is about creation.

A number of themes from ancient Near Eastern creation myths seem to be reflected in Genesis: the overcoming of chaotic, formless waters in the formation of the cosmos (Gen. 1.1-2), humans made from the earth with an infusion of the divine (Gen. 2.7), and a re-creation through flood (Gen. 6–9). Indeed, the scholarly consensus concerning the authorship and date of Genesis indicates influence from surrounding cultures, particularly Babylon. It therefore seems very likely that the composition of Genesis was significantly influenced by other ancient creation myths such as *Atrahasis* and *Enuma Elish*.[7] As we will see, however, it is the way in which Genesis differs from these other creation stories that reveals its distinctive contribution to the theology of creation.

The genesis of Genesis

So when was Genesis written? Of course, tradition holds that Moses wrote the Pentateuch, the first five books of the Bible, except the last chapter of Deuteronomy that gives an account of his death. According to Rabbinical Judaism, this would imply a date around the thirteenth century BC. However, modern critical scholarship suggests that Genesis was written or edited from various sources much later, sometime around the destruction of the temple in Jerusalem and the exile of the elite of Judah to Babylon, beginning in 597 BC.[8] Some scholars argue for a pre-exilic date because the language of Genesis seems old and is quite different to the language we find in texts that are known to be post-exilic, such as Chronicles. Others point out that Genesis seems to be dependent on prophetic literature that we know to be exilic or post-exilic. While there appears to be some consensus that Genesis is composed as a book some time after the Babylonian exile, perhaps in the fifth century BC, it is nevertheless the case that it is heavily influenced by traditions and texts from the ancient Near East that are much older.[9]

There is general scholarly agreement that two sources lie behind the opening chapters of Genesis, even if a single editor or author blended those sources to produce a unified work.[10] These sources are identified by their particular literary styles and their core thematic concerns. The first is known as the Priestly writer (usually abbreviated to 'P') because the text has a particular concern for the created order which reflects the religious calendar; the observance of the law, including the keeping of the Sabbath; and the pattern of temple worship in Jerusalem that would have been the concern of priests. For example, we read in Gen. 1.14 that the lights in the dome of the sky that separate day from night are 'for signs and for seasons and for days and years'. In other words, their purpose is to mark the ritual religious calendar which is dependent on solar and lunar cycles. It is usual to attribute Genesis 1.1–2.4a to the Priestly author. One distinguishing feature of this opening section of Genesis is that God is referred to as 'Elohim', a generic rather than a personal name for God. In the first section of Genesis, the Priestly author provides a view of God as the transcendent cosmic creator who brings order to the cosmos by distinguishing its various elements.

The order of creation described in Genesis 1 has a particular symmetrical pattern and beauty in which the latter three days of creation mirror the first three days.[11]

Day 1: 'Let there be light!'	Day 4: Creation of the heavenly lights (sun, moon and stars)
Day 2: Creation of sky and the separation of waters to create sea	Day 5: Creation of birds (sky) and sea creatures
Day 3: Creation of land and vegetation which will be food for humans	Day 6: Creation of land animals and humans

Day 7: God completes his work and rests

There are some distinctive thematic concerns in these opening verses of Genesis which mark its unique contribution to the theology of creation. The first is the peaceful nature of God's creative act. In myths such as *Enuma Elish*, creation is the result of a conflict between the gods; it is violent. Creation involves conquest and the threat of a return to chaos is always present. By contrast, in Genesis we read of God's creative word ('God said, "Let there be ..."') which brings light from darkness. In the beginning there is no time or motion, only flux and chaos. However, this is not portrayed as a violent chaos, or as a rival to God's power; it merely lacks purpose. God is not depicted as battling against opposing forces. To adopt a phrase of St Paul, he simply 'calls into existence the things that do not exist' (Rom. 4.17). Secondly, the heavens and the earth are declared 'good' on five occasions during the days of creation. On the sixth day, after the creation of man and woman, creation is declared 'very good' (1.31). So this is not a morally neutral or indifferent cosmic order. It exhibits what is commonly called divine providence: namely, God's provision for his creatures and their ordering towards particular good ends, such as the provision of food (vv. 29–30). Good is intrinsic to the rational order of the heavens and the earth. Creation is rational not simply because it follows predictable patterns (which is how contemporary science would see the matter), but because it is good.

The peaceful and rational order of the heavens and the earth described in Genesis 1 becomes crucial for later theological and philosophical reflections on creation. It implies that peace is creation's primordial state. Violence and evil are not necessary or intrinsic to creation; they are an intrusion that is alien to God's providential plan. This intrusion of violence and evil will become the focus of Genesis 3 and the story of the expulsion of the first man and woman from the Garden of Eden. Here, the orderly pattern of creation over six days implies that the heavens and the earth are rational – that is, we can relate the parts to each other and to the whole – because they are arranged according to their particular ends. The creation of time is particularly important because it structures the ebb and flow – the 'motion' – of the created order into days and seasons. We can therefore make sense of creation and its processes. Of course, the ability to make sense of an ordered cosmos is intrinsic to the practice that today we call science.

Finally, the seventh day of rest when God completed his work is 'blessed' and 'hallowed'. This marks the completion of creation. In his commentary entitled 'The Literal Meaning of Genesis', Augustine of Hippo (AD 354–AD 430) asks how it can be that God can 'rest'. Surely creation cannot be a labour which challenges divine omnipotence and makes God tired. Neither does God create and then simply stand back from his creation, for creation requires God's continual and gracious sustaining power. Similarly, we cannot conclude that God needs to create and is therefore somehow perfected by his act of creation, because God enjoys eternal bliss and fulfilment. In no sense does God *need* creation, even if God *desires* creation. So Augustine states that

> we take it that God so rested from all his works which he had made that from now on he set up no new kind of nature any more, not so that he stopped holding together and directing the ones which he had already set in place. Thus both statements are true: that *God rested on the seventh day* (Genesis 2.2) and that *he is working until now*. (Jn 5.17)[12]

Augustine points out that God's act of creation is complete in the sense that all that is and will be needed for creation's divinely ordained purposes is by the seventh day latent within the created order, even if it is yet to be realized. The foundations or principles of creation are in place. Thus Genesis makes a key claim concerning the created order: it is complete, whole and therefore 'one' (a *uni*verse), this being ritually expressed in the Sabbath rest. Genesis therefore announces creation's goodness in terms of its wholeness or completeness. It is sufficient and features no intrinsic lack.

Creation and worship

The six-day or 'hexameral' period of creation, followed by a seventh day of divine rest when the work of creation is completed, is perhaps the most striking and unique aspect of the Genesis creation story. It is a structure which is not shared with other ancient accounts of creation. We read of a pattern of creation that reflects the ritual priestly concern with order, placement and distinction. Indeed, associating the pattern of creation with the pattern of ritual worship led by priests in the temple in Jerusalem is a traditional way of understanding the opening chapter of Genesis, particularly in relation to the Sabbath day of rest and prayer. This connection, between temple worship and creation, has been recognized at least since the time of the Hellenistic Jewish scholar Philo of Alexandria (c. 20 BC–c. AD 50), who regards creation as God's Temple, and the Jewish Roman historian Josephus (c. AD 37–c. 100).[13]

What are we to make of the idea that creation is God's Temple? How are we to understand the link between temple liturgy and creation? As a first step, we need to recall the link between Moses, the recipient of the law that establishes Jewish temple worship, and the writing of Genesis. In antiquity Moses was thought to be the author of Genesis. But how could he know about the origins of the cosmos? Margaret Barker points to a clue in The Book of Jubilees, a Hebrew text dated to around the second century BC.[14] In large part, Jubilees is a retelling of Genesis and the first part of Exodus, hence later Greek translators referred to the book as 'Little Genesis'. It describes the division of the days of the Law 'from the moment of creation' as this is shown to Moses on Mount Sinai.[15] Distinct periods of seven days form the basis of the text's ritual division of time. The opening chapter mirrors the description of Moses's encounter with God on Mount Sinai, as this is reported in Exod. 24.15-18. In Exod. 24.15 and Jubilees 1.2-3 we read that Moses went up onto the mountain and a cloud covered the mountain for six days; on the seventh day God called to Moses. This six-day encounter has been interpreted as God showing Moses his six-day act of creation. Thus Chapter 2 of Jubilees explains that 'the angel of the presence spoke to Moses by the word of the Lord, saying, "Write the whole account of creation, that in six days the Lord God completed all his works and all that he created. And he observed a Sabbath the seventh day, and he sanctified it for all ages. And he set it as a sign for all his works."'[16] Immediately after Moses's encounter with God on Mount Sinai, we read in Exodus that Moses is commanded to gather an offering for the building of a sanctuary, so that God may dwell with the people: 'In accordance with all I show you concerning the pattern of the tabernacle and of all its furniture, so you shall make it' (Exod. 25.9). The tabernacle is to be the place where God will meet his people, and where the people will worship. It seems that the vision of a six-day creation is expressed in the liturgical six-day cycle of divine worship in the tabernacle, punctuated by the seventh day of rest. Moreover, the construction of the tabernacle reflects the relative ordering of creation as described in Genesis 1.[17] As well as Exodus 25 and the description of the first arrangement of the tabernacle and sanctuary, in Exod. 40.16-33, the final chapter of the book, we learn the details of God's command to Moses to arrange the tabernacle. This begins on the first day of the first month and is therefore representative of the new year and the renewal of creation. What follows is a seven-stage process, each stage concluding with 'as the Lord had commanded to Moses'. On the first day, Moses sets up the tabernacle, covering it with a tent (Exod. 40.17-19). The space within the tent is not yet separated into distinct areas, as it will be later, each with its particular meaning in relation to the others. This first day of the construction of the tabernacle corresponds to the first day of creation in Gen. 1.3-5, in which there is no distinction within creation except light and dark. On the second day, Moses takes the covenant and places it into the ark and places the mercy seat over the ark. He places the ark in the tabernacle and sets up the curtain which separates the ark of the covenant from the remainder of the tabernacle (Exod. 40.20-21). Moses therefore distinguishes between different spatial regions: that which is holy and that which is the Holy of Holies. Thus the tabernacle is now divided in two, just as creation is divided into the sky above and the waters beneath the dome on the second day (Gen. 1.6-9). So the pattern continues until Moses completes his work on the seventh day and a cloud covers the tent and the glory of the Lord comes to fill the tabernacle (Exod. 40.33-34).

While Moses's authorship of the Pentateuch is not credible on historical grounds, the link between the pattern of creation in Genesis and the pattern of Jewish worship as described in Exodus and other Old Testament texts is long established.[18] Indeed, other ancient Near Eastern cultures also made explicit links between cosmology and temple worship.[19] Passages such as Isa. 66.1-2 point to creation as God's Temple and dwelling place:

Thus says the Lord:
Heaven is my throne
and the earth is my footstool;

what is the house that you would build for me,
and what is my resting-place?
All these things my hand has made,
and so all these things are mine,
says the Lord.

Similarly, Psalm 104 proclaims creation to be like the tent erected by
Moses or the temple built by Solomon: 'You stretch out the heavens
like a tent. ... You set the earth on its foundations, so that it shall
never be shaken.' The sevenfold structure of the psalm also closely
mirrors the pattern of Genesis 1.[20] Indeed, the psalmist indicates
that the appropriate response to creation is worship:

In his hand are the depths of the earth; the heights of the
mountains are his also. The sea is his, for he made it, and the dry
land, which his hands have formed. O come, let us worship and
bow down, let us kneel before the Lord, our Maker!' (Ps. 95.4-6)

Likewise, the response of Moses to the vision of creation on Mount
Sinai is the construction of the tabernacle for the worship of the
creator. Creation elicits praise of the creator.

So what are we to conclude from the connection between Genesis's
account of creation and the ritualized worship of God? Modern
biblical scholarship points to Gen. 1-2.4a as a text that reinforces
the priestly temple ideology focused on Jerusalem in the aftermath
of the return from exile in Babylon. The concern is apparently to
focus on the central political importance of the temple for Jewish
identity as they re-establish a home in Jerusalem. Beyond this, we
can identify a number of explicitly theological implications of the
link between creation and temple worship in the Old Testament.

First, the link between temple and creation suggests that, before
God dwells with his people in the temple, he dwells first within
creation. Creation is described by Isaiah as God's throne and
footstool. With great poetic beauty, Psalm 139 tells of the presence
of God in the farthest reaches of creation:

Where can I go from your spirit? Or where can I flee from your
presence? If I ascend to heaven, you are there; if I make my bed
in Sheol, you are there. If I take the wings of the morning and
settle at the farthest limits of the sea, even there your hand shall

lead me, and your right hand shall hold me fast. (Ps. 139.7-10)

Psalm 19 proclaims, 'The heavens are telling the glory of God; and the firmament proclaims his handiwork,' suggesting that the worship of creation is cosmic as well as human. If God is to be met in the temple made by human hands, this is only because he is first met in the temple of divine making: creation itself. This implies that God's creation is not simply a 'product' for our use or abuse; it is the place of God's dwelling and the manifestation of his glory. In other words, Genesis 1 is not concerned with the prosaic details of 'how God did it'. The text teaches that creation has an intrinsic meaning and purpose: the revealing and sharing of God's life.

Secondly, the link between creation and temple worship indicates that they share a symbolic or 'sacramental' order. What does this mean? In Christian theology, a sacrament is classically defined as an outward and visible *sign* of an inward and spiritual reality.[21] The Christian sacraments such as Baptism and the Eucharist are clearly derived from Jewish liturgical practice. However, a sacrament or liturgical ritual is not *merely* a sign, because it is inextricably linked to the reality it signifies; the sign carries with it and donates the thing that it signifies. For example, the signs of bread and wine in the Eucharist bear within themselves in the most immediate fashion the reality that they signify, namely the body and blood of Christ. Similarly, the sacrifices, feasts and anointings of the Jewish temple brought with them God's blessing, healing and peace. More generally, the order of Christian sacraments and the rituals of the Jewish temple – the signs of God's grace and purposes – reveal the sacramental order of all creation. They reveal the created order as an order of signs. Why? The symbolic or sacramental nature of the liturgy in worship is not arbitrary, but rests on the sacramental nature of creation itself. The tent of meeting raised by Moses enveloped a system of signs that were bearers of meaning and could therefore be read and interpreted, just as the sky envelopes the system of signs within God's creation which point to its creator. The tabernacle, the ark, the mercy seat, the oil for anointing, the altar, bread, incense and washing basin were not simply functional tools for worship. They were symbols which pointed to God, his ordering of creation and all that he provides for his creatures. They bore in them that which they signified, namely the living reality of God's covenant with his people. Similarly, creation signifies God's blessing and providence. The sacramental order of the tabernacle structured by Moses, and its successor, the Jerusalem temple built by Solomon, were only possible because they were derived from the sacramental order of creation itself. An implication of all this is that creation is an ordered system of signs that can be 'read' like a book. This becomes crucial to the so-called 'two-books' tradition in the early and medieval church, in which the book of nature was to be read and interpreted alongside God's other text, the book of scripture.[22] We will discuss this in more detail in Chapter 4.

Thirdly, the axis of the liturgical cycle in the tabernacle and temple was the Sabbath. Likewise, the conclusion of creation is the seventh day which God blesses and hallows as the Sabbath. It is therefore crucial to both the order of creation and the order of worship. How are we to understand the Sabbath? Numerous commentators, from Augustine to the present day,[23] point out that the seventh day in Gen. 2.2-3 is the only day not to have an evening. The Sabbath is perpetual and ongoing; it is indicative of God's eternal rest.[24] The Sabbath marks the completion of God's work of creation, but its open-ended nature also characterizes the ongoing work of hallowing and sanctifying creation, achieved through God's providential care (Exod. 31.13).[25] In the New Testament and later Christian theology, the incarnation – specifically Mary's fiat,[26] when creation welcomes God's invitation – will become the pivotal moment of sanctification when God unites creation to himself in the single person of Christ. The life of Christ is understood in the Gospels as akin to the 'sixth day' in which the Father and Son by the Spirit continue to work in the redemption of creation. For example, Jesus tells his disciples 'My Father is still working, and I also am working' (Jn 5.17). Jesus heals and ministers even on the liturgical Sabbath because creation has not reached its final rest (Jn 5.15-18). There is an important sense in which the resurrection of Jesus on the dawn *after* the Sabbath is the renewal and completion of that Sabbath through participation in the eternal life of God. The risen Christ is the morning star (Rev. 2.28 and 22.16): always new, reconciling creation to God and drawing creation into God's eternal Sabbath. This is also the first day of the new creation.

Importantly, the Sabbath in Genesis belongs to God; it is not merely a product of creation's temporal cycles. Only later, during the exodus from Egypt, does humankind come to share in the Sabbath as God's gift. How? This is an intimation of, or participation in, God's eternal rest. Humankind is given a ritual Sabbath every seventh day which is mediated through, and measures, the worship of the tabernacle and temple (Exod. 16.29; 20.8-11). Jesus teaches that he is Lord of the Sabbath and it is a gift for humankind (Mk 2.26-27). The Sabbath orders humanity towards its proper end: the divine rest. So humanity is not for the service of the Sabbath, but the Sabbath is for humanity (Mk 2.27). Beyond the first gift of creation, the Sabbath is God's 'second gift' by means of which we have a share in God's life. Moreover, wider creation, both land and animals, comes to share in the Sabbath (Lev. 25.4; Deut. 5.12-15). As R. R. Reno points out, in a sense, creation is being drawn into the eternal Sabbath by the work of the Father and Son in sanctifying and hallowing the created order.[27] So the weekly Sabbath is the anticipation of creation's final end in which creation finds its rest.

The significance of humanity's share in the Sabbath can be seen if we recall that in other ancient Near Eastern creation myths, including *Enuma Elish*, human beings are a by-product of conflict between the gods. They are created specifically to labour for the gods; by contrast, rest is exclusively divine. The God of Genesis has no such need of human labour. Man and woman are formed to share in God's life through his creation. Indeed, the Sabbath may be particularly significant with respect to one of the most important and radical teachings in the Old Testament, namely the view that humanity is made in the image of God. While the Bible is clear that there can be no idol or likeness of God (Exod. 20.4), humankind is made in the image of God (Gen. 1.27). This understanding of humanity's relation to God later acquired the Latin term *imago dei* (image of God). It has been understood in numerous ways. Some argue that humanity must share a specific quality with God that is not shared by other creatures, such as rationality. Others suggest that humanity's exercise of dominion over creation constitutes the *imago dei*, for humanity shares in God's care for creation (Gen. 1.28). For now, we can speculatively suggest that an aspect of the *imago dei* is humanity's share in that which had previously been understood as purely divine, namely rest. To rest on the Sabbath is to share in God's life. It is an aspect of human dignity and identity as formed in the image of God. The implication is that the cult of work and the exploitation of labour, so characteristic of our contemporary culture, are inhuman.

The Yahwist writer: The intimacy of God

The Priestly writer of Gen. 1-2.4a portrays God as the transcendent creator of a cosmic temple that is ordered and good. By contrast, the depiction of God and creation in the remainder of Genesis is rather different. These portions of Genesis, often dated earlier than those of the priestly writings, come from what biblical scholars usually label the Yahwistic source (abbreviated to 'J' from the German 'Jahwe'). They provide us with an account of creation which has additional emphases and priorities. The writer (or writers) refers to 'Yahweh', the personal name of God revealed to Moses on Mount Horeb as God prepares to deliver the Israelites from captivity in Egypt (Exodus 3).[28] In contrast to the cosmic creator of the first chapter of Genesis, in Genesis 2 and 3 Yahweh is more intimate: he addresses humanity, issues commands and walks in the Garden of Eden to be present in, rather than beyond, his creation.

While Genesis 1 contains a brief account of the creation of man and woman in God's image, the human drama which we encounter in Genesis 2 and 3 is altogether more elaborate. God forms the first man from the dust of the earth, thus indicating humanity's intrinsic and intimate connection with the earth and wider creation.[29] Only when the breath of God is breathed directly into man does he become a living being, so from its inception human life also has a particular divine origin. Christ's breathing of the Spirit over his disciples in the post-resurrection appearance recorded by John (Jn 20.22) clearly evokes the creation of humanity in Genesis 2. It indicates the Christian understanding that the gift of human life in the beginning was already orientated towards the second gift of new life in the Holy Spirit at the resurrection. This second gift brings the first gift to perfection.

In the first chapter of Genesis we saw that God rested on the seventh day, when creation was whole and complete in the sense that everything was present within the divinely prescribed order, even if only potentially. In the second chapter of Genesis we read about creation's yearning need for fulfilment. God uses one part of the cosmic order to meet the need of another part. This stresses the interdependent nature of the different parts of creation. For example, the earth needs to be tilled (Gen. 2.5; 2.15), the vegetation needs water (2.5), the man needs the breath of life (2.7), the man needs food that is also beautiful (2.9) and the man needs a companion and helper (2.18). There is a providential order to creation in which one part supplies the needs of another.

At the heart of this narrative is the Garden of Eden, planted 'in the east' with trees that are 'pleasant to the sight and good for food'. Two of these trees are given particular mention: the tree of life and the tree of the knowledge of good and evil. The man is placed in the garden to till and keep it. Coupled with the man's naming of the creatures, this is often interpreted as an aspect of the *imago dei*: the care and governance of creation which humanity shares with God. The naming of creatures is significant because it indicates an authority in which the man classifies creation and relates its different parts to one another. There is an exercise of judgement in which the man orders creation, but always in obedience to a latent ordering of things already given by God in the beginning. This naming or classification of creatures in Genesis 2 later provides significant theological context for the practice of observing and classifying the natural world philosophically and scientifically.

In tilling and keeping the earth, it is important to note that man is not serving God in quite the way that the humans were created to serve the gods in other ancient Near Eastern creation myths.[30] At no point does Genesis describe God as in need of man's labour; in the Jewish and Christian traditions God's life is eternally replete. Need belongs only to creation. Humanity is an integral part of meeting that need, in the attentive and careful work of 'keeping the earth'. The man is to work with the grain of creation to bring about its fruitfulness. Equally, the man also has needs: first for food provided by the earth and secondly for a companion who is not found within the animal kingdom; instead, God draws something new from the man's rib, namely woman. Man declares his partner to be 'bone of my bones and flesh of my flesh' (Gen. 2.23) in a way that allows them to 'become one flesh' (2.24). The creation of woman is the completion of the man because God had declared that he should not be alone (2.18). This also suggests that the *imago dei* does not subsist simply in the individual human person, but in the human community which is constituted of both female and male.[31]

Tragedy: The expulsion from Eden

Of all the stories in the Old Testament, the drama of the man and the woman and their expulsion from the Garden of Eden, later to be known as 'the Fall', is one of the best known and most frequently depicted in Christian art. The experience of sin and evil in creation is often explored with reference to this ancient story of tragic destruction and disobedience.

God first placed two trees in the Garden of Eden: the tree of life and the tree of the knowledge of good and evil. The man and woman were commanded that they might eat the fruit of any tree in the garden – except the tree of knowledge. The cunning serpent, however, tempts the woman specifically with the idea of 'becoming like gods, knowing good and evil' (Gen. 3.5).[32] As the man and the woman eat the fruit of the tree of knowledge, a chain of events begins, which issues in a kind of death brought about by sin. This is followed by expulsion from the Garden of Eden and the toils and burdens of human life (Gen. 3.14-24). These events are also the beginning of the Christian story of salvation, which reaches its pivotal moment in Christ as 'the second Adam' (1 Cor. 15.45); his cross comes to be understood by later Christian theologians as 'the tree of life' which redeems the consequences of eating the tree of the knowledge of good and evil.

There has been much debate concerning the nature of this first sin. For example, was it covetousness, envy or pride? It seems to be a pre-ethical decision to take the fruit because the woman and man did not yet know the difference between good and evil when they ate the fruit, although paradoxically it was clearly an act of disobedience in the face of God's command (Gen. 2.16 and 3.3, in which the woman also states that it was prohibited to touch the tree).[33] One attractive interpretation of this stage of the narrative concerns the need for human maturity before the acquisition of the knowledge of good and evil. We find this, for example, in the work of the second-century apologist Irenaeus of Lyon (c. 130–c. 200).[34] Elsewhere in the Old Testament, the knowledge of good and evil is an aspect of human maturity (Deut. 1.39) and we commonly accept that children need time to be taught right from wrong as they grow up. Patristic interpreters of Genesis, such as Irenaeus, certainly regarded the first man and woman as like children because of their physical innocence prior to eating the fruit of the tree of knowledge; only after eating the fruit are they conscious of their nakedness in a way that we associate with adulthood. So, might the fruit of the tree of the knowledge of good and evil have been meant to be reserved for a time when humanity, after due growth and maturing, was capable of receiving such wisdom? In taking the fruit of the tree of knowledge, does humanity seize this wisdom prematurely, with disastrous consequences of corruption and lost innocence?

Taking the fruit is an assertion of autonomy in the face of God's command. It is an attempt to achieve a divine status by force, which suggests that the man and the woman regard the gift of their human nature and God's provision for them through creation as inadequate or incomplete. It is thus an implicit rejection of the view that creation is continually reliant for its flourishing on the divine providential goodness which includes God's commands. Genesis 3 thus points to two important aspects of the human experience of sin: its delusional and bewildering nature and the sense of the forceful, even violent, assertion of self-sufficient autonomy in the face of God's providence. What God provides and commands is insufficient, says the serpent; you can surely do better, becoming like the self-sufficient and autonomous gods you were meant to be. In other words, this first sin consists in humanity forgetting that it is *created*. To be created is to receive the sustaining power and providence of the creator as sufficient without the need for self-assertive greed that comes from a sense that what one has is insufficient. The sin about which we read in Genesis 2 and 3 is the prideful assertion of independence from God who is the necessary source of creation's goodness and humanity's freedom. The Christian theological tradition up to the late medieval period is concerned to avoid any sense that creation is autonomous or stands alongside God as another 'thing'; this concern begins in a reading of the first chapters of Genesis.

However one interprets the decision by the first man and woman to break the command of God and eat the fruit of the tree of the knowledge of good and evil, the narrative illustrates something very important about the appearance of sin and evil in creation: its bewildering inexplicability. Exactly *why* do the man and woman eat the fruit? Are they victims, deceived in their innocence by the serpent? Or are they fundamentally responsible? For much of his career, the great Western theologian Augustine of Hippo sought an answer concerning why evil is present within creation, particularly given that creation is announced as 'good' in Genesis 1. Does sin's source lie in material nature and the temptations of the body? Is it good that some fail to follow God's commands, in order to teach the righteous? Is the sin of the first man and woman somehow inevitable, simply because they are created and therefore are always open to weakness, confusion and the possibility of evil? Augustine considers all these possibilities. When reflecting on why God allowed the man and woman to be tempted, he is frank: 'So then, if you ask why God allowed the man to be tempted, knowing beforehand that he was going to consent to temptation, I have to confess that I am quite unable to plumb the depths of his purpose and plan, and that it is far and away beyond my powers.'[35] Augustine goes on to point out that sin is at least helpful in teaching the righteous and he argues that a humanity which *of necessity* always acted according to the good would be of less worth than a humanity which was genuinely wise concerning good and evil. Still, this seems like an insufficient reason for, or justification of, the entry of evil and sin into creation.

Augustine's wider theology provides an important context for these reflections on sin and evil in Genesis. In the light of Genesis 1, Augustine regards creation as good. Following a tradition of thought that we can trace to Plato (c. 427–c. 347 BC), he sees creation as having a share in divine existence that is eternally good. In this wider context, evil and sin are not regarded as having a positive existence in themselves. Rather, they are absences of the good. Just as darkness is not something in itself, but is the absence of light, so evil is not something in itself but is the absence of goodness. This Augustinian tradition refers to evil as *privatio boni*, the privation of the good.[36] The implication is that evil is literally 'nothing': not in the sense that it has no power or influence (quite the contrary), but in the sense that it is always parasitic on a prior and more fundamental good.[37] Evil is the absence or dissolution of the good, in the same way that illness is the absence of health. According to Augustine's view, the decision by the man and woman to eat the forbidden fruit is not a positive willing, but a failure or absence of willing. It is a *dis*order:

a thing which does not make sense in itself, but only in relation to the order of which it is a corruption. Eating the fruit of the tree of knowledge is the *absence* of a properly ordered will.

Elsewhere in his writings on Genesis, Augustine comments that prior to the first humans eating the fruit of the tree of knowledge, 'there was a tranquil avoidance of sin; and, as long as this continued, no evil of any kind intruded, from any source, to bring them sadness'.[38] At first, humanity cleaves easily and naturally to the good; the human will is readily orientated towards the good and it requires no special effort. In this interpretation, the entry of sin into the world through the temptation of the man and woman represents a radical change: it is the introduction of the idea that the good is an option. In other words, the good is something we have to choose by laboured deliberation rather than something to which our wills are readily orientated. For Augustine, the introduction of 'deliberative choice' did not represent an enhancement of human freedom but its demise. Why? Because freedom consists not simply in the ability to will, but the ability to will the good. It was this latter ability, to will the good in tranquillity, which was lost as a result of human sin. The remainder of human history, for Augustine, is an attempt to discern the good amid a fog of sin and foolishness.

For Augustine, it is the good which is intelligible and rational because we can make sense of it. When we say of someone 'she was a good friend to me', we are suggesting that her actions made sense; she acted as a friend ought to act. When we say 'that's a good apple' or 'that's a good house', we are saying that these things are intelligible as apples and houses because they are what apples and houses *ought to be*. Goodness is rational and intelligible because it refers to the proper ends or purposes of things. By contrast, evil is intrinsically unintelligible. In the face of human wickedness or natural disaster, we rightly ask 'why?' because we cannot make sense of such experience with reference to our more basic intuition concerning the way things ought to be. Of course, we can sometimes give a certain kind of explanation for human sin or evil in terms of prior events or conditions. For example, we might say of a violent man that he developed a disposition to violence because he was a victim of violence as a child. But can we make sense of evil and sin in creation in this way, with reference to purpose and justification? We can only do so by implying that evil and sin in creation are in some strange way actually good in the long run – but this is not to take our experience of sin and evil with full seriousness. If we could provide a rational justification or reason for cancer in a child, for example, we would indeed live in a wicked world. Augustine maintains that evil and sin within creation are strictly speaking unintelligible. So while he acknowledges evil and sin in creation, Augustine always regards them as unintelligible intrusions into a good creation. They are alien to God's intention of the way creation ought to be. This is why, then, a rational justification for the first humans' eating of the fruit of the tree of knowledge cannot be given. It may be ascribed to the influence of Satan via the serpent, but eating the fruit of the tree serves only a destructive purpose; therefore it cannot be deemed intelligible.[39] The narrative of the first man and woman in Genesis 2 and 3 is therefore not an attempt to justify or explain the strife that we witness in creation. Instead, it points to the unintelligibility of sin and evil and to its radical consequences. It establishes the beginning of the story of salvation, the drama of history – setting in motion not a *justification* of sin and evil but God's *response* to sin and evil. Fundamentally, it points to the human sense that creation is not what it ought to be; it requires God's saving grace and it is yet to be brought to full perfection (Rom. 8.18-23).

These opening chapters of the Bible point to a number of important and distinctive teachings. First, creation is symbolic or sacramental. Its purpose is to share in the divine life and an important expression of that participation is ritual worship and the liturgy of the Sabbath rest. Secondly, creation is fundamentally good and ordered; evil and disorder are an alien intrusion and parasitic on the fundamental goodness and intelligibility of creation. The goodness and order of creation opens the possibility of making sense of the natural world through the various methods of rational, human enquiry, of which modern science is one example. At first glance, therefore, we do not have an obvious conflict between creation as depicted in Genesis and the natural world as described and analysed by science. Or do we? It depends on how we understand and interpret the text of Genesis.

Interpreting Genesis

The Christian theologians of the first centuries generally regarded Genesis as an historical narrative. After all, it was a scriptural book and therefore ultimately divine in origin, though also a human work. There were no serious alternative accounts of the origins of creation, even though philosophical accounts from ancient Greece – such as Plato's cosmology *Timaeus* – might also illuminate our understanding of the cosmos. Despite these historical assumptions, early Christian theology approached biblical texts with a sophisticated method of interpretation which extended well beyond the literal or historical sense of the text. They derived this method from ancient Greek philosophy and from the work of the Jewish philosopher Philo of Alexandria.

The most important theologian in the development of this hermeneutic is Origen of Alexandria (c. 185–c. 254). Origen takes the broadly Platonic view that creation is an elaborate system of signs which can be used for the edification of humanity concerning the eternal and divine realm, rather like the sacramental order of creation we encountered above. Likewise, scripture is a system of signs requiring careful interpretation beyond their simple surface or historical meaning. There are many layers of meaning, which can be uncovered in order to teach us about the deeper truths of creation, human nature and our life with God. In his commentary on the Song of Songs, Origen writes, 'This relationship [between the visible and the invisible] does not obtain only with creatures. ... The Divine Scripture itself is written with wisdom of a rather similar sort.'[40]

Origen developed a famous threefold method for interpreting scripture according to the image of body, soul and spirit. The first sense – the 'body' of scripture – is the literal sense. This might refer to the historical or obvious sense of the text and provides the most straightforward and accessible interpretation.[41] For example, the literal sense of Genesis would simply refer to the events of the days of creation rather than their meaning. The second sense of scripture – the 'soul' of scripture – refers to the moral teaching of the text.[42] It points to scripture's teaching concerning how we ought to live with one another and with God. The moral sense of Genesis 2 might refer to the need for obedience in relation to divine teaching and command. The third sense – the 'spirit' of scripture – is the most important and became known as allegorical or spiritual interpretation. This layer of meaning contains timeless theological truths concerning God and our life with God. The tree of life becomes an allegory of the cross of Christ by which the gift of eternal life is offered to humanity. To this threefold interpretation of scripture, an 'anagogical' interpretation was added by other theologians in the early church. This refers to what scripture teaches about the eschaton or the end times.

The fourfold interpretation of scripture – the literal, moral, anagogical and allegorical senses – remained the centrepiece of Christian hermeneutics until the Reformation. It allowed a positive spiritual or moral interpretation of certain passages of scripture which, when taken only literally, would not make sense. Thus, when reading Gen. 3.8, ought we to interpret God walking in the garden in the evening breeze literally? Surely not, given that God is incorporeal and eternal. Through allegorical interpretation, a relaxed evening's walk becomes an allegory of God's intimacy with creation and his enjoyment of, and delight in, all that he had made. In Genesis 3, that relaxed enjoyment and delight was about to be disturbed.

Although theologians of the early church regarded Genesis as a historical narrative, this was not the most important sense of the text. Its allegorical or spiritual teaching was where the most important theological truths were to be found. Indeed, the earliest Jewish and Christian interpretations of Genesis recognized that the text had to be taken figuratively if it was to make any sense at all. When compared to a straightforward experience of the natural world, portions of the text made little sense when taken only literally. Origen writes,

What man of intelligence, I ask, will consider it a reasonable statement that the first and the second and the third day, in which there are said to be both morning and evening, existed without sun and moon and stars, whilst the first day was even without a heaven? And who could be found so silly as to believe that God, after the manner of a farmer, 'planted trees in a paradise eastward of Eden', and set therein a 'tree of life', that is, a visible and palpable tree of wood, of such a sort that anyone who ate of this tree with bodily teeth would gain life. ... And further, when God is said to 'walk in the paradise in the evening' and Adam to hide himself behind a tree, I do not think anyone will doubt that these statements are made by scripture in a figurative manner, in order that through them certain mystical truths may be indicated.[43]

Augustine, writing in the fifth century, is equally forthright when it comes to a comparison between Genesis and natural history or natural philosophy. He recognizes that there can be knowledge about the natural world which is the fruit of natural philosophy – or roughly what today we would call science. Such knowledge can be substantiated via observation and reason. Christians should not claim to pit the teachings of Genesis against the knowledge of the world gleaned from natural philosophy *as if it were the same kind of knowledge*. This will only lead to the ridicule of the scriptures. Augustine writes,

> Now it is quite disgraceful and disastrous, something to be on one's guard against at all costs, that they [the natural philosophers] should ever hear Christians spouting what they claim our Christian literature has to say on these topics, and talking such nonsense that they can scarcely contain their laughter when they see them to be *toto caelo*, as the saying goes, wide of the mark.[44]

From the earliest days of Christian theology the literal reading of Genesis was not regarded as the most significant. The text, though viewed as historical by many (but by no means all) theologians, held much deeper and more significant truths concerning the meaning of creation. It was not the kind of text that could be compared straightforwardly with the knowledge of the natural world gained from other disciplines, whose methods focused on observation rather than interpretation of the natural order. Origen realized this in the third century, Augustine in the fifth century, and countless theologians held the same view before and after.

The friction between the account of creation in Genesis and the description of the natural world which we find in ancient natural philosophy or the modern natural sciences has its origins in the increasingly exclusive focus on literal interpretations of scripture that we encounter in the Reformation. Increasingly elaborate use of allegory in the medieval period meant that Christian theologians of the sixteenth and seventeenth centuries sought a more straightforward interpretation of scripture which focused on the text's natural or surface meaning. We will examine the consequences of this focus on the literal sense of scripture in relation to the rise of natural science in much more detail in Chapter 4. For now, we can note that this had a considerable effect on the perceived significance of Genesis, particularly on which parts of the text were regarded as most important. When read literally, it became increasingly important to establish the historical or factual credentials of Genesis, in order to establish its truth and authority. For theologians in antiquity and the medieval period, factual issues such as the location of Eden or the date of creation were hardly important; the allegorical meaning of the text was far more significant. When a literal reading took precedence, the historical facts needed to be established by observation according to the methods of natural history. The historian of science Peter Harrison remarks,

> In the early modern period, the geography of paradise, to take one example, took on an unprecedented significance. Whereas for medieval and patristic exegetes the Garden of Eden had been a potent idea, laden with psychological or allegorical meaning – paradise was thus placed in the third heaven, the orb of the moon, or in the human mind – now considerable efforts were expended on attempts to identify the earthly location of Eden and in describing its physical features.[45]

The historical facts of the matter had to be established in order to shore up the credibility and value of Genesis. By contrast, for early Jewish and Christian theologians the credibility of Genesis did not lie in its credentials as a literal and historical account; its credibility lay in its theology of creation. In other words, Genesis was not primarily teaching us a history lesson in what happened, but a theological lesson concerning the meaning of the created order and our place therein.

In this new world of literal prioritization, the apparent conflict between Genesis and alternative accounts of the natural world seemed to reach its most critical moment when Darwin published *On the Origin of Species* in 1859. His theory of evolution by natural selection presented the greatest ever challenge to the account of creation in Genesis. Quite simply, in a world dominated by literal interpretation the two texts could not both be true. One described creation in seven days, the other over millions of years. Genesis was put side by side with Darwin's work and found wanting. Thus emerged the creationists: those who hold to the literal truth of Genesis contra the account of evolution provided by Darwin. However, the conflict between the two accounts makes a startling assumption: that these two texts – Genesis and *On the Origin of Species* – are the same kind of account, such that they can be compared like for like. Can we compare a text from the fifth or sixth century BC ancient Near East with a nineteenth-century work of natural history? This seems implausible. Yet the situation is even more troubling. The debate concerning the relationship between Genesis and Darwinian evolution makes a further assumption: it implicitly takes the method of Darwin's *On the Origin of Species* as the norm for any truthful account of creation and the natural world. This debate assumes that the only knowledge of creation and nature worth having is empirical and historical. In other words, the account must be literal or it is of no value. The debate between creationists and evolutionary biology thus occurs on terrain established by Darwin: the terrain of natural history. Having accepted the terms of the debate, the creationists are obliged to argue – against all the available evidence – that Genesis is better natural history than Darwin's *On the Origin of Species*.[46] Clearly Genesis is not the same kind of text as *On the Origin of Species*. Its methods and priorities are wholly different. This is not to suggest that the texts cannot speak to each other; nor is it to assume a happy synergy between the two. Rather, it is simply to point out that any straightforward comparison must recognize the possibility of different approaches to our exploration of creation and nature.

Conclusion

So, how are we to receive Genesis today? As we have seen, the historical origins of the text are enormously complex. Its meaning in relation to other texts of scripture is rich and deeply suggestive with respect to the goodness and purpose of creation. But is it 'just a myth'? To describe Genesis as *just* a myth reveals a typically modern preference for literal or purely historical truth. If we want to suggest that something is false or misleading, we describe it as a myth. But our deep intellectual history is replete with myths, which are able to deliver a certain kind of allegorical truth which is of more value and significance than factual or literal accounts. In concluding this chapter, I would like, therefore, to explore what it means to describe Genesis as myth.

Around the time that Genesis was written and compiled, Greek thought was making an important distinction between different kinds of discourse. History emerged in the work of the fifth-century Athenian historian Thucydides (c. 460–c. 395 BC) and the argumentative method of philosophy developed as an investigation into nature, particularly in the work of Alexander of Miletus (c. 610–c. 546BC). These were naturalistic alternatives to the more traditional discourse of poetry and myth. Nevertheless, a myth was a story that conveyed truth, albeit in a form that was figurative, imaginative and therefore more accessible. In his dialogue *Protagoras*, Plato makes a distinction between *muthos* (myth) and *logos* (reason), *muthos* seeming to refer to a narrative story, whereas *logos* refers to a reasoned argument. In the *Republic*, Plato appears to be sceptical about the value of traditional mythical stories, on the grounds that they do not offer the reasoned arguments which belong to philosophy. Indeed, he makes reference to an ancient quarrel between philosophy and poetry.[47] Yet Plato uses myths and figurative images throughout his dialogues, including the *Phaedo*, *Phaedrus* and *Timaeus*. The *Republic* contains two of his most famous allegorical images, the cave and the sun. He frequently interweaves myth with argument in order to persuade his audience concerning the demanding truths that lie at the very edge of human reason's abilities. This is particularly true of his cosmology, *Timaeus*, in which he seeks a truthful account of the origins of the universe and concludes that only myth will suffice to explore the mysteries that are not amenable to the raw use of philosophical reason. The *Timaeus* is only a 'likely account' rather than a literal account that delivers the facts; it is a myth concerning a cosmos that, when compared to divine eternity, is itself 'mythical'. Nevertheless, Plato sees no ultimate opposition between *muthos* and *logos*. The two can be interwoven, although *muthos* is particularly useful for the persuasion of non-philosophical audiences.

With our much more restrictive modern sense of what counts as truthful, inevitably the mythical tends to be accorded little value. Taking a longer view of our intellectual history, in which the methods of modern natural science are accorded their proper place without assuming their hegemony, to describe a text as mythical may be to identify its character and intentions more clearly. Plato, whose thought so influenced Jewish and Christian interpreters of Genesis, saw no opposition between *muthos* and *logos*, between a narrative account of creation and a philosophical account. Genesis certainly contains the drama of a mythical narrative – into which is woven an argument concerning the goodness of creation, its sacramental purpose in the praise of its creator, God's providence and judgement, the nature of the human person and the tragedy of human sin. These are dramatic reflections on some of our most perplexing questions concerning the meaning and purpose of existence, not just the prosaic facts of existence. As such, Genesis teaches its readers at the very boundaries of our intellectual capabilities, where both *muthos* and *logos* are required.

2

God and Creation *ex nihilo*

The first verse of Genesis tells of the time when God created the heavens and the earth. The earth was a formless void, darkness covered the face of the deep and the spirit of God swept over the waters. At first glance, it seems that God created out of a chaotic material realm that already existed. A broadly similar view can be found in the tradition of ancient Greek philosophy. Plato's mythical cosmogony, *Timaeus*, describes the creation of the cosmos from chaotic material by the god-like craftsman known as the demiurge.[1] That material resists the attempts of the demiurge to fashion it according to rational, mathematical principles. Aristotle's view was rather different: the universe has always existed and is therefore of everlasting time.[2]

Given this scriptural and philosophical background, it is remarkable that a very different consensus gradually emerges among Jewish and Christian theologians from at least the first century AD, followed in due course by Islamic scholars.[3] These three traditions claim that if we are to speak of God's creative act, we must not speak of God fabricating the cosmos out of some kind of pre-existent material. Rather, we must speak of God creating *ex nihilo*, 'out of nothing'. What does this mean? As we will see in this chapter, in many ways it is easier to see what creation *ex nihilo* does *not* mean. Creation out of nothing does not mean that 'nothing' is some special stuff that God uses in his act of creation. Nor is 'nothing' a vacuum because a vacuum still requires space and has significance.[4] Put simply, creation *ex nihilo* means that God does not create the universe out of something else. God does not take chaotic matter and fashion it into an orderly and rational universe; there are no prior materials out of which God fashions the universe. There is not even a pre-existent space within which God creates. Instead, we are to think of God creating everything, including matter, space and time. Aside from that absolute act of creation, there is nothing.

Creation *ex nihilo* is remarkable for a number of reasons. First, it clearly contradicts the classical philosophical maxim first articulated by Parmenides (fl. late sixth century BC): *ex nihilo, nihil fit.* Out of nothing, nothing comes. Because nothing could come from nothing, the ancient Greeks thought that something had always existed, whether a chaotic material realm which was brought into order (Plato) or an orderly cosmos which has no beginning (Aristotle). By contrast, creation *ex nihilo* suggests that the cosmos has some kind of absolute beginning or origin. Secondly, creation *ex nihilo* differs from an important view of the origins of the cosmos that we find in the tradition known as Neoplatonism (literally, the 'new Platonism'), a broad variation on Platonic philosophy whose first exponent is usually thought to be Plotinus (AD 204/5–270). In his *Enneads*, Plotinus writes of an 'overflow' of creation from the divine first principle, which he calls 'the One'.[5] This overflow later came to be labelled 'emanation'. The emanationist view suggests that creation flows or emanates from God (or, for the pagan Neoplatonists, 'the One'), much as light emanates from a candle or a stream flows from its spring. Early Christian theologians were uneasy about emanation as a way of understanding creation because it suggests that creation is not a free and voluntary act; it implies that creation just happens, eternally and necessarily, by virtue of the divine nature – much as the stream necessarily flows from the spring. Following scripture, Christianity's first theologians wanted to maintain that creation is God's totally free and voluntary act, not something which pours forth by necessity or compulsion from the divine. While some later theologians, notably Aquinas, describe creation as an emanation from God, they always qualify such emanation as freely willed and not necessary or constrained in any way.

In the background to creation *ex nihilo*, we can therefore see three alternative views of creation. First, we have the Aristotelian view that the universe is of everlasting time and sits alongside God, mirroring his eternity. Secondly, we have the constructivist view, apparently seen in Plato's *Timaeus*, in which a demiurge makes the cosmos from pre-existent material. Having no ultimate beginning or origin, this pre-existent material chaos always sits alongside

God. Thirdly, we have the emanationist view in which creation emerges from God by necessity, like the stream from the spring, albeit without a temporal beginning. For the Jewish, Christian and Islamic traditions, all three views share a common problem: they make it difficult to distinguish between God and creation. In the case of the Aristotelian and constructivist views, there is always something that sits alongside God, challenging his eternal nature. In other words, there is a material nature (whether orderly or chaotic) which is always present and which does not seem to have an *ultimate* origin in God's creative act. This material nature seems to be like God insofar as it is not bound by time. In the case of the Neoplatonic emanationist view, there is also a danger of seeing creation as the 'stretching out' of divine being in such a way that creation and God become continuous, much as the stream is continuous with the spring. This could lead to a view known as pantheism – the idea that God and the universe are coterminous.

If there is one crucial issue that dominates the theology of creation in the ancient and medieval worlds, it is this: how do we distinguish between God and creation? This is important because, if we fail to identify with precision the absolute *difference* between God and creation, there is always a danger that we will conceive God as *part of* creation, or creation as part of God. And once God is understood as in any way like a creature we lapse into idolatry because we confuse God the creator for something created. [6] Moreover, for God truly to be the absolute source of creation he cannot be understood as *like* a creature in any univocal sense because then God himself would need some kind of explanation. That is, we could legitimately ask the question: 'Who created God?'[7] So before all else, God must be understood as totally self-subsistent, having no attribute that implies a need of something further. Indeed, theologians of the ancient and medieval periods were also adamant that God does not need to create and gains nothing by creating. Rather, creation is a purely free, completely unique, totally gratuitous and wholly unnecessary act. The three views of creation mentioned above – the Aristotelian, constructivist and emanationist views – all present a similar problem with respect to this divine freedom: the apparently necessary existence of something other than God. In the case of the Aristotelian view, there has always been an orderly universe. In the case of the constructivist view, there has always been a material realm which God draws from chaos to order. In the case of the emanationist view, creation necessarily flows from the divine. In all three cases, it seems as if there is something other than God of which God is not the *ultimate* source.

In this chapter, we will examine the meaning of creation *ex nihilo*, the way in which it establishes the distinction between God and creation and its relation to scientific cosmologies such as the Big Bang. It will be seen that creation *ex nihilo* is not, in fact, first and foremost a theory about how God created the cosmos. Creation *ex nihilo* emerges first from what the monotheistic traditions profess about God. On the basis of that profession, certain claims are made concerning creation. To begin with, we will examine the biblical and historical background to creation *ex nihilo*.

The origins of creation *ex nihilo*[8]

Although the consensus among early church theologians concerning the centrality of creation *ex nihilo* is remarkable,[9] there is allegedly no obvious verbatim instance of this teaching in scripture. At first glance, the crucial early verses of Genesis imply that there is a temporal beginning to creation and that God creates by manipulating formless matter. The New Revised Standard Version renders the first two verses of Genesis as follows: 'In the beginning when God created the heavens and the earth, the earth was a formless void and darkness covered the face of the deep, while a wind from God swept over the face of the waters.' The implication is that *when* God creates, at that moment there is *already* a formless void, a 'deep', and a wind sweeping over the waters. This seems to imply pre-existent matter from which God creates. Such modern translations refer to the Hebrew text of the Bible produced by Jewish grammarians and Torah scholars known as Masoretes between the seventh and tenth centuries AD.[10] The oldest manuscript we possess comes from around the ninth century AD. For very good reasons, Biblical scholars refer primarily to the Masoretic text. However, there are different interpretations and translations of these verses, some of which more clearly suggest creation *ex nihilo*.[11] As well as a number of modern translations of the Hebrew text,[12] the Greek translation of the Old Testament known as the Septuagint or LXX, produced around the third century BC, offers a slightly different sense of 'beginning': 'In the beginning (*en archē*) God created the heavens and the earth.'[13] The 'when' of some translations of the Hebrew Masoretic text is not included in the Septuagint version. To understand the significance of this difference, we should note two senses of 'beginning'. First, we might think of a temporal beginning in statements such as 'at the beginning of the journey' or 'when I began to eat'. This sense of beginning refers to a moment in time in which there is a 'before' and an 'after'. Some modern translations of the first verse of Genesis imply this temporal sense of beginning; God creates at one moment within the flow of time, at this moment rather than that moment. It seems that creation is located in time. Another sense of beginning refers to something's rationale or foundation. For example, we might say 'the beginning of wisdom is the fear of the Lord' (Ps. 111.10) or 'justice is the beginning of peace'. This is a different kind of beginning that is not temporal but metaphysical: 'beginning' refers to the root, principle or purpose of something. If this is the kind of beginning which the Septuagint translators had in mind, not to mention some traditional scholarly renderings of the Hebrew, it is more consistent with the beginning proposed by creation *ex nihilo*: an absolute origin of all things *including* time, rather than a beginning *within* time.

The first verse of St. John's gospel, in repeating the phrasing of Gen. 1.1, appears to offer a gloss on Genesis and creation's origins which refers clearly to the fundamental origin or 'beginning' of all things in God's eternal Word: 'In the beginning (*en archē*) was the Word, and the Word was with God, and the Word was God. He was in the beginning with God. All things came into being through him, and without him not one thing came into being.'[14] Indeed, the New Testament consistently refers to creation in terms of a fundamental origin of *all* things: 'For from him and through him and to him are all things' (Rom. 11:36); 'yet for us there is one God, the Father, from whom are all things and for whom we exist' (1 Cor. 8:6); 'and to make everyone see what is the plan of the mystery hidden for ages in God who created all things' (Eph. 3.9); 'for in him all things in heaven and on earth were created, things visible and invisible, whether thrones or dominions or rulers or powers – all things have been created through him and for him' (Col. 1.16); 'You are worthy, our Lord and God, to receive glory and honour and power, for you

created all things, and by your will they existed and were created'
(Rev. 4.11).

If it seems difficult to decide the precise meaning of the opening
verses of Genesis, we must allow for different priorities among the
Priestly authors of the Hebrew text and the Hellenized Judaism
which produced its Septuagint translation. For the Priestly writers,
the precise metaphysical basis of creation and its causal origin are
not the central concern; what matters is that the world that God
creates is good, beautiful and providentially ordered. Though not
the focus of the Priestly writers' attention, a world devoid of this
divine imprint would, in a sense, be 'nothing'. The teaching that
God is the creative source or 'beginning' of all things also seems
to lie behind the wisdom literature of the second century BC.[15]
Another oft-cited text comes from the second book of Maccabees, a
deuterocanonical work written in Greek in the late second or early
first century BC. It concerns the warrior Judas Maccabeus and the
Jewish revolt against King Antiochus IV and his empire beginning
around 169 BC. This was a period of oppression for the Jews that
included the desecration of the Temple; it produced many martyrs
and deep hostility towards Hellenistic culture. The experience of
oppression and martyrdom gave rise to debates concerning the
resurrection of the dead. This theme is reflected in the seventh
chapter of the second book of Maccabees in which seven brothers
and their mother are arrested by the king and compelled to eat
food contrary to Jewish law. Six of the brothers are martyred in
gruesome fashion. Their mother encourages her sons, evoking the
themes of creation, life and resurrection:

> I do not know how you came into being in my womb. It was
> not I who gave you life and breath, nor I who set in order the
> elements within each of you. Therefore the Creator of the world,
> who shaped the beginning of humankind and devised the origin
> of all things, will in his mercy give life and breath back to you
> again, since you now forget yourselves for the sake of his laws.
> (2 Macc. 7.22-23)

Following the brutal death of six of the brothers and with only one
remaining, King Antiochus urges the woman to persuade her child
to turn from the law and the ways of his ancestors. But the woman
says to her son:

My son, have pity on me. I carried you nine months in my womb, and nursed you for three years, and have reared you and brought you up to this point in your life, and have taken care of you. I beg you, my child, to look at the heaven and the earth and see everything that is in them, and recognize that God did not make them out of things that existed. And in the same way the human race came into being. Do not fear this butcher, but prove worthy of your brothers. Accept death, so that in God's mercy I may get you back again along with your brothers. (2 Macc. 7.27-29)

Turning to the New Testament, an important text similarly invokes the themes of creation and life. When writing to the Christians of Rome around AD 55, St. Paul considers the life that was brought from Abraham and the faith which is the promise and gift of God.

For this reason it depends on faith, in order that the promise may rest on grace and be guaranteed to all his descendants, not only to the adherents of the law but also to those who share the faith of Abraham (for he is the father of all of us, as it is written, 'I have made you the father of many nations') – in the presence of the God in whom he believed, who gives life to the dead and calls into existence the things that do not exist. (Rom. 4.16-17)

Insofar as the Jewish and Christian scriptures reflect on creation and cosmic origins, they are particularly concerned with God's power, providence, presence and fidelity to his creation as well as creation as an absolute beginning of all things (Gen. 1 and 2; Prov. 8.22-30; Ps. 104; 121.1-2; 148.4-5; Job 38.4–39.30; Isa. 45.7-14; Jn. 1; Col. 1.15-17). These passages hardly constitute a clear and consistent statement concerning the metaphysics of creation; that is not their purpose. They do, however, reflect particular convictions concerning God's supreme authority and freedom, even in the face of an apparently ultimate and unavoidable power – the oblivion or 'nothingness' of death. Whether the woman depicted in 2 Maccabees witnessing the brutal martyrdom of her sons had creation *ex nihilo* in mind hardly seems relevant or decidable. What is important is that the tradition preserves her plea to her son in terms which reflect the conviction that God's freedom and power are such that all creatures have a fundamental source in God's creative act. In contrast to the teaching of the Greek philosophers, *this* Greek text, the second book of Maccabees, is clear that God did not create out of things already in existence.[16] Nothing rivals the creator and death is not the ultimate horizon; God even calls things to life from nothing. These are the seeds of what was to become the more thoroughly worked-out metaphysical teaching that God creates out of nothing.

As well as these scriptural origins, scholars also find traces of creation *ex nihilo* in the works of the Hellenistic Jewish thinker Philo of Alexandria (c. 20 BC–c. AD 50) [17] and its clear expression in Christian thought occurring at least as early as the second century, in texts such as *The Shepherd of Hermas*.[18] We find a concise statement in a work by Tatian, an Assyrian convert to Christianity who wrote his anti-Hellenistic 'Oration to the Greeks' around AD 160. He stated, 'For matter is not, like God, without beginning, nor, as having no beginning, is of equal power with God; it is begotten, and not produced by any other being, but brought into existence by the Framer of all things alone.'[19] Theophilus, bishop of Antioch from around AD 169, wrote to a pagan named Autolycus, 'And all things God has made out of things that were not into things that are, in order that through His works His greatness may be known and understood.'[20] By the mid-second century, then, expressions of creation *ex nihilo* were clear and explicit, even if not formulated in precise metaphysical language.

So it seems that the idea of creation *ex nihilo* was distilled over a long period as Jewish and Christian thinkers developed a distinctive scriptural monotheism that had clear consequences for how one should speak theologically of God's creative act. The standard scholarly narrative of the emergence of creation *ex nihilo* implies that, while this doctrine 'corresponds factually with the Old Testament proclamation about creation',[21] it is not demanded by the scriptural text and only emerges clearly in second-century Christianity, as a response to the challenges of ancient Greek cosmology – particularly Platonism and Stoicism – and Gnosticism.[22] However, in surveying this doctrine's scriptural basis and its early history, we have seen that creation *ex nihilo* is more than a product of Christian theological apologetics in the second century, even if it achieved a new clarity in this period. The biblical conviction that God's creative act establishes a fundamental beginning of all things including time and matter leads Janet Soskice to aptly describe creation *ex nihilo* as 'a *biblically compelled* piece of metaphysical theology'.[23] Creation *ex nihilo* is therefore much more than a philosophical invention. In an important sense, it has its fundamental basis in scripture, elucidated in the delicate interweaving of theology and philosophy.

The scriptural foundation of creation *ex nihilo* extends beyond those texts that deal explicitly with God's creative act. As we will see, what emerges in the development and clarification of this doctrine is a teaching that does not simply begin and end with creation per se, but also draws conclusions concerning creation from a more fundamental doctrine of God. The wider, scripturally derived doctrine of God gives rise to the need to speak of God creating *ex nihilo*, as distinct from understanding the created order as timeless, as constructed from always existing material, or as emanating from the divine. Given scripture's profession of God as sovereignly free (Ps. 103.19), one (Exod. 3.14; Deut. 6.4), eternal (Deut. 33.27; Ps. 90.2; Isa. 40.28; Rev. 22.13) and omnipotent (Rom. 1.20), creation *ex nihilo* becomes a way of expressing a distinct monotheism, as well as a particular doctrine of creation.

So how are we to understand the teaching that God creates out of nothing? To explore the meaning of creation *ex nihilo* further, we turn now to examine this teaching within the context of the doctrine of God as this is represented in the work of some of the greatest Christian thinkers of the ancient and medieval periods, particularly Augustine of Hippo (AD 354–430) and Thomas Aquinas (c. 1225– 1274).

Creation *ex nihilo*: Divine simplicity

As we have seen, an overriding concern of Christian theology is the need to establish the distinction between God and creation. Relevant to this are certain attributes of created existence: creatures are finite, temporal and contingent. To refer to creation as *contingent* is to point out that it might not exist. In other words, there is nothing about a creature that is sufficient to ensure its existence. Furthermore, by its very nature a creature, because it does not explain its own existence, points to something whose existence requires no further explanation, that is to say, it is uncreated.

One way in which traditional theology establishes this difference between the created and the uncreated is with the notion of divine simplicity. Augustine draws a clear connection between divine simplicity and creation:

There is, then, a Good which alone is simple, and therefore alone immutable, and this is God. By this Good all other goods have been created; but they are not simple, and therefore are not immutable.[24]

To understand the concept of simplicity, it is easiest to begin with creatures because this is the realm with which we are familiar. A creature is composed of parts that are assembled to form a whole; it has a structure that is often very complex. For example, there are parts of the human body or parts of a plant. In addition to their material parts, creatures are also composed of qualities or attributes. In the case of human beings, we might point to power and knowledge. However, my particular power and knowledge are not essential to my nature but are *additions to*, or *qualifications of*, my human existence; I *possess* them. In other words, I can acquire my power and knowledge through growing and learning or I can lose my power and knowledge through illness, forgetfulness or ageing, but I would still exist. So a creature may acquire certain attributes and lose those attributes and this implies that creatures change. This also suggests that a creature has a structure that includes existence – for example, existence plus knowledge plus power. To put it another way, a creature is *composed* of existence plus certain attributes that may change over time. Recalling that we can even speak of existence is something a creature *receives* and *possesses* – because the source of its existence lies elsewhere and not within itself – there is nothing about a creature that suggests that it must exist. Ultimately, a creature also comes into existence and out of existence. Therefore, according to Augustine, creaturely reality is identified by a fundamentally composite structure, which we can express in terms of the distinction between what something *is* and what something *has*. I *have* the ability to speak French, but I *am not* that ability. I could forget how to speak French and I would still be me (although of course I would have changed). To put that matter another way, creatures have an existence to which is added accidental qualities to make it this or that *kind of thing*.

In referring to God as simple, Augustine wishes to claim that there is no distinction between what God *is* and what God *has*. So God's attributes (what God *has*) and God's existence (what God *is*) are one and the same. God does not possess anything because possession implies the possibility of loss and contingency and this is characteristic of the creaturely realm. With reference to God the Trinity, Augustine writes:

> It is for this reason, then, that the nature of the Trinity is called simple, because it has not anything that it can lose, and because it is not something different from what it has, in the way that a vessel is different from its liquid or a body from its colour or the air from its light or heat, or the mind from its wisdom. For none of these things is what it has: the vessel is not liquid; the body is not colour; the air is not light or heat; the mind is not wisdom.[25]

God simply *is* his wisdom, power, knowledge and so on. These are not merely attributes that God might or might not have. God *is* these attributes and is therefore not subject to change. One implication of this is that God has no structure; divine simplicity is the metaphysical expression of God's perfect unity and oneness.

Writing more than eight centuries later, the Italian Dominican theologian Thomas Aquinas clarified the concept of divine simplicity by pointing out that creatures are subject to a most fundamental composition: essence and existence. In other words, it is not of a creature's essence – it is not essential to it – that it exist. Existence is not essential or definitive of a horse, a tree or a person; these things might or might not exist. In that sense they are contingent. This means that, within the order of creation, things receive and possess their existence as an addition to their essence, to what they are. This is not the case with God and this is how we distinguish God from creation: it is of God's essence that God exists. So in God, essence (*what* God is) is perfectly continuous with God's existence (*that* God is).[26]

Aquinas's view of divine simplicity can also be explained using two categories he inherits from Aristotle: 'substance' and 'accident'.[27] A creature's 'substance' is its essential nature, what makes it what it is, for example a 'cow' or 'man'.[28] By contrast, an 'accident' is a quality or attribute that something possesses that is not definitive of what that thing is; it is possessed 'accidentally'. [29] For example, my substantial nature is human male but my brown hair is accidental. I ould dye my hair red and I would still be the same human person. Qualities such as height, weight, colour or physical fitness are not definitive of who or what I am; I may gain or lose such qualities but my substantial nature would remain the same. The categories of substance and accident allow Aquinas to distinguish between an accidental change and a substantial change. An accidental change occurs to a tree when its accidents are altered – the colour of its leaves during autumn, for example. When the woodsman fells the tree to turn it into timber for the construction of a house, this would constitute a substantial change – an alteration in what something is, in this case a change from tree to timber to house.[30] According to Aquinas, God is animmutable and eternal substance, lacking all accidents. This is not to say that God is *a* substance, a 'this' rather than a 'that', because God is not a type of thing.[31] Rather, 'the substance of God is therefore his existence.'[32] This is another way of saying that in God there is no composition of substance plus existence; existence *is* the very substance of God.

So the concept of divine simplicity allows Augustine and Aquinas to distinguish between God and creation. On the one hand, creatures possess their attributes and can therefore be distinguished from those attributes. They can gain or lose them. In fact, even existence itself is something that does not belong *properly* (i.e., intrinsically or by nature) to a creature; it is received, possessed and may be lost. As such, creaturely existence is composed or structured. By contrast, God does not receive or possess existence. It is of God's essence to exist; essence and existence are one and the same in God. God therefore exists by necessity and is totally *uncaused*. Aquinas expresses this by referring to God as *ipsum esse per se subsistens*, 'self-subsistent being itself'.[33]

By establishing God as simple in this way, Aquinas shows us that God is the source of *all* created being because God is 'being itself'. There is nothing that exists that does not owe its existence wholly and immediately to God. As such, God is 'the principle and cause of being to other things'.[34] Because God is the source of *everything* that is *not* God, this suggests that we must not speak of God creating the universe from some always-present material stuff that does not owe its existence to God. We might say that, according to creation *ex nihilo*, the universe does not have a material cause; there is not some stuff out of which God fabricates the cosmos. God is the source not only of particular things, but also of existence per se. The consequence of viewing God as the ultimate source and principle of existence itself – or the *archē* of all things, to use the Greek of the Septuagint – is that we must speak of God creating 'out of nothing', because there is no thing whose existence is not caused by God.

The claim that there is no material cause to creation (there is no matter upon which God works to form the universe) marks an important distinction between our acts of making and God's act of creation. When we make something, say a pot or a car, we work with existing material to reform it into something else. One thing – a lump of clay or some metal and rubber – becomes something else – a pot or a car. The material with which we work resists us to some degree; we have to mould it by force into something else. The material restricts us in the sense that we can make some things with our particular material, but not others. For example, I could make a pot out of clay but I could not make a car or a hammer out of clay. Unlike our acts of making, God is not restricted in his creation by the characteristics of some pre-existent material stuff. There is no limit to God's creativity because it is the origin of existence itself, including matter. There is no material stuff to resist God. So creation *ex nihilo*, in denying that there is a material cause to creation, preserves the divine freedom in the act of creating. Our acts of creativity participate in, or presuppose, God's creation of all things out of nothing.

This concept of participation – sharing in God's primordial creativity – points to another important way in which Aquinas distinguishes between God and creation that we will encounter again in later chapters. Whereas God exists essentially (*ens per essentiam*), creation exists by participation (*ens per participationem*).[35] He puts it this way in the *Summa Contra Gentiles*.

> Every thing, furthermore, exists because it has being. A thing whose essence is not its being, consequently, is not *through its essence*, but *by participation* in something, namely, being itself. But that which is through participation in something cannot be the first being, because prior to it is the being in which it participates in order to be. But God is the first being, with nothing prior to Him. The essence of God, therefore, is His own being.[36]

In this dense passage, Aquinas wishes to claim something quite straightforward: creation does not exist of its own power or by its own right. It is not self-standing. In other words, existence is not *proper* to creation. Instead, creation's being is 'borrowed' from God via participation in God. Creation exists because it participates in that which exists in and of itself, namely God. There are two important corollaries of this view. First, as we will see in more detail in the next chapter, when we speak of God's act of creation, we are not to think of there being some entity called 'God' to which we add another entity alongside God that we call 'creation'. For Aquinas, it is not a matter of there being 'God' and then suddenly at the moment of creation 'God plus the universe'. There is only one focus of existence, namely God. Everything else exists by sharing in God's existence just as terrestrial things are warm or visible not in their own right, but because they participate in the light of the sun. Secondly, strictly speaking creation *in itself* is nothing because it is in continual receipt of its being from God. It is held in existence at every moment by God's gracious donation of being. This brings us to a vital aspect of creation *ex nihilo*: as well as creating without any pre-existent material stuff, God sustains creation in existence 'out of nothing' *at every moment*. Creation hovers over nothingness at every instant, held in existence only by God's sustaining power. This moment now, as you are reading this book, is just as much *ex nihilo* as the very first instant of creation.

Creation *ex nihilo:* The relation between God and creation

For Aquinas creation is wholly contingent because it exists only by participation in God's eternal simplicity. This has yet another important consequence: there is a radical and irreducible asymmetry between God and creation. It is not that God is a bit like a very powerful and very creative person. The difference between God and creation is not a difference in degree or even a difference in kind. It is a sheer and utterly unique difference because God exists in himself, whereas creation exists always and only by participation in God, by virtue of God's creative gratuity. This leads Aquinas to describe the relation between God and creation in a way that has often been a source of misunderstanding and controversy: while God creates, knows, governs and loves creation, the relation between God and creatures is real in creatures but not in God.[37] This does not mean that God is unrelated to creation or that God is indifferent to creation. Although the discussion of relations in ancient and medieval philosophy is very complex and the concept is technical, what Aquinas has in mind with regard to God and creation can be stated succinctly. Let us start with the first of Aquinas's three kinds of relation: real relations.

Two subjects can be related to each other in such a way that they are mutually constitutive and have something in common. This might be a shared characteristic; for example, Alice can be taller than Clare because they have height in common. Also, an action between two terms might cause them to be related. For example, a company can hire a worker and, by this action, the two terms – the company and the worker – become related and mutually constitutive, as employer and employee. Similarly, a couple can be related via a mediating action such as a hug or a kiss. Aquinas calls such relations 'real' because they bring about a change in *both* terms. In such real relations one term always implies the other. Where there is a wife there is a husband and vice versa; where there is an employer there is an employee and vice versa. Such relations are symmetrical in that the terms constitute each other in a particular way, for example as husband and wife or employer and employee.

Aquinas also identifies a variety of relations which are 'logical' or 'relations according to reason'.[38] Such relations occur only in the mind and do not change either term. For example, we might relate Black Beauty to the equine species. Another example would be the relation between two future beings such as the relation between my grandchildren and me. At the time of writing (and, I hope, for some time to come) this is a relation only according to reason and not a real relation.[39] Such logical relations are a kind of association or classification in the mind.

As well as real relations and relations according to reason, Aquinas also describes a third kind of relation, one which involves both real and logical elements. These are 'mixed relations'. A good example of a mixed relation would be my relation to the city of Prague when I visit as a tourist. I come to know about Prague and, as such, my relation to Prague is real in me because it changes me. Prague's relation to me, however, is merely logical because my knowledge of the city does not change Prague. The relation between a knower (in this case, me as a tourist) and something known (in this case, Prague) is one of Aquinas's examples of a mixed relation.

In describing the relation between God and creation as 'logical' in God and 'real' in creation, Aquinas is describing a mixed relation.[40] As such, he wishes to make some important claims about the *asymmetrical* relation between God and creation. First, creation is a reality wholly in the creature but not in God. In other words, God's act of creation immediately constitutes a creature's very existence, but creation does not constitute, establish or define God in any way. God would be God and creator whether or not creation existed. The act of creation does not realize any potential in God. This means that, even though God wills creation, God does not need to create in order to fulfil himself. At first glance this appears coldly logical as a way of describing God's relation to creation. It is important, however, to recognize that it helps us to understand creation as an act of free and selfless love. Imagine I have creative potential as an artist or musician. In practising my skills I realize something in myself; there is a benefit to me as well as to those who (against all the odds) appreciate my painting or musicianship. I *need* to practise my skills in order to fulfil myself. There is a degree of obligation: to realize myself as an artist or musician I must paint or play the piano. In God's act of creation, he gains nothing; he is therefore in no way compelled or obliged to create. There is, as it were, no ulterior motive. God creates as a pure selfless act of donation. There is only one beneficiary of God's creative act: creation itself. For this reason it is a pure and free gift, a theme to which we will return in the final chapter.

In describing God's relation to creation as real in creatures, Aquinas also wants to point out that the relation between creatures is not like the relation between creatures and God. For a start, while it is the case that all our creaturely relations together help to comprise our identity, none of those relations, of themselves, entirely constitute what a creature is. For example, I am related to many people and institutions, but none of those relations is *wholly* constitutive of what I am. I might be related to a particular company as its employee and I could leave that company's employment, but I would still be the same person, albeit a changed person. We might say that such relations, although very important and precious, are accidental to who and what I am. But there is one relation that is wholly constitutive of a creature and, as it were, 'non-negotiable': a creature's relation to God. Every relation between creatures assumes a most fundamental prior relation which constitutes a creature's very being, that between the creature and God.

Finally, in describing the relation between God and creation as logical in God but real in creatures, Aquinas is able to describe the unmediated intimacy between God and creation. In any real relation between creatures there is always something held in common between creatures (e.g., a shared humanity) or a mediating act (e.g., the act of marriage). In the relation between God and creation, there is nothing held in common between the terms and neither is there a mediating act *besides* the very act of creation *ex nihilo*. God and creation do not share 'existence' or 'being' in common because God is existence itself, in which creation participates. As a result, God's relation to creation is more intimate and immediate than relations between creatures – precisely because of the sheer difference between God and creation. God can be infinitely close to creation because there is no mediating principle or act between the terms besides the very act of creation itself. Yet at the same time God remains wholly transcendent because of the sheer difference between God and creation. To reiterate, the asymmetrical relation between God and creation is not a difference of degree or a difference of kind; it is a sheer difference in which God's transcendence is at once God's immanence.

In describing the asymmetry of the relation between God and creation, we saw that God does not benefit from creation. There is no 'ulterior motive' in the sense that God does not realize himself in creating because God is eternally and fully realized. As Aquinas would say, God is 'pure act' because there is no potential in God to be other than he is. God is not required to create in order to achieve a goal or realize a potential. So why does God create? If there is no need or benefit, if God is eternally replete and fully actual, why bother? If creation is *ex nihilo*, there is nothing to benefit from creation – no potential to be realized in some pre-existent material nature, no partially made stuff waiting to be fashioned into something more orderly and beautiful. If there is no reason to create, does this mean that creation is an act of pure caprice, a sort of random decision by God to establish a created order? Because creation is from nothing, there is nothing for God to control, overcome or realize, so it looks as if creation has no basis or foundation except the inscrutable (we might even say 'random') will of God. The difference between God and creation that is established *ex nihilo* seems to be impenetrable to reason.

Following a number of patristic theologians including Augustine, this is not the way that Aquinas understands God's act of creation. The act of creation *ex nihilo* is the act of God the Trinity and it is

crucial to remember that what Aquinas writes about the difference
between God and creation has its origins in his analysis of the
difference between the divine persons who are named in scripture
as Father, Son and Holy Spirit (Mat. 3.13-17; 28.16-20).[41] God is
love (1 Jn. 4.16), love is a relation and the three divine persons
are in a triadic eternal relation that is pure love. The processions
of the persons of the Trinity establish the eternal relations of the
Godhead. The Son is eternally begotten of the Father and the Holy
Spirit proceeds from the Father and Son. The Father eternally
communicates the fullness of divinity to the Son, and the Father and
Son communicate the fullness of divinity to the Spirit. The eternal
relations of the Trinity are real relations in the sense that the persons
are wholly mutually determinative: the Father is only Father in
relation to the Son and the Spirit; the Son is only Son in relation to
the Father and the Spirit; the Spirit is only Spirit in relation to the
Father and the Son.[42] So the difference between God and creation
is not a random and inscrutable difference; it is a participation in,
or trace of, the eternal differences and relations of the Godhead.[43]
For Aquinas, the emanation of creation from God, which is freely
willed and in no sense necessary, is an image of, or a participation
in, the eternal emanation of the persons of the Trinity.[44] So God's
act of creation is not simply a result of the divine will, impenetrable
to reason. It is an expression of the very nature of God himself
as eternally self-giving. As the Father communicates himself in
the procession of the Son, and the Father and Son communicate
their love in the procession of the Holy Spirit, so God's love is
communicated in the freely willed communication of created being
in creation *ex nihilo*. Aquinas writes, 'Hence also God the Father
made the creature through His Word, which is His Son; and through
His Love, which is the Holy Ghost. And so the processions of the
Persons are the type of the productions of creatures inasmuch as
they include the essential attributes, knowledge and will.'[45]

So creation *ex nihilo* is not simply an act of the divine will. It
is also an expression of God's eternal nature as self-donating love.
The real relation of creation to God is a participation in the real
relations of the persons of the Trinity. In pointing to this connection
between God's act of creation and God's eternal and revealed
nature, Aquinas is reflecting a crucial principle which can be traced
to Aristotelian and Neoplatonic theology and philosophy: effects
resemble their causes.[46] In order to understand what this means,

consider an artist who produces landscape paintings. The effect – the painting – will resemble the cause – the artist. Of course, this does not necessarily mean that the painting will *look* like the artist, although there are some cause–effect relations in which the effect does look like the cause (biological reproduction, for example). In the case of the artist and her paintings, it means that the painting will reflect something of the artist's training, skill, style and visual interpretation of the world. Any given effect will, at least in this sense, resemble or represent its cause. The same is the case with creation understood as an effect of its cause, God. Creation *ex nihilo* resembles God's freedom, power and eternal relations of love.

Creation *ex nihilo*: Motion and time

God's act of creation *ex nihilo* is the origin and basis of all events within the created order. As such, it must be distinguished from natural processes. If it were a natural process, it would also require some kind of explanation. So creation is not just another event; it is the *archē* or principle of all things. In order to distinguish creation itself from events *within* the created order, Aquinas insists that creation is not a motion.[47] By 'motion' he means any kind of change – including change of place (locomotion), change of quality (e.g., learning) or change of quantity (e.g., growing). Motion involves succession – one thing becoming another. It is a process by which something that already exists realizes its potential. By denying that creation is a motion, Aquinas wishes to claim that creation is not a process. That is, it is not one thing becoming another. Such processes belong only *within* the natural order. To reiterate: because the act of creation is the very principle of the natural processes which occur within the natural order, it cannot itself be a process – otherwise the act of creation itself would require further explanation in terms of something else. So creation *ex nihilo* is the absolute beginning and origin – if you like, the ontological 'point zero' – which is the basis of creation's motion.

In turn, motion is clearly linked to time, although the nature of time has been disputed in ancient, medieval and modern physics. For thinkers such as Augustine and Aquinas – who followed the precedent set by Plato and Aristotle – time is the measure of motion. By means of time, we can measure different motions relative to each other – the fraction of a second for the beat of a bird's wing, the twenty minutes it takes us to walk a mile, the three years it takes us to learn a new language. In the seventeenth century the question of absolute time and space arose in the classical mechanics of Isaac Newton (1643–1727): Would time pass in the absence of motion? In the twentieth century, a new physics particularly associated with Albert Einstein (1879–1955) introduced the notion of relative time. Creation *ex nihilo* presents us with a very important and tricky question with respect to time: if creation is the origin or beginning of everything, does it mean that time itself had a beginning? This is how creation *ex nihilo* is often interpreted, as meaning that there was a 'time zero', akin to the Big Bang, that is the absolute temporal beginning of everything. Contrary to Aristotle's teaching, there was a moment of creation. The universe has not always existed. Time is not everlasting.

A philosophical problem arises, however, because 'beginning' is itself a temporal concept. If creation *ex nihilo* means not only that God sustains creation in existence *ex nihilo* at every instant, but also that there was a first instant, can we ask what happened prior to that first instant? We cannot, because there is nothing before creation or before time itself. The notion of there being a first instant of time seems philosophically confused because any instant of time, even the first instant, is framed or defined by a 'before' and 'after'. But if there were a 'before' to the first instant of time, it would not be the first instant; it would follow something else.[48]

The question of the nature of the universe's beginning is, of course, one of the most fundamental and enduring in theology and philosophy. Many Greek philosophers, observing the unchanging and cyclical nature of the heavens, believed matter to be eternal. The circle has no beginning or end, yet is finite. This seemed to rule out an absolute temporal beginning to the cosmos. The Epicurean and Stoic philosophers challenged Aristotle's view on the grounds that we observe perishability in parts of the cosmos, so the whole must be perishable too. On this view, time would have an end, if not a beginning. Later Neoplatonic philosophers, including Plotinus, argued against the Christian view that the universe had a beginning on the grounds that a temporal origin (non-being temporally succeeded by being) would imply that God had changed in deciding to create – and change cannot be predicated of the divine. Following Anselm in his *Monologion*,[49] most thinkers of the thirteenth century argued that creation *ex nihilo* does not simply deny a material cause of the universe, but must also refer creation's temporal origin. According to Bonaventure (c. 1217–1274) and Aquinas's teacher Albert the Great (d.1280), the universe began to exist after not existing and the doctrine of creation *ex nihilo* is incompatible with the view that the universe is eternal.

Aquinas took a more subtle approach. He argued that there is nothing inherently contradictory in the view that the universe is eternal, although we should be cautious about the use of the word 'eternal'. When applied to God, 'eternal' does not mean that God simply goes on and on and on. It means that God is beyond time. God's existence is not a matter of succession (one thing after another) but is 'one'. So God's 'time' is singular and simple. We are not supposed to be able to imagine what such existence might be like. It is unimaginable because our existence is temporally divisible; we live in the moment between before and after. So this concept of 'eternity' when applied to God is negative in the sense that it tells us what God's existence is *not*: it is not divisible according to time. By contrast, when applied to the universe 'eternal' denotes that time has no beginning or end. It is in this sense that Aristotle believed that the universe is eternal. Aquinas thinks Aristotle's view is probable (what he calls 'relatively demonstrable') but not subject to strict philosophical proof because God does not will creation's existence necessarily. Creation might not be, so it is not necessarily of everlasting time.[50]

Aquinas's view is that we know by faith that there is creation, but creation can also be demonstrated by reason. He distinguishes creation from making something because whereas making something implies pre-existent material, creation means 'to produce a thing into being according to its entire substance'.[51] In addition to this, creation *ex nihilo* has a twofold meaning. First, it means that the creator is the source of the entire being of the creature, including its material nature, in such a way that 'the causality of the creator extends to everything that is in the thing'.[52] Secondly, non-being is prior to being not in a temporal sense but by a 'priority of nature'. What Aquinas means is that when a creature normally receives something – say a lump of clay receiving the form of a pot – something comes before what is received. In other words, there is a recipient. In the case of creation *ex nihilo*, it is not the case that something is already there, which then receives being. There is nothing prior to the creature's receipt of its very existence. Left to itself, creation would not lack something; it would simply cease to exist. Aquinas sums this up in a passage in his treatise *The Power of God* (*De Potentia Dei*):

> We should say that God does not by one action bring things into existing and by another preserve them in existing, since the very existing of permanent things is divisible only incidentally, as it is subject to movement, and it is as such instantaneous. And so God's action intrinsically causing a thing to exist does not differ insofar as it causes the beginning and the continuation of existing.[53]

So Aquinas does not interpret creation *ex nihilo* to mean that God starts creation off from nothing and then, by a secondary act, sustains creation in being. The beginning and continuation of creation's existence are one and the same creative act of God. Yet revealed faith requires that we add a further interpretation of creation *ex nihilo*, namely 'that the creature should have non-being prior to being [even] in duration, so that it is said to be "out of nothing" because it is temporally after nothing'.[54] The notion that creation *ex nihilo* concerns a temporal beginning to the universe is an article of revealed faith which cannot be demonstrated and is therefore not granted by the philosophers.

In the end, Aquinas agrees that creation *ex nihilo* means that creation had a temporal beginning or a 'time zero', but as a matter of faith rather than philosophical demonstration. This does not mean that faith contradicts reason, but that faith adds an extra dimension of understanding that enhances the rational exploration of creation by philosophy. What does faith add?

> Things are said to be created in the beginning of time, not as if the beginning of time were a measure of creation, but because together with time heaven and earth were created.[55]

Aquinas is stating that creation *ex nihilo* means there is no 'before' and 'after' to God's creation. Nevertheless, God is the absolute source of everything that is not God, including time. In faith, we must therefore talk of time itself having a beginning. At that beginning, the absolute origin of everything that is not God, we have reached the edge of our words.

Creation *ex nihilo*: Contemporary science

At the turn of the twentieth century, the most popular cosmology among physicists was known as the 'steady-state' theory. On this view, the universe is in more or less the same state at any moment. As it expands, matter is created. The French priest and physicist, Georges Lemaître (1894–1966), proposed a different approach to the expanding universe that he called 'the hypothesis of the primeval atom'. Lemaître suggested that the universe began with an explosion from what later became known as a singularity, the 'primeval atom'. In 1949, the Cambridge cosmologist Fred Hoyle (1915–2001), who preferred the steady-state theory, coined the phrase 'Big Bang' to describe Lemaître's view. The 'Big Bang', now a very familiar term, suggests that the universe expanded and cooled from a primordial hot and dense condition around fourteen billion years ago.

The idea of a 'Big Bang' immediately drew comparisons with creation *ex nihilo*. Did this finally provide scientific evidence for the theological view that creation came from nothing? More recently, scientists have been keen to explain how the universe could come from nothing without the need to involve God.

A moment's thought reveals that Big Bang cosmology and creation *ex nihilo* are not one and the same view of the origins of the cosmos. The reasons why they cannot coincide are both scientific and theological. The first reason concerns the nature of scientific enquiry. Science deals with processes *within* the natural order – one thing becoming another. Whenever cosmologists attempt to define creation from nothing in scientific terms, it always turns out to be something coming from something else.[56] Recall that 'nothing' in creation *ex nihilo* is not a vacuum of any description, not even a quantum vacuum. 'Nothing' means just that: 'nothing'. If science were to say anything about this 'nothing' and what comes from it, it would stop being science and would become metaphysics. This is precisely Aquinas's point when he says that creation is not any kind of motion. In other words, creation is not one thing becoming another. While contemporary cosmology might not contradict creation *ex nihilo*, they are not coterminous.

The second reason why Big Bang cosmology cannot be one with creation *ex nihilo* is because the latter is more about the nature of God and creation's relation to God than it is a description or explanation of 'how or when God got the universe running'. As we have seen, creation *ex nihilo* is about the absolute ontological priority of God and the asymmetrical relation between God and creation. It preserves the distinction between God and creation and establishes what we *do not* mean by 'creation' – a process of manufacture or a necessary overflow of divine being. Moreover, creation *ex nihilo* is concerned not only with a temporal beginning of creation, but also with creation's utterly contingent nature at every moment. Creation exists 'suspended' over nothingness, sharing in God's eternal existence. There is, therefore, no competition between contemporary cosmology and the theology and metaphysics of creation *ex nihilo*. Their origins and implications are quite different.[57]

Conclusion

Creation *ex nihilo* is a distinctive mark of the Jewish, Christian and Muslim understanding of God's creative act. It emerges from certain convictions concerning what we must say of God if we are to preserve the distinction between God and creation. God is the absolute source of all that is not God, including matter, space and time. Creation *ex nihilo* is also what the theologian John Webster calls 'a distributed doctrine': it appears throughout Christian theology's treatment of its central topics.

> Our understanding of creation is amplified and deepened by this frequent recurrence, for its full scope and meaning become apparent in relation to what is said about other divine works of nature, such as preservation and governance, and, most of all, in relation to what is said in the works of grace which culminate in the missions of the Son of God and the Holy Spirit.[58]

One of the key implications of creation *ex nihilo* is that creatures, in themselves, are nothing. The relation between God and creation is radically asymmetrical. Creation only exists by participation in God's sustaining power, an idea we will explore further in the next chapter. For some critics of creation *ex nihilo*, this renders the creature wholly debased, having no intrinsic worth. To reduce the creature to nothing *but* its relation to God seems to evacuate the creature of any true significance.[59]

Such a criticism represents a deep misunderstanding of creation *ex nihilo*. It is certainly the case that creation from nothing points to the radically *gifted* nature of created being, an idea to which we will return in the final chapter. Creation is, however, a pure act of gratuitous love precisely because God gains nothing by creating. In fact, one of the perplexing questions for Christian theology is why, given God's eternal perfection and repletion, he would create. As we have seen, it cannot be due to any lack or need because God realizes nothing in creating. The act of creation, therefore, can only be described as a primal instance of *utter* gratuity with no 'ulterior motive'. It is the pure donation of existence by love that includes the donation of integrity and value: '*Because of* (not *in spite of*) the non-reciprocal character of the relation of creator and creature, the creature has integrity.'[60] Creation is not an act of coercion, compulsion or even persuasion. It is the purely peaceful, totally free and unnecessary donation of existence from nothing. Creation's participation in God, the source of its being and fount of its integrity, is the subject of the next chapter.

3

God and Creation: Participation and Providence

When attempting to identify the fundamentals of the natural world, today's sciences tend to focus particularly on temporal origins or beginnings. Cosmologists can roll back the clock to consider mathematically the physical conditions of the universe just the tiniest fraction of a second after the so-called 'Big Bang'. Biologists seek to understand evolution across millions of years by returning to the most primitive forms of life and 'the origin of species'. It seems that if we can return to temporal origins – to the beginning of the universe or the critical early stages of primitive evolution – we can unlock the secrets of the universe or grasp the essence of life. Given this privileging of origins, it is no surprise that the theology of creation in the modern period, under the heavy influence of the natural sciences, has focused particularly on the question of 'when and how it all began' or the conditions established by God at the beginning of time by which the universe continues to work like clockwork. In exploring Genesis and creation *ex nihilo* in the first two chapters of this book, we seem to be following this tendency to focus on temporal origins. The theology of creation, however, is not simply about how creation began. It is more concerned with the present order and purpose of creation. God's ordering and continual care for creation and God's loving guidance of creatures towards their proper end is known as the doctrine of providence. It is concerned with the way that God continually provides for creation. This is the subject of the present chapter.

In the previous chapter we examined the concept of divine simplicity and Aquinas's distinction between God who exists in himself (*ens per essentiam*) and creation that exists by participation (*ens per participationem*).[1] We also noted the asymmetrical relation between God and creation. That relation is real in creatures but not in God. This means that creation is wholly reliant on its relation to God who creates *ex nihilo*, while God realizes nothing in himself by his act of creation. God has no need of creation, so creation is an act of pure loving donation with no self-interest. In the act of creation there is not one thing (God) and then suddenly two things (God plus creation). There is only one focus of existence – God – and everything else exists in a relation of participation in God. We will continue to focus particularly on Aquinas in the present chapter because so many subsequent theologies of creation are elucidations of, or responses to, Aquinas's thought on this matter. His works synthesize patristic theology, Aristotelian philosophy and Neoplatonism in order to expound the meaning and implications of scripture's witness to God's creative act. Before proceeding to examine the doctrine of providence and the order of causation within creation, we need to clarify further the relation of creation to God and the nature of creaturely participation in God as understood by Aquinas. To do this, we will start at an unexpected place, namely his discussion of theological language towards the beginning of the *Summa Theologiae*. How we talk about God is not simply a matter of convention. It reflects our relation as creatures to God who created us. Exploring Aquinas's view of the way we *speak* analogically of God will allow us to understand in more detail the way we *exist* in analogical relation to God.

Having clarified further the relation of creation to God in Aquinas's thought, we will be able to explore the idea that God provides for creation. Providence implies that God acts within creation to achieve his purposes. How are we to understand divine action in relation to creaturely activity? Because God is the source of existence and not just another item in a long list of things that exist, neither can God be just one more cause among other causes. If God were one among a series of causes, he would be part of the created order and not the source of the created order. In order to understand the relation between divine and creaturely causation, we will explore the concept of creation's participation in God and the analogy between divine existence and creaturely existence. This relation is, in turn, the basis of the analogy between God's providential action and creaturely action.

At the heart of the doctrine of providence is the idea that creation is ordered to certain ends or goals. In other words, creation exhibits purpose. You read this book in order to learn more about the doctrine of creation. The sculptor hammers at the marble in order to make a statue that will decorate the hall. The flower is brightly coloured in order to attract pollinating insects. The phrases 'in order to' or 'for the purpose of' indicate orientation towards a certain end or goal. In ancient and medieval theology and philosophy, such ends – the objects of purposive activity – are understood as causes. The goal of understanding causes you to read this book; the goal of decorating the hall causes the sculptor to hammer at the marble; the goal of satisfying my hunger causes me to go to the shop. These 'goals' are known as 'final causes' and the study of final causes is known as 'teleology', from the Greek *telos* meaning 'goal' or 'end'.[2] God provides purposes for creatures and the identification of these goals help to explain creaturely activity. Theologians also identify the way in which God provides the means for the achievement of creaturely ends. We will see that, for Aquinas, ever-deeper participation in God's goodness is the final goal or purpose of his creation.

The claim that God orders creation to certain good ends raises a number of crucial questions. For example, how are we to understand the occurrence of evil and suffering within a providentially governed creation? Does God eternally will such evil and suffering as a means of achieving his good purposes? Are creation and its history determined? Or are we to say that evil is not caused or willed by God but that, despite their rebellion, God eternally wills the good of creatures and redeems their fallen nature? It will become apparent that the distinction between what God wills and what God permits is crucial to the doctrine of providence. In this chapter, we will gradually sketch a picture of God's loving providence as infinitely present to creatures, but not at the cost of creation's integrity and freedom. First, however, we will examine Aquinas's understanding of how we speak of God by analogy in order to understand the nature of creation's analogical relation to God.

Speaking of God and creation: Participation and the analogy of being

For Aquinas, it is not at all obvious that we are able to speak of God, because our words are orientated towards finite things – the natural world, human beings and so on – and using those same words to refer to the infinity of God would surely stretch them beyond breaking point. Whenever we speak about God we would seem to use words more properly suited to creatures. Such speech must surely be futile because God infinitely exceeds any thought or conception we might have of him. Yet we do speak about God, whether in schools, universities, seminaries or the liturgy of the church. The observation that we apparently cannot speak of God and yet we do speak of God is the beginning of Aquinas's consideration of theological language and the naming of God. How, for Aquinas, can we speak of God? In answering this question, Aquinas is not providing us with a theory of language that we might then deploy in speaking about God. Rather, he is beginning with some comments about how we happily get on with the business of speaking about God. His key question is this: how can we be sure that we are speaking about *God* and not, say, an angel – that is, something created?

There is one crucial observation that Aquinas makes prior to his consideration of theological language and it is important that we are aware of this context. However we speak of God, we must use words that we more commonly associate with finite creation. As Aquinas says, we name God from creatures.[3] We are permitted to do this because of a principle that Aquinas accepts from Aristotle and Neoplatonism that we encountered in the last chapter: effects resemble their causes.[4] Think of a cause–effect relation, say a potter (the cause) who makes a pot (the effect). Does Aquinas mean that pots look like potters? Obviously not. He only wishes to say that any effect will express something of the character or 'style' of its cause. So a pot reflects the potter's skill, intention, imagination and creativity. In a somewhat similar sense (although qualifications apply), because God is the cause of creation, creation will express something of the character of God, however faintly or obliquely. In one of his early works, Aquinas makes the striking comment that 'every knower knows God implicitly in whatever thing he knows' precisely because creation resembles God, its creator.[5] This is the basis on which we name God from creatures. In some sense, creatures are like God, so when we use creaturely words to refer to God those words are not completely out of place. At a more pragmatic level, Aquinas simply wishes to note that, when we speak of God, we use words that are more readily used of creatures. Nevertheless, deploying words that are usually used of creatures when we speak about God is not straightforward. For example, we know what it means to call a dog or a recipe 'good'; we should not be so quick to think that we can identify or define divine goodness, because such goodness is infinite and of a wholly different order. In order to identify what we mean by 'a good dog' or 'a good recipe', we must know what kind of thing a dog or a recipe is, because they exemplify goodness in different ways according to their natures. However, we do not know what God is, for God is not a type of thing. God is not just one among others, classifiable under genus or species. Yet because God is the cause of creation, creation will express something of its divine origin. Aquinas writes:

> Now it was shown above that in this life we cannot see the essence of God; but we know God from creatures as their principle, and also by way of excellence and remotion. In this way therefore He can be named by us from creatures, yet not so that the name which signifies Him expresses the divine essence in itself.[6]

One of the most obvious ways in which we speak of God is figuratively or metaphorically. The Bible is replete with metaphorical speech about God: for example, when we say that 'God is my rock'. We might understand metaphor in a number of ways, but most generally it should be observed that metaphors are *literally* false (God is not literally a rock). Yet they certainly carry a weight of truth that we would struggle to express in purely literal speech. Metaphorical speech, in already being somewhat indirect and tentative, does not seem to present us with such an acute problem when used to refer to God, for there is no pretence to be speaking literally or directly. Some would say that simple metaphorical speech about God (of which there are countless examples in the Bible, such as God walking in the garden in Genesis 3) is most appropriate, because such speech could not be mistaken for literal reference to God. It is a constant reminder that literal speech about

God is problematic. Yet we clearly speak of God using more than metaphor. It is surely not straightforwardly metaphorical to call God 'good' or 'wise'. So how else might we speak of God?

There are two ways of speaking of God that Aquinas dismisses for a number of reasons. The first suggests that, when we make statements such as 'God is good', we *only* mean that God is the cause of goodness. In other words, God is good simply because he causes goodness in others. This, however, is problematic: God is also the cause of bodies, yet God is not a body. The difficulty that Aquinas is trying to avoid is the notion that goodness is caused by God in creatures but does not belong to God himself. Aquinas wishes to maintain that goodness belongs primarily to God. Alternatively, we might think that when we speak of God we do so negatively. So when we say God is good we are not suggesting that we have any positive purchase on what it is for God to be good; we are merely saying that 'God is not evil'. Broadly speaking, this is the basis of what is sometimes known as negative theology or the *via negativa* (the negative way). At one level, Aquinas is deeply attracted to this tradition that refers to God not by a process of positive ascription, but by negating our conception of God due to its infinite inadequacy. However, Aquinas's reason for not opting wholeheartedly for the so-called *via negativa* is that in some instances we do speak of God positively and we apparently mean what we say. So how might we best make sense of this positive speech about God?

Pursuing this question, Aquinas begins by pointing out that the words that we use of God might be deployed equivocally or univocally. When we equivocate, we use what is apparently the same word but in utterly unrelated ways. For example, we might refer to 'the pitcher of beer' and 'the baseball pitcher', thus using the word 'pitcher' equivocally to the point where we might wonder whether we are, in any meaningful sense, using the same word. When we use words 'univocally' – literally 'with one voice' – the use is identical. For example, we might refer to 'John's wisdom' and 'Peter's wisdom', using the word 'wisdom' univocally. For Aquinas, when we speak of God we do not equivocate, but neither do we speak univocally. When we say 'God is good' and 'Benedict is good' we are using the word 'good' neither equivocally (in completely different senses) nor univocally (in identical senses). We are not speaking univocally because what it means for God to be good is not what it means for Benedict to be good, even though Benedict's goodness might be an expression of, or a faint reflection of, divine goodness. What it means for a human person to be good is not what it means for God to be good, just as what it means for a dog to be faithful is not what it means for a husband to be faithful. Yet we are not using these terms equivocally, so there appears to be a relation between our use of terms such as 'good' and 'faithful' when applied in different circumstances with reference to different things. Does this suggest that there is an intermediate path between equivocation and univocation?

That middle path is known as analogy. When we speak of God, we do so analogically. Thirteenth-century logic borrowed from Aristotle the view that analogy is a kind of proportion between two things. Within this broad definition, there are a number of understandings of analogy which might meet Aquinas's needs in describing the way in which we speak of God, but he clearly opts for what is known as analogy of attribution (*analogia attributionis*). Let us consider Aquinas's example: health.[7] We could refer to many things as 'healthy' – Aquinas mentions a complexion, a diet and urine. They are healthy in different but not totally unrelated ways. What they share is a common focus. A complexion, for example, is not healthy in itself, but is indicative of health in a person. Likewise, urine is not healthy in itself, but indicates the health of a person. A diet is not healthy in itself, but insofar as it brings about health in a person. Indeed, a particular diet may be healthy for one person but not for another. A high-fibre diet rich in wheat, for example, may be healthy for one person but disastrous for someone suffering from coeliac disease. So a person is healthy in herself and other things (such as a diet) are called healthy by virtue of their relation to that person. The person who is healthy is the common focus of other things – complexion, diet and so on – to which we ascribe 'health' by analogy because of their relation to a common focus, namely a person. Health is ascribed *primarily* to the person and *secondarily* to other things (diet, complexion) by virtue of their relation to that person. It is important to note that we do not use the word 'health' in relation to a person, a complexion and a diet because they are similar kinds of thing; they belong to different genera. Rather, 'health' is used because of a relation of causality (a diet brings about the health of a person) or signification (a complexion is a sign of a person's health) to one common focus. So diets and complexions, although not healthy in themselves, are called 'healthy' because of a relation to those things (in this instance, human persons) that are healthy 'properly speaking', that is, in themselves. This is how Aquinas defines analogy:

> For in analogies the idea is not, as it is in univocals, one and the same, yet it is not totally diverse as in equivocals; but a term which is thus used in a multiple sense signifies various proportions to some one thing; thus 'healthy' applied to urine signifies the sign of animal health, and applied to medicine signifies the cause of the same health.[8]

Analogy is a way of relating things as varied as diets and complexions (things of different genera) to a single common focus.

So how does this relate to speech about God? Our language in relation to God is particularly tricky because God is not a type of thing. God cannot be classified within a particular genus. God transcends all categorization because he is the source of the categories or types into which creatures fall. Yet the radical difference between God and creatures that we earlier described in terms of the distinction between 'being through its essence' (*ens per essentiam*) and 'being through participation' (*ens per participationem*) is the basis of the connection between God and creation: God is the causal principle of creatures. We name God from creatures because God is the surpassing principle of creatures. As Aquinas puts it:

> Thus whatever is said of God and creatures, is said according to the relation of a creature to God as its principle and cause, wherein all perfections of things pre-exist excellently.[9]

What Aquinas wishes to say is that we speak of God and creatures analogously because the perfections of creatures – for example, goodness or life – pre-exist in God in a more excellent and universal way. So when we say that 'Ben is good', 'the dog is good', 'the cherry tree is good' and 'God is good', we are using the word 'good' analogously because of a likeness of the creatures (Ben, the dog and the tree) to God. What is the nature of that likeness? It is imperative that we discount one way of understanding that likeness. It is not that there is a thing called 'goodness' that hovers between creatures and God to which both creatures and God measure up. No: the common focus that allows us to name people, dogs and trees as good by analogy is

God who is supremely and transcendentally good *in himself*. Creatures are like God in being good *in their own particular way*, for example as a person, a dog or a tree, through participation in a certain likeness of God. But God is good transcendentally in himself, beyond all type and categorization. God is not good in a particular way as this or that kind of thing, but is *the Good*. By contrast, creatures are good because they participate in the transcendental source of goodness, namely God. It is not that creatures share in common an abstract quality or form that enables us to name them all as 'good'. Rather, it is God as the source and common focus of their goodness that allows us to name diverse creatures belonging to utterly different genera with the analogous name 'good'. So just as a diet, complexion and urine can be called 'healthy' by virtue of their relation to a common focus (a 'healthy' person), so a person, a dog and a tree are called 'good' by virtue of their relation to a common focus, namely God who is eternally and transcendentally (i.e., without categorization or qualification) good in himself.

For Aquinas, therefore, we name God from creatures because God is the source and common focus of creaturely existence and perfection and creatures thereby have a certain likeness to God because they are effects of divine creativity. Within our speech about God, Aquinas makes a distinction between our use of perfection terms such as 'good', 'true' and 'living' and our use of other terms that are deployed metaphorically in relation to God. Terms that are used metaphorically such as 'rock' are predicated first of creatures and secondarily of God. When applied to God, the term 'rock' is a metaphor for his steadfastness. Perfection terms, on the other hand, are predicated primarily of God and secondarily of creatures. So when we say that God is 'good' or 'wise', these perfections belong primarily to God and secondarily to creatures because these perfections flow from God to creatures. It is not that we refer to God as good or wise simply because he brings about goodness and wisdom in creatures, as when we say that a diet is called 'healthy' because it brings about the health of a person. If that were the case, God would become 'good' only when he brings about goodness in creatures. Aquinas's thinking is quite different: the perfection, which is found eternally and primarily in God, flows from God to the creature by virtue of God being that perfection in himself and the creature's participation in a likeness of God. When we call Benedict 'good' and God 'good', we are saying that Benedict's goodness is derived from God's goodness; the perfection of the good flows from God to Benedict and is received by Benedict in a finite and particular form according to his human nature – namely, as the goodness of a man.[10]

Although Aquinas claims that we can refer to God using perfection terms, he does not think that we have a firm grasp of those divine perfections themselves. When we name God as good, *what* we are referring to is certainly God's goodness as this flows to creatures. Nevertheless, *the way* we use the word 'good' is in accordance with how we know and conceive of goodness in the created realm. So Aquinas makes a distinction between *what* a word signifies (*res significata*, the thing signified), in this case goodness which belongs really and primarily to God, and *the way* in which we use that word to signify God's goodness (*modus significandi*, the mode of signification). We refer to God's goodness or wisdom, but we do so in a creaturely way as we conceive of these perfections and encounter them in the structure of our language.[11] Regarding the *res significata*, words are used primarily of God and secondarily of creatures. Regarding the *modus significandi*, words are used primarily of creatures.[12] To put the matter another way, we name God from creatures, but the perfections themselves flow from God to creatures by his creative power.

So let us recap. Perfections – good, living, true, wise – belong first to God. He is these perfections in himself without restriction or qualification. Unlike a creature, God does not *have* goodness, life and wisdom. God *is* his goodness, life and wisdom; in the simplicity of God, these perfections are one. By God's creative power, creatures receive goodness *in particular and diverse manners* as it flows from God to creatures. This means that creatures, as effects of God's creative power, resemble God as perfections flow to them and are received according to their particular natures. So the Good is received by a dog according to the nature of a dog and a tree according to the nature of a tree. Because of the likeness of creatures to God, we can name God from creatures by analogy. We can say 'God is good' or 'God is life' because we know about goodness and life in creation because goodness and life are derived from God. Yet we recognize that, although we use these terms as we encounter them in creation, they belong first to God who is their proper source. Creatures have these perfections not in themselves, but by participation in the divine perfections.

Aquinas deploys a very helpful example in order to explain the nature of participation and the likeness of creatures to God. If a cause and its effect – for example, a mother (the agent) and her child (the effect) – belong to the same species, there will be a likeness in form between the agent and the effect. To put it simply, a mother and her child are the same kind of thing, namely human beings, so the cause simply repeats itself in the effect. They are alike because they share the same form or species. There are, however, instances where a cause and its effects do not belong to the same species or even to the same genus. Aquinas uses the example of the sun. The sun's light and heat generate plants and animals and, in this remote sense, plants and animals are 'like' the sun because they participate in the sun's causal power. Plants and animals do not receive the form of the sun specifically (they are not hot, light-emitting gaseous bodies), but they share in its power according to their particular form or mode of being and therefore resemble the sun in a remote way. The sun is a universal cause in the sense that it extends its power to many different things of a lower nature. Those things participate in a diminished likeness of the sun. But what if, unlike the sun, the cause is not classifiable in any genus or species? What if the cause is not a type of thing, but is God?

> Therefore if there is an agent not contained in any 'genus', its effect will still more distantly reproduce the form of the agent, not, that is, so as to participate in the likeness of the agent's form according to the same specific or generic formality, but only according to some sort of analogy; as existence is common to all. In this way all created things, so far as they are beings, are like God as the first and universal principle of all being.[13]

Aquinas is making a very important claim. There is an analogy between creaturely perfection and divine perfection. The basis of that analogy is the flow of perfections from God to creatures. These perfections are received in a finite way by creatures according to their particular mode of being. So we do not say that the dog and the tree are good properly in themselves, but insofar as they participate in, and therefore resemble very remotely, a likeness of that which is good in itself, namely God.

Aquinas now extends this understanding from the use of terms such as good, wise and living into the realm of existence itself. His claim is that it is not just words that are analogical; 'being' (*esse*) is analogical.[14] What this means is that creation does not exist in itself, but analogically through its participation in a likeness of that which does exist essentially in itself, namely God. Being flows from God to creation but is proper only to God. To clarify the stages of the argument further, think back to the example of health. We can name a diet and a complexion as 'healthy' by analogy not because a diet and a complexion have a common characteristic, but because they share a common focus in the healthy person. It is by virtue of their relation to the healthy person that we name a complexion and a diet 'healthy' by analogy. Similarly, we can name a dog and a tree as good not because they share a common quality (what it is for a dog to be good and a tree to be good are quite different), but because they share a common focus in divine goodness. It is by virtue of their relation to God, the source of goodness, that a dog and a tree are 'good'. Extending this to being, Aquinas wishes to say that creatures have being because they share a common focus in God who is the source of being. Whereas God exists in himself (*ens per essentiam*), creation exists 'analogically' by virtue of its relation to God. The nature of that relation is one of participation (*ens per participationem*).[15]

The implication is radical and reflects very clearly the theme of creation *ex nihilo*: there is only one focus of being, only one true existent, namely God. Creation, in itself, is nothing. It exists by sharing in or borrowing God's existence according to its own finite mode of being. Creation is not outside or alongside God as an alternative focus of being, as if God and creation were separate *things*. In an important sense, creation is 'in' God and yet radically distinct because God, who is being itself, is the only source of what Aquinas calls *ens commune* – 'being in common' or 'created being'.[16] To put the matter succinctly, God and creation do not share an abstract thing called 'being' in common. Creation has a participation in God's being. Whereas God's being is simple and one, it is received in creation in many different and divided ways. This is the basis of what later became known as the analogy of being or the *analogia entis*. Creation exists by analogy to God who exists eternally in himself.[17] This marks the participation of our categorical domain – that is, the created domain of categories or types of thing – in the transcendental perfection of being as such – that is, God in his universal simplicity and perfection beyond all type or categorization.

The analogy of being, however, presents us with a potential problem. If there is only one focus of being, only one true existent that we call God, and all other things only exist in relation to God, does that lead us in the direction of pantheism? Pantheism is the view that everything, in the end, is an aspect of God. In one version of pantheism, the world is, as it were, God's body. In the case of the analogy of being, does creation have any integrity or does it exist only as an aspect of God? An answer to this question will need to describe with precision the nature of the difference between God and creation to avoid, on the one hand, pantheism, and on the other hand, the idea that God and creation are two things standing alongside each other. There are two possible responses. We encountered the first in the previous chapter and it begins with the realization that a creature participates in its particular way (e.g., as a human being) in that which is universal (being itself). At the heart of a creature there is a composition between the creature's essence or nature (*what* it is) and the universality of the being in which it participates (*that* it is). So the man participates in being *as a man* whereas the horse participates in being *as a horse*. In neither case does the man or the horse exhaust the possibilities of being, because there are infinitely many other ways of participating in being – for example, as a tree or a cow. So there must be a *real distinction* between the essence of the creature (in our examples, the essence of horse or man) and the creature's existence (the share it has in being or the fact of its existence). So what a creature is (its essence or nature) is really distinct from its existence, because the creature's essence does not demand or require its existence, because creatures are contingent. In creation, being in its universal generality is contracted or limited to an essence to form the particular creature; in the creature, being and essence are really, and not merely conceptually, distinct.[18] This marks the difference between creatures, in whom essence and existence are distinct, and God, in whom essence and existence wholly coincide in divine simplicity. Creation receives existence by participation. God is the source of that existence because God is existence itself.

The second answer to the question concerning whether creation has integrity as other than God puts the matter in a similar but slightly more straightforward way: while creation is really distinct from God, the difference between God and creation is not like the difference between creatures. Why not? Take the example of the desk at which I am sat. The difference between the desk and me belongs to both the desk and me. Our material natures – the wood of the desk and my body – constitute us as individual creatures standing alongside each other. The difference between the desk and me is symmetrical: the desk constitutes itself as this desk and I constitute myself as this human person. The difference between God and creation, however, is not symmetrical. Creation does not establish itself as other than God in the way that the desk establishes itself as other than me. Why not? Because that would imply that creation has a self-standing, autonomous existence outside its relation to God. Rather, the source of creation's difference from God is God's creative act. It is God who holds creation as other than himself. In other words, unlike the desk's difference from me, the difference that creation has from God is not properly creation's own; it is given by God. So God grants to creation an improper participation in his own substantiality. It is 'improper' in the sense that it does not belong to creation to be other than God *except insofar as God grants that otherness*. Rather than picturing creation as standing alongside God and *then* receiving his gracious gifts, we are better to think even of the capacity to be a recipient of God's gifts, including the gift of existence, as itself a gift of God. There is nothing in the relation of creation to God that lies outside God's infinite gratuity. It is God who holds creation as other than himself so that creation can receive a participation in his likeness. If we follow the implications of creation *ex nihilo* faithfully, we cannot ground the difference between God and creation anywhere except in the gratuity of God's act of creation, for outside that divine gratuity there is *nothing*. We can say that creation has its own existence and integrity, but it is an existence and integrity that is received from God's gratuity.

Having now examined in more detail Aquinas's account of the analogical relation of creation to God, focused on the *analogia entis* and participation, we can now turn to examine the analogical relation of creaturely action to divine action in the work of providence. This will focus on the crucial distinction between what theologians and philosophers of antiquity and the medieval period term primary and secondary causation. The key point we will explore in the next section is the way in which we can talk of the non-competitive relation between divine causation and creaturely causation. Any event within the created order is not caused either by God or by creatures, as if they competed in a zero-sum game, but by both in very different ways. We will see that creatures are real and potent secondary causes by virtue of their participation in the primary causation of God.

Providence: Primary and secondary causation

Scripture is rich in talk of the divine governance of creation.[19] How is that divine governance ordered and brought to effect? How does God act in creation in relation to the action of creatures? Does God guide creation? If so, how? Does God act alongside creatures, as an alternative source of action, or in a completely different way? These are the issues we will be considering in this section.

Let us begin with a simple example: if I move a glass across a desk, is it me who moves the glass or God? On the one hand, we might be tempted to think that God is omnipotent (all powerful) and, in the end, when all is said and done, God is really the principal agent of any and every action in his creation. Absolutely speaking we might be tempted to say that it is really God who moves the glass. But this seems to deny the reality of any created cause because it reduces me to the status of a mere puppet in moving the glass. The medieval supporters of this view, whom Aquinas opposed, saw God's action as so immediate that it cancelled all created causes, to the point where, for example, it is not fire that heats the saucepan but God in the fire.[20] This is sometimes known as 'occasionalism', because created causes are merely the occasion for God's action. More generally and with respect to human action, this picture of divine causation has the unfortunate consequence of absolving human agents of any responsibility for their actions, because their actions are really God's actions.

The alternative is to insist that it is obviously me who moves the glass. But this seems to render God obsolete within the created order, in a fashion reminiscent of deism. So how are we to understand the movement of the glass? The trick is to understand that God's causal action and my causal action are *not of the same kind*. The movement of the glass is not caused by *either* me *or* God, as if we compete to move the glass. To put the matter another way, God's causal action and creaturely causal action are not univocal (i.e., different degrees of the same kind of causal power). Rather, we are to think of both God *and* me as causes of the glass being moved across the desk, but in totally different ways. How can this be?

Lying behind Aquinas's view of divine action, which we will explore in more detail below, is the notion of a hierarchy of different causes. At the risk of oversimplification, to grasp this idea consider a football team with a very wealthy owner. The owner, having bought the club, appoints a prominent and successful coach who is given a large transfer budget to buy and train some of the world's best players. The players arrive and are trained by the coach. They are so successful that they win the championship title in their first season together. Who caused the team to win the championship? Was it the owner who bought the club and supplied the funds to hire the coach and buy the players? Or was it the coach who trained the team and provided the tactics? Or was it the players who went onto the pitch and scored the goals? The answer is that all these agents combined to win the championship, but they caused that victory in very different ways. There is an important sense in which the owner of the club, in providing the necessary funds, *enabled* the coach and players to become real and potent causes in their own right. We might say that the owner is the primary cause of the club winning the championship, in the sense the she has a universal causal power that enables the coach and players to do their job. This in no way denigrates the power, skill and dedication of the coach and players who, in their own way, are secondary causes of the club's victory. Quite the contrary – we would be quick to praise the players as the *immediate* cause of the club winning the championship while the owner remains hidden in the executive entertainment suite. While recognizing that this simple example is in many respects wholly inadequate to a consideration of divine providential action, it introduces us to the crucial idea of a differentiated hierarchy of causes.

For Aquinas, an intelligible account of divine providential action in creation must involve a hierarchy of differentiated causes, in which God is known as the primary cause and creatures as secondary causes. [21] This means that God is not a cause among causes, but is the basis of all causation in creation, because God creates and sustains every causal agent. In other words, God enables created secondary causes to be real and potent because he creates and sustains them. All other causes participate in God's causal power. This does not mean that God's causal power is added to our causal power to make a very big causal power. It is not as if we are pulling in a tug-of-war and all of a sudden God joins in at the back to add an extra bit of pulling power. This would imply that God's causal power is a very big version of our own. Rather, God's causal power is of an utterly different order. Creaturely causes are causes by analogy with God's causal power by means of participation. God makes creatures to be causes in their own right. This means that in no sense do God's primary causal power and creaturely causes compete with or displace each other; they are of a wholly different order. There are real and potent secondary causes in creation, but only by participation in the primary causation of God.

How does Aquinas explain this? A passage from his treatise 'On the Power of God' (*De potentia dei*) indicates God's threefold causal power.

> Therefore, God causes each action inasmuch as he bestows the power to act, preserves it, and applies it to action, and inasmuch as every other power acts by his power. And when we have added to these things that God is his power, and that he is within each thing as what holds the thing in existence, not as part of the thing's essence, we will conclude that he acts directly in each active thing *without excluding action by the will and nature*.[22]

So God gives creatures their natural powers in three ways: first, by creating them with a particular nature that gives them the power to act in a certain way; secondly, by preserving them in being; and thirdly, by applying them to action. Regarding the first, a very simple example of God providing a nature by which a creature can act might be the colour of a flower that enables it to attract insects for pollination. We might also think of the heaviness of an object by which it moves to a low place or the human intellect that allows the motion of learning. The second way of God giving natural powers to creatures concerns their preservation. Here, Aquinas likens God's action to a medicine that preserves sight and therefore causes seeing. Similarly, God preserves creatures in being and is therefore the cause of their action. Finally, God applies creatures to action as a chef applies the sharpness of a knife to the slicing of food. The crucial claim, however, is in the final line of the previous quotation: God gives creatures the power to act and, in a sense, is the cause of all action, but 'without excluding action by the will and nature'. To understand what this means we have to refer to the first proposition of an anonymous Neoplatonic treatise that fascinated Aquinas and upon which he wrote a commentary, the 'Book of Causes' (*Liber de Causis*): 'Every primary cause infuses its effect more powerfully than does a universal second cause.'[23] This means that the primary cause – God – pours itself into every secondary cause by creating, sustaining and applying it to action. This primary cause is universal and therefore most intimate and powerful because without this primary cause there would be no secondary causes in existence.

To grasp this point, think of the universal causality of the sun. It is the source of our energy and provides motion. As such, its causal power extends to everything on earth. Without it, there would be no motion and life. In other words, the sun is like a universal primary cause that enables secondary causes on earth. Indeed, this is the analogy Aquinas uses when he refers to 'a heavenly body' such as the sun:

> Therefore, divine power needs to be present in each active thing, as the power of a heavenly body needs to be present in each active physical element. But there is a difference in that the divine essence is wherever there is divine power, but the essence of a heavenly body is not wherever its power is. And again, God is his power, but the heavenly body is not.[24]

Notice how Aquinas qualifies the analogy. Unlike a heavenly body that acts at a distance, God is most intimate to created secondary causes because he sustains their very being. Moreover, God *is* his power (because there is no alternative source of God's power beyond God himself) whereas the heavenly body *possesses* its power as an attribute (because it has that power from God by virtue of its creation). Aquinas can talk of God being so immanent to created secondary causes without the risk of God being confused with those secondary causes because of the absolute difference between God and creation. There is not a difference of degree between God and creation. God is wholly other. This means that God can be immanent to creation – infused in created causes – precisely because God is transcendent – wholly other and therefore not at risk of becoming one with his creation. God's immanence (his closeness) *is* God's transcendence (his otherness).[25]

We can now relate primary and secondary causes to our earlier discussion of analogy. Created secondary causes are real and potent because of their analogical relation to a common focus, namely God's primary causation. That relation is one of participation. Secondary causes are made real and potent by their participation in God, the primary cause. That primary cause infuses itself most intimately and powerfully because without it there would be no other causes. God's causation is immediate and immanent in all causal powers; it flows into secondary causes. Yet this does not mean that secondary causes are mere instruments or extensions of the primary cause. Aquinas is quite clear that it is an aspect of God's power and goodness that he is able to make secondary causes real and potent, and providentially govern creation through those causes.[26] He writes:

> There are certain intermediaries of God's providence; for He governs things inferior by superior, not on account of any defect in His power, but by reason of the abundance of His goodness; so that the dignity of causality is imparted even to creatures.[27]

So God is not one cause among others. To return to our original question concerning who moved a glass across the desk, we are not to think of God moving me so that I then move the glass in a kind of domino effect, as if God were a cause within a chain of causes. Rather, God creates and sustains the glass and me. God applies me to action through my form or essential nature so that I can participate in his providential power as a real, potent, immediate and free secondary cause of the movement of the glass. So God is the primary cause of all my actions because he creates me, sustains me and applies me to action through my nature, but this does not obliterate or obscure my real, potent and free causal efficacy.

This view of God's providential power allows Aquinas to adopt an interesting approach to miracles. Ordinarily, we think of miracles as the addition of an extra cause, namely God. We think of miracles as a divine intervention in such a way that God acts where he was not previously acting. For Aquinas, miracles are not a matter of divine intervention in this sense and they are not brought about by the addition of an extra cause. Given our discussion of primary and secondary causation, this view would make no sense, because God is not one cause among others in such a way that his causal power could be added to other causal powers – to give them a boost, as it were. Instead, miracles occur when secondary causes are absent. So the cure of a disease can be brought about by real and potent secondary causes, namely a physician using medicines. A miraculous cure occurs without the mediation of those secondary causes. So when someone is miraculously cured of an illness, the causal power of God is especially significant for us because it is not mediated by secondary causes. The otherwise-veiled causal power of God is revealed in a way that causes wonder because of the absence of secondary causes.[28] An important implication of this view is that miracles do not constitute a *breaking* of the natural created order, although they do occur outside the order of secondary causes.[29] So a miracle is an event that might happen within the natural order by means of secondary causes (e.g., recovery from illness through medical care) but is brought about by God without mediation.

So Aquinas's view of providence seeks an intelligible description of the way in which God acts with respect to created causes. This, however, is only part of the story. Central to the doctrine of providence is the view that God governs creation towards particular ends, according to his loving purposes. Indeed, it is fundamental to Aquinas's view of the natural order that every agent acts for an end. The purpose of an action – its goal or end – is what makes the action intelligible. So we now turn to examine the purposiveness of creation.

Providence and creation's ends

Aquinas was living and working in the thirteenth century when the works of Aristotle (384–322 BC) were reintroduced to the Christian West.[30] He wrote many commentaries on Aristotle's works and critically adopted this philosophy in the service of Christian theology, blending it with elements of Neoplatonism that so heavily influenced ancient Christian thought. One aspect of Aristotle's philosophy that influenced Aquinas is its account of causation. In his *Physics* and *Metaphysics*, Aristotle describes four modes of cause.[31] To understand these four modes, let us consider the causes of a sculpture that is being made to decorate a hallway. First, there is the marble from which the sculpture is fashioned. Aristotle's ancient and medieval commentators label this *the material cause*.[32] Secondly, there is the sculptor's art that, through the action of the hammer and chisel, effects most immediately the change in the marble. This is known as *the efficient cause* and Aristotle describes it as the primary source or principle of motion or change. Further examples of an efficient cause are a man fathering a child or a doctor healing a patient. Thirdly, there is *the formal cause*. When we think of the form of something, we tend to imagine its shape. For Aristotle, however, form is far more than something's shape. It is the 'what it is to be' something, what we might call something's inner essence. The form of something is its nature; it indicates how that thing will change or the direction in which it will develop. For example, a caterpillar through its form develops in the direction of a butterfly, while a seed through its form develops in the direction of a flower. A form can be held actually or potentially. For example, a boy has the form of boy *actually* and the form of man *potentially*. Aristotle would say that the boy is in potency to becoming a man – just as, for example, an acorn is in potency to becoming an oak or a cygnet a swan. The principle of the movement of the boy towards manhood is within the boy – it is his form that will be actualized as he develops into adulthood. In the case of natural objects such as trees and animals, the form is immanent within the creature. For example, it belongs to the essence of a seed to become a flower or a fawn to become a deer. A sculpture, on the other hand, is not a natural object but a work of human artifice. The form resides first in the sculptor's mind and, through the exercise of the art of sculpting, comes to reside in the marble as it takes the form of the sculpture. The fourth mode of causation is the end or goal, what Aristotle calls 'that for the sake of which' an action is undertaken. For example, a bird builds a nest for the sake of protection, a lion hunts for the sake of food, or a person studies for the sake of understanding and wisdom. In the case of the sculpture, the sculptor creates his work of art for the sake of decorating the hallway. That is the goal or end (in Greek, the *telos*) of this particular work of artifice and it makes intelligible the action of the sculptor. It answers the question 'why?' The goal or end of an action was later labelled *the final cause* and the study of final causes or purposes is known as 'teleology' – the study of the *telos* or 'goal'. The form and the final cause are two ways of referring to the dynamic striving after a goal. The form of a boy indicates a dynamic striving after the goal of adulthood. The form of the sculpture in the artistry of the sculptor's mind indicates the dynamic striving after the creation of works of art.

All these modes of causation – labelled by later commentators as the material, efficient, formal and final causes – help to explain natural phenomena.[33] For Aristotle and Aquinas, however, the final cause is the most important, because it refers to the 'why?' of things. Indeed, for Aquinas every agent acts through its form towards some purpose or end.[34] The heart beats in order to pump blood around the body, the whale migrates in order to breed, you are reading this book in order to understand more about the theology of creation. These are examples of purposive, goal-orientated or teleological behaviour. But natural kinds do not just reach after any old goal. For Aquinas, all things seek a particular goal: their own good and flourishing. In seeking that good, they are in fact seeking a deeper participation in that which is universally and absolutely good in itself, namely God.

> All things desire God as their end, when they desire some good thing, whether this desire be intellectual or sensible, or natural, i.e. without knowledge; because nothing is good and desirable except forasmuch as it participates in the likeness to God.[35]

So in being most fully itself, a creature is striving after its own particular good – in an important sense, by striving after that good it is imitating God, who is the universal Good. Because the idea of creaturely perfection is present in the divine mind, as creatures attain their own good they become more God-like, in their own particular way. So, Aquinas writes,

> everything tends through its motion or action toward a good, as its end. ... Now, a thing participates in the good precisely to the same extent that it becomes like the first goodness, which is God. So, all things tend through their movements and actions toward the divine likeness, as toward their ultimate end.[36]

It is important to remember, however, that this striving after purposes and goals belongs both to living things and to inanimate things such as rocks. Even a lifeless object is orientated towards certain goals. A rock, for example, belongs in a low place – it will fall by virtue of its heavy form. The whole of the created order is purposive, as things strive for their goodness and perfection. Even the lowliest inanimate object seeks its proper place in the cosmos. By striving in this way, all created things are seeking to imitate or participate in the divine goodness that is the ultimate goal of all things.[37]

In our modern scientific culture, this providential and teleological view of creation may strike some as quite strange. It is easy to grasp the idea that we, as conscious human beings, are orientated towards certain ends and goals because we are deliberative. In other words, we can set goals for ourselves because we have free will. We might even allow that certain animals such as dolphins or lions are goal orientated because they use strategies to achieve certain ends, such as catching their prey. But can we think of trees and rocks as orientated towards certain ends? Ancient and medieval philosophers and theologians were adamant that we can and that the universe is intelligible only in terms of the ends towards which created things strive. Christian thinkers such as Augustine of Hippo and Thomas Aquinas argued that God creates things by giving them a form or nature that sets them on a path towards a certain goal, whether that be the tree bearing fruit or the rock falling to the ground. Any creature, animate or inanimate, expresses its nature precisely by striving for a certain goal that is the fulfilment of that nature. Crucially, the creation is not meant to escape or overcome its finitude or creatureliness in order to fulfil itself and become more God-like. Quite the opposite: it is in becoming more fully itself that the creature enters more deeply into the life of God.

We will discuss teleology with respect to the concept of design in more detail in Chapter 4. For the moment, the view of providence sketched so far in this chapter presents us with two important questions. Does God strictly determine the unfolding of creation, including human history, in his providential ordering of creation? What are we to make of the failure of creation to attain good ends, for example in the experience of suffering and evil?

Providence: Suffering and evil

It is undeniable that within the created order we experience the failure of creatures to achieve good ends and, in particular, the horrendous suffering of animals (including human beings) in a way that makes it difficult to understand God's providential guidance of creation. At its very root, scripture is concerned with the so-called 'Fall' of creation and its need for restoration, particularly the healing of human sin and its consequences. The

Christian theological tradition is replete with considerations of the wickedness and suffering that beset creation and human history, not least in the cross of Jesus Christ. Most recently, articulations of the so-called 'problem of evil', the apparent contradiction between the existence of an omnipotent and omnibenevolent God and evil and suffering in creation, have resulted in attempts to give reasons for that suffering and evil. Such theodicies – attempts to 'justify the ways of God to man' – generally try to find a greater good to the pattern of suffering and evil and vary in sophistication and cogency. In concluding this chapter, however, we will not consider modern philosophical theodicies; the topic has been discussed relentlessly elsewhere.[38] Instead, using a more traditional metaphysics and doctrine of creation, we will examine the way in which the doctrine of divine transcendence and providence articulated in this chapter help us to avoid some potential problems and to think more clearly about divine governance of the created order.

One approach to the experience of evil and suffering finds its roots in Platonic philosophy but was given particularly potent Christian expression by Augustine of Hippo in the early fifth century.[39] Augustine takes Genesis as his starting point and argues that creation is good. As we have seen in this chapter, creation's existence and goodness are derived from God by means of participation in the infinite and unqualified divine goodness. Goodness and striving after the good are basic to the order of creation. Through its narrative of sin, Genesis teaches that evil and suffering are not basic to the order of creation; they are an alien intrusion. More importantly, evil is not an entity in itself. It is, rather, the absence of the good. Just as darkness is not something in itself but is only the absence of light, so too evil is nothing in itself but is the absence or privation of the good. To take two further examples, sickness is the absence of health and vice is the absence of the virtue that is proper to true humanity. This tradition of thought concerning evil is frequently labelled *privatio boni* – the privation of the good. Because evil is not something in itself but is the absence of the good, evil may be described as parasitic on the good. Outside a relation to the good as the good's absence, there can be no evil. Augustine's mature doctrine of creation is opposed to the view, derived from the followers of the Persian gnostic philosopher Mani (c. 216–274), that he held earlier in his career. Known as the Manichees, Mani's followers understood evil and good as basic and opposed cosmic forces, rather like Star Wars. Augustine came to the view that evil is not a force in its own right opposed to the good, but is only the absence of the good. It is the good that is ontologically basic.

Importantly for Augustine, it is only the good that is intelligible. How are we to understand this? Take the object on my desk: it is made of china and has a handle. It is about 9 cm high, cylindrical in shape with a diameter of 8 cm and is open at one end. In other words, it is a mug. It is intelligible as a mug rather than, say, a cereal bowl because it is a *good* mug. It is what it ought to be and, precisely because it is a good mug, I know it as a mug rather than a bowl or a vase. Of course, I could use the mug as a bowl or a vase, but it would not be particularly good in either usage – hence it is most intelligible as a mug. I could smash the mug on the floor and then it would become a collection of broken pottery that is neither one thing nor another. It would then lack intelligibility, precisely because it is not a good anything. To put it in the metaphysical terms we used early, it would now lack the form of a mug. For Augustine, there is a critical link between goodness and our ability to make sense of things. Insofar as things are good, they are what they ought to be and they are intelligible as such. So the truth of something – its intelligibility – is intrinsically bound up with its goodness. We retain traces of this way of thinking when we say, for example, 'she was a true friend'. What we mean is that she was a good friend: what a friend ought to be. The goodness, truth and intelligibility of things are inextricably bound together.

The implication of this line of thought is that, whereas the good is what we can make sense of because we can give reasons for it, evil is unintelligible. As the absence or lack of the good, evil is precisely the absence or lack of intelligibility. We cannot make sense of it. This way of considering evil is reflected in scripture when Job refuses the attempts of his so-called 'comforters' to find intelligible reasons or justifications for his extreme and unmerited suffering. Properly speaking, we cannot give reasons for evil.[40] If we were to give reasons for evil, we would in effect be treating evil as if it were something of which we could make sense. In other words, we would be treating it as good. Indeed, certain theodicies do precisely this.[41]

Understanding evil as an absence or a lack is for some inadequate because it does not do justice to our experience of evil as a devastatingly destructive force. To refer to cancer merely as the absence of health seems trite. It is important, however, that the tradition of

understanding evil as *privatio boni* is not an empirical thesis about
how we experience evil and suffering, but a metaphysical thesis about
the nature of evil and suffering in relation to a more ontologically
basic good. As one contemporary theologian puts it, *privatio boni*
'refuses to allow evil a foothold in being'.[42] Strictly speaking, evil
does not exist in its own right, but only as the absence of that which
truly exists, namely, the good. According to the view that evil is a
privatio boni, there could not be *pure* evil, because for something to
be pure evil would require its total absence or lack – including an
absence of being. Insofar as something exists at all, its bare existence
is in some measure a share in the good. Take the example of a man
whose life is full of wickedness and completely lacking in virtue. He
is good in the sense that he exists. The man's being is in relation to
God. In terms of what a man ought to be, however, he is evil because
he *lacks* the virtue that is proper to human beings.[43]

   The accidental and contingent nature of evil and its intrusion
into the created order raises an obvious question: does God will
such evil? For some theologians, the doctrine of providence means
that the history of creation consists in a kind of universal teleology
in which God *directly* wills or permits every event in the world. To
deny this claim would apparently be to suppose that creatures could
lie outside God's immediate causal influence and thwart his will.
On this view God is the primary efficient cause of every particular
event (including each individual sin) in the sense that God infallibly
and eternally predetermines such acts. So providence is simply the
dialectical unfolding of a plan eternally decreed and determined by
God and anything else would constitute the thwarting of the divine
will. The creature's will and action is potentially a threat to the
divine will, so the divine will eternally decrees the movement of
that creature towards good or evil. Meanwhile, a relative absence
or lack of God's grace means that creatures, who are nothing in
themselves, are unable to sustain their drive towards the good and
therefore dissolve into relative non-being and the unintelligibility of
evil. Lying behind this view is the supposition (or superstition) that
creation, simply because it is not God, is almost bound to lapse into
evil if it is not propped up by an additional causal power that we call
God's grace. At its most extreme, this understanding of providence
issues in the doctrine known as double predestination: God eternally
determines some to damnation and others to salvation. According
to its proponents, this is the only way of ensuring the absolute

providential sovereignty of God over creation. Suffering and evil are the result of creaturely action and yet they are eternally willed as the necessary means of God realizing his eternal purposes in creation.

As David Bentley Hart has so forcefully argued, this view of providence represents a profound misunderstanding of the metaphysical distinction between primary and secondary causation and a failure to preserve the proper understanding of the difference between what God wills and what God permits.[44] It also fails to do justice to the scriptural witness to God's will for the ultimate good of all creation (Ezek. 33.11; 2 Pet. 3.9; Eph. 1.7-12; 1 Tim. 2.4). Why is this the case? Think back to the example of me moving a glass across a table. It was pointed out that I move the glass and in that sense I am responsible for this particular act. God, who is the primary cause, sustains created things in existence and I participate in God's primary, creative causal power. I am made a cause by God because God brings creatures into being, sustains them and, through their form, applies them to action. My causal power is related by analogy to God who is the fount and source of all causation. But it is crucial that an absolute difference must be preserved between God's primary causal power and creaturely secondary causes, just as one must preserve the absolute difference between God's being and created being. It is not that God eternally decrees that I will move the glass and therefore determines my will to act in this way. If that were the case, God would become just one member in a single chain of univocal causes – God, me, the movement of the glass. My will would be seen as a threat to the divine will, so the sovereignty of God's will would be preserved by the eternal decree that I will move the glass. We would be left with mere determinism or fatalism. The picture of God's providence that we find in Aquinas is quite different. God's primary causal power pertains to creation *ex nihilo*, the sustaining of all things in being and the appointment of their proper ends as a participation in the Good. This is the crucial thought: the proximity of God to creation does not have to be guaranteed by the view that God determines every particular act and event in the created order – even sin and death – as if he were driving a machine. The proximity of God to creation is maintained by the claim that God sustains creation in being, orders creatures to certain ends by virtue of what creatures are (their form), and makes them real, potent and free secondary causes by giving them a share in his utterly unique and wholly originate primary causation, that is, the creation of causal agents other than himself.[45] God is the primary cause that infuses itself most deeply *into* secondary causes. The act of creation donates to creatures a nature or form by which they act freely in and for themselves as secondary causes. That freedom is not a wild and indifferent indeterminism, but the ability of a creature to participate in the fulfilment of its own nature. It is the freedom not to be just this or that, but the freedom of the creature to be fully itself by fulfilling its own nature in which it acts. Indeed, it is in no sense a diminishment of God's power that he bestows the free power of causation on creatures. Quite the opposite is the case. If God were the eternally determining cause of every particular event in creation's history, such that secondary causes were merely instrumental, then 'the order of cause and effect would be taken away from created things: and this would imply lack of power in the Creator: for it is due to the power of the cause, that it bestows *active power* on its effect'.[46] So Aquinas sums up providence in this way:

> Two things belong to providence – namely, the type of the order of things foreordained towards an end; and the execution of this order, which is called government. As regards the first of these, God has immediate providence over everything, because He has in His intellect the types of everything, even the smallest; and whatsoever causes He assigns to certain effects, He gives them the power to produce those effects. Whence it must be that He has beforehand the type of those effects in His mind. As to the second, there are certain intermediaries of God's providence; for He governs things inferior by superior, not on account of any defect in His power, but by reason of the abundance of His goodness; so that the dignity of causality is imparted even to creatures.[47]

We therefore have a picture of creation's freedom which is exercised within God's loving guidance of his creatures towards their end in the Good, despite the rebellion of sin and the dissolution of created existence caused by suffering and evil. What God permits in history may be, in itself, contrary to his eternal will. As Hart puts it, 'To believe in divine and unfailing providence is not to burden one's conscience with the need to see every event in this world not only as the occasion of God's grace, but as the positive determination of God's will whereby he brings to pass a comprehensive design that, in the absence of any single one of these events, would not have been possible.'[48] Yet through the preservation of creation's otherness and his love for creatures, God's eternal kingdom will in the end be established through his peaceable governance of creation. This is not a justification of evil and suffering within the order of providence, nor is it an explanation of why evil and suffering occur in the created order. For example, any courage, generosity, hope, patience and spiritual growth shown by a young person dying of cancer maybe a response born of hope in God and the fruit of God's grace shown in the care and love of family and medical staff, but it is no justification of the wickedness of this disease nor an outworking of an eternally determined plan that demands *this* person die of *this* disease. This is, however, a suggestion that, rather than seek *a priori* justifications for evil and suffering, the Christian theologian must attend to what God actually does within the providential order of creation so as to bring about his loving purposes. In the end, attention to what God providentially provides will entail attention to the person of Jesus Christ who is the incarnation in history of the Word through whom and for whom all things are created (Col. 1.16). As the revealing of God's saving providence, Christ is the appearance of creation's end in the midst of creation's way to God.

Conclusion

The need for a clear and intelligible understanding of the creator–creature relationship is nowhere more evident than in the doctrine of providence. Through the analogy of being (*analogia entis*), we have examined creation's participation in God and God's simultaneous immanence and transcendence with respect to creation. In turn, this allows a proper distinction between primary and secondary causes which points to creaturely freedom and integrity while maintaining creation's utter contingency and dependence on God. That freedom and integrity is exercised in the natures God gives to his creatures and the ends to which they are ordered.

In the next chapter, we will shift to a more historical mode in order to examine the relationship between theology and natural science as it arose in the early modern period. We will see that by the sixteenth century a considerable change had taken place in the understanding of the relation of creation to God. This had the effect of rendering the notion of divine providence increasingly anthropomorphic and therefore unintelligible.

4

Creation, the Rise of Science and the Design of the Universe

The theologies of creation and providence that we have outlined thus far are particularly concerned with creatures and their relation to God. Specific claims are made about the meaning and purposes of nature. As such, theology is often thought to share a subject matter with science: the natural world. Contemporary cosmology makes claims about the origins of the universe; physics and chemistry make claims about the constituents of that universe; and biology makes claims about the nature and development of life. According to one view, science and theology offer fundamentally different accounts of that world, one rational and the other mythical and superstitious. They are therefore engaged in a fight to the death. Science is perceived as representing a wholly new level of knowledge that establishes plain matters of fact according to publicly agreed criteria for rational enquiry. Moreover, science is alleged to have a moral as well as intellectual superiority over religion; because these criteria for the establishment of matters of fact are publically agreed, we are told that science is more democratic. It instils virtues of objectivity and fairness in its practitioners. Science thus replaces the superstitious, romantic and naïve speculations of theology; every scientific triumph is also a blow to religion. We commonly associate this 'conflict thesis' with the so-called New Atheists, but it can be found in slightly different guises at least as far back as the scientist John William Draper (1811–1882) and the American historian and educationist Andrew Dickson White (1832–1918).[1] On the opposing side of the 'conflict thesis' are creationists. They argue that theology founded on a proper (i.e., literal) reading of the

Bible discounts scientific theories such as evolution. The creationists are, in many ways, the mirror image of scientistic atheists in their literalism and dogmatic commitment to a single way of accessing fundamental truth.

An alternative view sees science and theology as representing two completely independent ways of understanding nature and reality. According to the biologist Stephen Jay Gould, they represent non-overlapping magisteria.[2] Between the view that science and theology are engaged in battle and the view that science and theology are ships that pass in the night is the view that science and theology offer methodologically different but compatible accounts of nature and its origins. On this understanding, scientific discoveries are consistent with, or even provide evidence for, God's creative activity as proclaimed in scripture and in the order of creation.[3]

The relationship between the science of nature and the theology of creation is complex and there are a variety of ways in which theologians, scientists, philosophers and historians understand that relationship. The purpose of this chapter is to put the relationship between science and theology (specifically the doctrines of God and creation) into historical perspective by examining the theological context of the rise of natural science from the sixteenth century and its effect on the Christian doctrine of creation. We begin by considering what is meant by 'science' and how it developed from the natural philosophy of the early modern period. After examining the so-called 'scientific revolution' of the sixteenth and seventeenth centuries, we will explore in more detail the Reformation as the theological context of the rise of scientific investigations of creation.

What is 'science'?

When examining the history of science, it is important to note that the term 'science' is not applied exclusively to the empirical study of nature until the nineteenth century. The first example of the use of the term 'scientist' as we would understand it today is found in William Whewell's 1834 review of Mary Somerville's *On the Connexion of the Physical Sciences*, published in the *Quarterly Review*. In the Latin of the medieval period, a *scientia* was any body of knowledge. The different *scientia* of human learning – music, arithmetic, geometry, metaphysics and so on – were hierarchically ordered according to their different principles. For example, the science of optics was subordinate to the more abstract and higher science of geometry, because optics used geometry in its investigations of the behaviour of light. The highest *scientia* was the Christian theology that Thomas Aquinas called the 'holy teaching' of the church (*sacra doctrina*). What today we would broadly recognize as 'science' was, in the sixteenth to eighteenth centuries, known as 'natural philosophy' or 'experimental philosophy'. Today, English is the only European language that restricts the meaning of 'science' to the natural sciences. In other European languages, 'science' – for example, 'wissenschaft' in German – refers to any body of critical knowledge.

Today, we tend to associate natural science with an evidence-based and rational approach to the study of nature. Of course, it is the case that nature was investigated rationally using empirical and philosophical methods in the academies of ancient Greece and in the schools and communities of medieval Christianity and Islam. What, then, was the special character of early modern science or 'natural philosophy'? Natural philosophers, particularly those in England such as Robert Boyle (1627–1691), Robert Hooke (1635–1703) and Isaac Newton (1643–1727), studied nature in two innovative ways that distinguished their enterprise from the *philosophia naturalis* of medieval Scholasticism. First, whereas the observation of nature (rather than mere philosophical speculation) had long been advocated, the natural philosophy of the early modern period regarded experiment as a key feature of its method. Experiment involved not merely the observation of natural events, but their control and measurement. In other words, such observation was contrived, in the sense of being conducted under controlled conditions – eventually the conditions of the laboratory. Crucially, an experiment was conducted in order to falsify or confirm a particular hypothesis about nature. The provision of clear evidence that is in principle falsifiable by an identically repeatable experiment was, and continues to be, a crucial part of the production of scientific matters of fact. General conclusions were drawn appropriate to the data gleaned from limited but repeatable experimental observations.[4] In this way, the experimental and empirical character of British natural philosophy is sometimes (but too simplistically) distinguished from the speculative and rationalist natural philosophies of continental thinkers such as René Descartes

(1596–1650), Gottfried Wilhelm Leibniz (1646–1716) and Baruch Spinoza (1632–1677).[5]

The second distinctive feature of natural philosophy in the early modern period, and one found across Europe, was the increasing and innovative use of mathematics to study and measure nature. For Aristotle, mathematics was an abstraction and of no real worth in studying physical phenomena. It had a particular subject matter – the unchanging abstractions of arithmetic and geometry – whereas physics studied substances that change and thus required a different kind of investigative procedure. Mathematics takes us in the direction of quantification, whereas Aristotle was interested in the real natures and qualities of things. Aristotle's predecessor and teacher Plato, by contrast, had advocated the use of mathematics in studying nature (particularly harmonic proportion and geometry) because he understood the visible realm to be a participation in, or approximation to, a real and unchanging mathematical realm. In Plato's cosmological treatise *Timaeus*, we see the clear application of mathematics to the understanding of natural phenomena. For example, Plato describes the harmonious proportions of the distances between planets and the changes to the elements of earth, air, fire and water via an analysis of the geometrical solids.[6] Yet the *Timaeus* was only known to medieval natural philosophers through partial Latin translations by Cicero (106 BC–43 BC) and Calcidius (fl. fourth century). It was not until a translation by the Italian Renaissance scholar and priest Marsilio Ficino (1433–1499) in 1484 that the full text of the *Timaeus* became available.[7] The influence of this work on thinkers such as Johannes Kepler (1571–1630) was considerable and provided an important encouragement to the mathematical exploration of planetary motion.

Nevertheless, the newly available complete translation of the *Timaeus* is not alone sufficient to explain the extensive early modern use of mathematics in the practical spheres of mechanics and dynamics as well as the formulation of laws of nature.[8] Already in the fourteenth century there had been particular interest in the possibility of quantifying qualitative changes so that they might be analysed using the techniques of mathematics and logic. Many of those engaged in this enterprise were fellows of Merton College, Oxford, including Walter Burley (c. 1275–1344/5), Richard Swineshead (fl. c. 1340–1354) and Thomas Bradwardine

(c. 1290–1349). They became collectively known as the 'calculators' (*calculatores*). Their ideas were influential in European centres of learning in the fifteenth and early sixteenth centuries; Leibniz, for example, had the 1520 Venice edition of Richard Swineshead's *Liber calculationum* transcribed. Thus the ideas of a fourteenth-century 'calculator' remained influential in the work of one of the seventeenth century's leading mathematicians.[9] Extraordinary further developments in mathematics in the seventeenth century, particularly the calculus, formed the basis of Isaac Newton's classical physics.[10] The emphasis on the quantitative rather than qualitative exploration of nature was a key factor in the move from Aristotelian natural philosophy to the modern approach to nature that we would recognize as 'science'.

A scientific revolution?

When charting the rise of the collection of practices that today we call 'science', historians sometimes refer to a revolution in thought in the mid-sixteenth century. The Polish astronomer and mathematician Nicolaus Copernicus (1473–1543) is a particularly iconic figure. In March 1543, after decades of work refining and circulating his ideas and observations, an ailing Copernicus celebrated the publication of his book *De Revolutionibus Orbium Coelestium* (*On the Revolutions of the Celestial Spheres*) in Nuremberg. He was a long-serving Canon of Frombork Cathedral in north-eastern Poland and a third-order Dominican who dedicated his work to Pope Paul III. Copernicus died just two months later and saw little of the influence that his treatise would enjoy on later thinkers, the controversy his observations would provoke and the place his name would take in the history of Western ideas. The *De Revolutionibus* was based in many ways upon the work of the ancient Greek astronomer Ptolemy (c. 100 AD–c. 170 AD) and his treatise known as the *Almagest*. In that sense, it was a very traditional work. It contained one crucial difference, however: whereas Ptolemy offered a geocentric model of the cosmos – one in which the earth is stationary at the centre – Copernicus's model was heliocentric: the earth and other planets revolve around the sun and the earth itself rotates on an axis. The notion of heliocentrism was proposed in antiquity and had been discussed for some time in medieval Europe. Even the very notion of a centre of the cosmos was questioned by, among others, the German cardinal and philosopher Nicholas of Cusa (1401–1464).[11] Yet heliocentrism was controversial for a number of reasons, not least because it contradicted a literal interpretation of certain passages of scripture (Jos. 10.12-13; Ps. 19.4-6; 1 Chron. 16.30; Eccl. 1.5).[12] In many ways, as one of the last representatives of the Ptolemaic system of astronomy, Copernicus is not quite the iconoclastic figure he is often taken to be. Yet the publication of *De Revolutionibus* is sometimes described as the 'Copernican revolution'. Historians of science have traditionally regarded Copernicus and the early sixteenth century as the beginning of a scientific revolution that transformed Western thought.

According to one account of this Copernican revolution, the medieval period, sometimes labelled 'the Dark Ages', was dominated by ignorance and superstition concerning the natural world. This was the era of Western history that ran from the decline of the Roman Empire in the fifth century (often labelled 'Late Antiquity') up to the fifteenth century. Within this dark period some light was shed on the workings of nature by the theologians of the High Middle Ages, notably Robert Grosseteste (1175– 1253), Roger Bacon (c. 1214/1220–c.1292), Albert the Great (c. 1200–1280) and Thomas Aquinas (c. 1225–1274). Building on the legacy of the very powerful Islamic natural philosophy of the eighth to twelfth centuries,[13] particularly in the field of optics, these theologians used Neoplatonic philosophy and the newly available works of Aristotle to understand the natural world and humanity's place in the cosmos, all within the context of scripture's teaching on creation. In the thirteenth century during which these Christian thinkers flourished, Paris was Europe's leading intellectual centre; despite sporadic condemnations of Aristotle's works and various of his philosophical propositions in the University and Diocese from 1210 to 1277, Aristotelian natural history, natural philosophy and metaphysics began a period of enormous influence in European thought. Until the seventeenth century, Aristotle's works dominated the curricula in the universities of Bologna, Paris and Oxford. Aristotelianism was gradually replaced, however, by a fundamentally different way of conceiving the natural world and investigating its secrets. It is this transition, to the period we call modernity and to the so-called Enlightenment, that is associated with the beginning of modern science and its extraordinary success in predicting and manipulating the natural world. According to some historians, the revolution which began with Copernicus reached its zenith with the work of Isaac Newton (1643–1727) and the publication of his *Philosophiæ Naturalis Principia Mathematica*, or *Mathematical Principles of Natural Philosophy*, in 1687.[14] Over the following two centuries, the biblical and theological view of creation – replete with sign, myth and poetry and supported by ancient Greek philosophy – seemingly came to be replaced by an objective scientific understanding of nature.

Many historians of science, however, question whether there really was a scientific *revolution* in the sixteenth and seventeenth centuries.[15] Another important question about this period concerns why the practice of natural science was consolidated so successfully in early modern Europe, given that advances in the understanding of the natural world had been genuine and widespread, albeit sporadic, in the medieval period. Why did modern science not arise in Arabia or the Far East, where there had been equally strong and successful traditions of natural philosophy? These are complex historical questions, but recent research makes clear that the modern project of natural science was intertwined with Christianity and with significant theological changes in scriptural interpretation and the doctrines of God, creation and providence.[16] Contrary to popular perception, the relationship between theology and the new science was far from antagonistic. Quite the reverse: natural science developed precisely because it receives its rationale from a particular theology of God and creation – one that is quite different from the theology of the patristic theologians and Thomas Aquinas. Some historians of science therefore argue that it was the particular Christian context of Europe that allowed the consolidation of the practices and discoveries of modern natural science, as it became institutionalized and gradually acquired prestige in the public domain.

To understand the rise of modern science, its theological context and the changing Christian theology of creation, we must look at that other revolution of the sixteenth century, namely, the Reformation. Peter Harrison argues that, in order to grasp the importance of the Reformation for the rise of modern science, we must first understand the ancient method of reading scripture and nature and the importance of authority in their interpretation.[17] It was a change in the way in which scripture was read that unwittingly prompted a change in the way that nature was read. This, in turn, had a significant effect on the development of scientific methods for probing nature. Following Harrison, we will therefore continue this chapter with a consideration of the allegorical reading of nature and scripture in ancient and medieval theology and the effect of a more exclusive emphasis on literal readings arising from the Reformation of the sixteenth century. Accompanying this shift in interpretative method was a crucial development in the doctrine of God and the way in which creation is understood to relate to the divine, albeit one that had roots in the Late Middle Ages.[18] This prompted the rise of 'physico-theology' and the idea that God governs creation like a machine through the application of laws of nature. Despite what appears to be historical evidence of conflict between the disciplines, we will see that science and the new natural theology were in a tense but symbiotic relationship until the nineteenth century. This impoverished theology of creation that accompanied the development of natural philosophy and science in the early modern period will help us to understand more clearly the current context for the discussion between theology and the natural sciences, including the supposed conflict between these disciplines in their understandings of creation and nature. In concluding this chapter, I will briefly refer to a more daring and interesting proposal for understanding the relationship between theology and science, made recently by the American theologian Michael Hanby: in order to be truly scientific, science needs an adequate theology of creation. We begin, however, with the theological roots of the scientific approach to nature and cosmology.

The two books: Scripture and nature

To grasp the changing theological context in which modern science arose, Harrison argues that we need to look back in Christian history to the hermeneutical method employed by the early Christian theologians in their readings of scripture in order to understand how they interpreted nature. This history encompasses the transition from a symbolic world view in which creatures are understood as signs of spiritual truths that are to be read and interpreted, to a more literal reading in which creatures are not symbolic bearers of intrinsic meaning, but objects that meet humanity's material needs and provide occasions for the demonstration of divine power and design.

The hermeneutical method for interpreting scripture that was deployed in various guises during the patristic and medieval periods can be traced at least as far back as the Hellenic Jewish philosopher Philo (c. 20 BC–c. 50 AD) and the Christian theologian Origen (c. 185–c. 254 AD), both from the city of Alexandria.[19] As we saw in Chapter 1, Origen originally proposed that scripture has three senses or layers of meaning (pp. 28–9). These were developed by his successors into a fourfold scheme. The first and foundational sense was the literal sense that is often taken to be the obvious historical meaning of the text.[20] All the other senses of scripture rely on the literal sense. The second sense is the moral or 'tropological' sense of scripture. This concerns the teaching of scripture concerning how we are to live. The third sense of scripture was the 'anagogical' sense, or that meaning pertaining to the last things or that for which we should strive, such as the kingdom of heaven or the vision of God. Finally, the fourth and most important sense of scripture was the spiritual or 'allegorical' sense. The allegorical sense concerned those enduring theological truths about God and our life with God.

For theologians of the early church, scripture itself distinguishes its literal and allegorical senses. In Gal. 4.21-26, for example, Paul tells how Abraham had two sons, one by a slave woman and another by a free woman. The child of the slave woman was born 'by the flesh' and the child of the free woman was born 'through the promise'. This, says Paul, is an allegory of two covenants: Hagar, the slave woman and mother of Ishmael, is the present Jerusalem that stands in slavery. Sarah, the free woman and mother of Isaac, stands for the Jerusalem above, that is, the church. 'She is free', writes Paul, 'and she is our mother' because, like Isaac, the people of Christ are children of the promise. An allegorical reading of this kind was important in scriptural hermeneutics of the early church because of the relationship of the Old Testament to the New Testament. The Old Testament by its very nature intended more than its historical meaning; it pointed to fulfilment in Christ. As Denys Turner explains, the literal or historical sense of scripture stood to the allegorical sense as the promise of the Old Testament stood to its fulfilment in the New Testament.[21]

Patristic theologians, including Basil of Caesarea (c. 329–379), Ambrose of Milan (c. 340–397) and most importantly Augustine (354–430), developed the fourfold system of interpretation. It was applied not only to scripture but also to nature, particularly through commentaries on the six days of creation known as the 'hexaemeral literature'. God was the author of nature no less than scripture. The meaning and purposes of creatures were thus to be discerned using the same hermeneutical scheme. Natural objects, understood literally, were to provide for the body of man. In this sense, nature was functional with respect to humanity's basic material needs. However, this left open the question of the meaning and purpose of those countless creatures that appear useless or deleterious to humanity.[22] Yet, while some creatures are of no material use, they may be spiritually important, because nature more generally is a system of signs that teaches people about themselves and life with God. For example, Augustine interprets the taming of wild beasts as an allegory of the human passions and their subjection by moral reason. Just as humanity was to have dominion over creation and tame the animals, so too the wild human passions were to be tamed under the dominion of the appetitive and intellective soul. Augustine writes:

> Refrain from the ugly savagery of pride, from the slothly pleasure of lust, from all that lyingly bears the name of science, that the wild beasts may be tamed, the cattle brought to subjection, and the serpents made harmless. For these animals are an allegory for the movements of the soul.[23]

The meanings of creatures, particularly the moral lessons that could be drawn from their behaviour (i.e., the tropological readings), were described in a short but highly influential anonymous treatise known as the *Physiologus*, written in Greek around the second century.[24] This summarized ancient learning concerning animals, plants and fantastical animals, drawing out the moral and spiritual lessons to be learnt from them. Around the eighth century, the *Physiologus* was translated into Latin and many Middle Eastern, African and European languages. It was the forerunner of the very popular medieval catalogues of animals and their behaviour known as bestiaries.[25]

Reading nature symbolically and allegorically in this way was far from arbitrary.[26] Importantly, scripture itself commends it. In the book of Job, God tells Job: 'But ask the animals, and they will teach you; the birds of the air, and they will tell you; ask the plants of the earth, and they will teach you; and the fish of the sea will declare to you. Who among all these does not know that the hand of the Lord has done this?' (Job 12.7-9). One of the most popular symbols of the medieval period that one also finds in the *Physiologus* is the pelican feeding her young with her own blood. It can still be seen in many churches today, including the nineteenth-century lectern at Durham Cathedral. The pelican became a common symbol of Christ's atonement and the feeding of his people at the Eucharist.[27] There are also many moral lessons within nature that were commended by scripture. Christ himself used images from nature: the fish, the mustard seed, water, the grape, the lilies, sparrows, the vine and so on. The key motivation for investigating nature, therefore, was not to manipulate or utilize natural resources to meet material needs. Neither was nature investigated in a spirit of mere curiosity. Rather, nature was a resource for learning about humanity and its place in the cosmic hierarchy, the way we should live as part of the pattern of God's creation and the final goal towards which humanity is called. Nature had value because creatures were always in themselves orientated towards God. They shimmered with God's glory because they were symbols of that glory and participated in his life. Nature had a value with respect to the human intellect because that intellect was capable of discerning the meanings of creatures and thereby learning about God in order to enter into communion with God. This is very much of a piece with the analogical imagination described in the previous chapter: effects (creatures) resemble their cause (God) and, by participation in divine being, they become signs of God after their own manner of existence.

This fourfold interpretation of scripture expressed a fundamental doctrine of creation based on signs, which is important for how we understand the way in which words and objects bear meaning. Take the example of words: we might think that words are arbitrarily attached to things. If it were not for conventional linguistic usage, a shared language in which words are consistently and reliably used to refer to particular objects (e.g., 'tree' is reliably used to refer to tall, leafy green objects planted in the ground) would not be possible. When we worry about proliferating interpretations of scripture, this may be a concern that the use of words becomes chaotic as they are stretched beyond their plain conventional meaning. We might think that words are signs of things and that is where signification stops. If we can attach words to things in a controlled and limited way, language will be more stable and transparent. It will be literal. As we

have seen, however, for Augustine the layers of meaning in scripture
are not arbitrary and they are not the result of the stretched use of
words. Rather, the layers of meaning arise because *things themselves
are signs*. It is not that words are symbolic and potentially bear
arbitrary multiple meanings that need to be controlled; it is the
creatures to which words refer that bear meaning. This means that
there are layers of meaning in scripture not because we arbitrarily
multiply the meanings of words in our interpretations, but because
the creation to which scripture refers is itself the bearer of layers
of meaning.[28] So the literal sense of scripture lies in the plain,
univocal meaning of words. The allegorical sense of scripture lies
in the various meanings of *the things to which words refer*. To
use a common example, the word 'Jerusalem' refers to the city in
the Middle East, but the city itself through its place in scripture
may refer to the kingdom of heaven, the city of God, the church,
the people of Israel and so on. For two theologians separated by
nearly a millennium, John Cassian (c. 360–430) and Nicholas of
Lyra (c. 1270–1349), Jerusalem is the city of the Jews when taken
literally; allegorically, it is the church of Christ; anagogically, it is
the city of God, which is heaven; tropologically, it is the human
soul.[29] To take another example, the word 'dove' may refer to a
white bird, but the bird itself may refer to hope in God (Gen. 8.11)
or the Holy Spirit (Lk. 3.22). Finally, consider the lamb as a sign
of Christ in relation to the Passover. The word 'lamb' refers to the
animal that is sacrificed at the Passover. The lamb itself, not the
word, is the sign of Christ. So the word 'lamb' is not a metaphor
for Christ. It is the lamb itself, sacrificed at the Passover, that is
the sign of Christ. So the meanings of words are a function of the
meanings of objects. While we can use words as metaphors and
thereby devise meanings beyond their literal use, we cannot do so
with creatures themselves. Only God can invest creatures, persons
and events with intrinsic meaning because God is creator and this
is part of his providential guidance of creation. The meanings of
creatures are revealed in scripture; this is why nature must be read
alongside the book of scripture. This means that the literal sense
of the words of scripture is crucial and foundational, but scripture
also opens for us the symbolic order of creation, which points us
to God's providential care in the history of creation and salvation.

The implication of this pattern of reading nature and scripture
is that the whole of creation is a system of signs. God's creatures

are like the 'words' of creation, which are formed in and through *the* Word (Jn 1.3; Col. 1.16-17), giving a multilayered system of meaning that refers to God. The created order, on this view, is a song of praise that can be read and interpreted. An important theological corollary of this approach is that the symbolic language of the church that we call the sacraments – for Augustine, the outward and visible signs of spiritual realities – is possible precisely because creation is, in its very ontological structure, sacramental: it is a system of signs that is revealed as such by *the* sign who is Jesus Christ. As we saw in Chapter 1, creation is a liturgical text of praise, with layers of meaning that require discernment and interpretation. Within that text we find the more particular word of scripture that, in turn, opens for us the meanings of creation through its witness to the incarnate Word through whom all things were made.

In the symbolic world of early Christianity exemplified in the writings of Augustine, the sign (*signum*) and the thing signified (*res*) were understood as intertwined in such a way that the sign could mediate the reality of that which it signified. For example, the water in the sacrament of baptism is a proper and objective mediator of God's redemption and new birth into the church by the Holy Spirit. It is a sign of creation (Gen. 1.2), the passage of the people of Israel through the waters of the Red Sea towards the Promised Land (Exod. 13.17–14.29) and new birth (Jn. 3.5) following Jesus's baptism by John (Mt. 3.13-17; Mk 1.9-11; Lk. 3.21-23). None of this symbolism is arbitrary or merely conventional; it is part of the fabric and purpose of God's creation. Nevertheless, for the patristic theologians there was always a danger of dwelling too much on the sign (*signum*) rather than the spiritual reality to which it pointed (*res* or 'thing'). One could, in this sense, take the sign too literally. Augustine therefore made a distinction between 'use' (*uti*) and 'enjoyment' (*frui*) in his hermeneutics. Only God was to be enjoyed entirely in himself without any further referent. Created signs, by contrast, open beyond themselves to become mediators of God, but they are not ends in themselves. For example, the love of one's spouse is not to be understood as an end in itself, but as opening up the reality of the infinite divine love that is the relationship's source and referent. The love of one's spouse, the sign (*signum*), is intertwined with and mediates the thing signified (*res*), in this case, divine love. To treat the sign as an end in itself would constitute a form of idolatry, namely worshipping and enjoying the sign *only* for itself rather than as also disclosing its referent.[30] For Augustine, we rest only in God; the created signs of nature point us to that rest. Nevertheless, there is no arbitrary connection or dualism of the sign and the thing signified. The sign joins and unites us to that which it signifies.

Medieval theologians inherited the fourfold system of interpreting scripture and nature along with Augustine's theology of the sign. Aquinas draws inspiration from both scripture and Augustine when he states,

> Since, however, God's effects show us the way to the contemplation of God Himself, according to Rom. 1:20, 'The invisible things of God ... are clearly seen, being understood by the things that are made,' it follows that the contemplation of the divine effects [creatures] also belongs to the contemplative life, inasmuch as man is guided thereby to the knowledge of God. Hence Augustine says (*De Vera Religione*, xxix) that 'in the study of creatures we must not exercise an empty and futile curiosity, but should make them the stepping-stone to things unperishable and everlasting'.[31]

The contemplation of God's creatures and the allegorical interpretation of scripture and nature were expressed more particularly in the famous 'two-books' tradition. God had provided two books for humanity's spiritual edification, the book of scripture and the book of nature. They were both complete, unified texts and delicately intertwined. For theologians such as William of Conches (c. 1090–1154), Hugh of St. Victor (c. 1096–1141), Alain of Lille (c. 1128–1202), Robert Grosseteste (1175–1254) and Bonaventure (1221–1274), the created order was a trace of God written by his finger for our interpretation and edification.[32] Of the metaphor of the book of nature in the medieval period, Harrison writes:

> The image of the 'book of nature' went considerably further than alternative metaphors which expressed the unity of the cosmos, for it implied firstly, that nature was to be read, expounded, investigated; that those meticulous labours which had hitherto been expended on the methodological investigation of that other book [scripture] could now be directed towards the natural world. ... Nature was a new authority, an alternative text, a doorway to the divine which could stand alongside the sacred page.[33]

The book of nature was not merely a system of signs pointing 'upwards' to spiritual truth. It was a unified and coherent symbolic order that could be read and understood through observation and the parallel reading of scripture. Thus the exploration of nature was commended by the metaphor of the book of nature and this, coupled with the newly available Aristotelian learning in the twelfth and thirteenth centuries, led to a rich pattern of investigation in the High Middle Ages.

To a modern reader, this complex interpretation of scripture and nature may seem strange, arbitrary and convoluted. Yet it required considerable skill and training. The interpretation of the intricate beauty and complexity of the book of nature was undertaken through the controlling lens of the book of scripture. Scripture provided a hermeneutical framework that kept the interpretation of nature within intelligible bounds. There was, however, another hermeneutical lens that was crucial for the interpretation of the books of nature and scripture: the church's tradition of interpretation. Picking up a copy of the Latin Vulgate scriptures in the medieval period, one would have been presented not only with the biblical text, but also with the commentaries and glosses of the Church Fathers in the margins. This meant that when one read scripture one was never reading it alone. Scripture was encountered in the company of authoritative church teachers and, because nature was read through scripture, so too the meanings of creatures were discerned via a tradition of interpretation. The underlying conviction in patristic and medieval exegesis was that scripture constitutes a coherent unity – a series of books that form a whole – and that God had similarly created a *uni*verse, that is, a single creation whose parts blend to form a unity. The church past and present interpreted these texts together.

Nevertheless, the elaborate nature of allegorical interpretation was not beyond criticism. In particular, there was concern among twelfth-century theologians such as Thierry of Chartres (c. 1100– 1155) and Rupert of Deutz (c. 1075–1129/30) that the literal sense of the text and the valuable lessons it taught was being lost amid very elaborate symbolism.[34] From the beginnings of Christian scriptural exegesis, the literal sense of scripture was understood as crucial and the root of all theological interpretation. This meant that, while the allegorical sense was the most illuminating, the literal sense of scripture had to be established before all others. Aquinas, following

Augustine, was clear that the spiritual senses of scripture rest on the literal sense and presuppose it.[35] This does not mean that the theologians of the early and medieval church were literalists because, while the literal sense was the first in the order of interpretation, it was consistent with further layers of meaning within the created order. The literal sense was first but the allegorical sense was treated as the most important in the quest to deepen one's life with God.

The Reformation: Literal readings

The Protestant Reformation beginning in the sixteenth century radically changed the hermeneutical framework for the understanding of nature and scripture. This began with a shift in the understanding of authority. In the patristic and medieval church, the individual did not interpret scripture; that task belonged to the church through its authoritative tradition. The German reformer Martin Luther (1483–1546) took a different view.[36] In 1513 he was to lecture on the Psalms at the Augustinian house in Wittenburg. The usual procedure would involve lecturing with reference to a scriptural text that included the marginal commentaries and glosses of the great theologians of the early church. But Luther asked his printer to prepare an edition of the Psalter that left the margins blank. All that remained was the scriptural text, the reader and the teacher. So began a reading of the scriptures outside the authoritative teaching and interpretative tradition of the church, both past and present. This became enshrined in the Reformation slogan *sola scriptura* – the authority of scripture alone, not the church's interpretation of scripture. Under the guidance of the Holy Spirit, the individual Christian could now interpret the biblical text for herself. The political and theological implications were radical and, whether or not one sympathizes, it is easy to see why church authorities were concerned. Rather than authority being vested in the body of the church and its book, the Bible, with the individual trained in and submitting to established and communal practices of interpretation, there could now potentially be as many interpretations of scripture as there were readers of scripture. It is certainly the case that Luther, Ulrich Zwingli (1484–1531), Conrad Grebel (c. 1498–1526) and other reformers were not espousing the imposition of an individual's opinion or interpretation onto scripture. The reader was to discern God's word in its plain sense. Nevertheless, from the 1520s it became apparent that the reformers could not agree on the meaning of that plain sense.[37] The risk to Christian unity and even political stability was very clear. This apparently innocent gesture by Luther – the preparation of a scriptural text devoid of any aid from the church's tradition of interpretation – represented early signs of a shift towards individual liberty, private interpretation and self-determination which were to become central in modern philosophy and the Enlightenment in the seventeenth and eighteenth centuries.

In addition to shifting the focus of authority onto the plain biblical text, the Reformation began to dismantle the traditional pattern of scriptural interpretation. Faced with increasingly elaborate allegorical exegesis, the fourfold interpretation of scripture was reduced to the literal sense alone. Writing against his nemesis Jerome Emser (1477–1527) in 1521, Luther states:

> For the diligence and efforts of all teachers are directed solely to discovering the literal meaning which alone is valid for them too. Thus Augustine also writes that 'figures prove nothing'. This means that Emser's spiritual understanding counts for nothing; but the other one [the literal one] is the highest, best, strongest, in short, the whole substance, nature, and foundation of Holy Scripture. If one abandoned it, the whole Scripture would be nothing.[38]

Other reformers, such as Martin Bucer (1491–1551), Philip Melanchton (1497–1560) and John Calvin (1509–1564), also shared a clear preference for the literal sense of scripture and a dislike of allegorical interpretation. While it is the case that patristic and medieval theologians regarded the literal sense as foundational, they did not regard the literal sense as opposed to the other senses of scripture. Quite the contrary – the literal sense of scripture prompted and enabled the discernment of further layers of meaning in the things to which scripture referred. For the reformers, the literal sense of scripture was preferred to the exclusion of the spiritual senses. Only the plain, historical sense of the scriptural text was to be discerned.

Harrison argues that this shift in the interpretation of scripture, towards a more exclusive focus on the literal sense, had unintended but far-reaching consequences for the interpretation of the book of nature. As we have seen, the allegorical interpretation of scripture was based on a symbolic view of the created order. Words referred to creatures, which, in turn, were resemblances of other creatures and vessels of theological meaning. The network of signs that composed the book of nature was read through the network of signs that composed the book of scripture. During the sixteenth century, the primacy of the 'plain sense' was extended from scripture to nature. No longer did birds, beasts and the celestial bodies *mean* anything. They were simply objects whose structure and design revealed the creator's ingenuity and power. The world was no longer replete with creaturely symbols and allegories. It was simply full of *things* that were not bearers of meaning but occasions for the display of God's power and intricate design.[39] Harrison writes:

> As an inevitable consequence of this way of reading texts nature would lose its meaning, and the vacuum created by this loss of intelligibility was gradually to be occupied by alternative accounts of the significance of natural things – those explanations which we regard as scientific.[40]

The theological developments of the Reformation, particularly the drive to investigate nature not as a text that bore meaning but a series of objects whose workings were to be probed by empirical methods, provided a crucial context for the rise of modern natural science. The view that creation is a sacramental order of signs conveying theological truths was replaced with the view that the universe is the product of an infinitely powerful manufacturer whose techniques can be probed in much the same way as the techniques of a human artisan. Francis Bacon, who provided one of the most influential accounts of the modern method of natural philosophy, wrote in 1623: 'For as the power and skill of a workman are seen in his works, but not his person, so the works of God express the wisdom and omnipotence of the Creator, without the least representation of his image.'[41] Nature could now be investigated literally and for its own sake rather than interpreted for the higher, spiritual truths it conveyed as part of a cosmic symbolic order. According to Harrison, this represented a radical contraction of the sacred: only the scriptural text – *sola scriptura* – was regarded as the vessel of divine truth. It was not, however, that the metaphor of the book of nature withered, but that the book was now written in a different language: the language of mathematics. The things of nature could be ordered according to literal taxonomic systems rather than patterns of symbolic meaning.

As well as the move from the fourfold interpretation of scripture and nature to an exclusive emphasis on the literal, we have also explored the changing nature of authority during the early stages of the Reformation. The sixteenth-century reformers relocated authority away from tradition and the church's interpretation of its sacred text to the literal sense of the Bible. Combined with access to the Bible in the vernacular and the easier availability of copies following the invention of the printing press, this opened the possibility of proliferating readings of scripture based on individuals' interpretations and opinions. This sheds some light on an event that is often taken to epitomize the conflict between theology and science: the famous trial of the Italian astronomer Galileo Galilei (1564–1642) by the Roman Catholic Inquisition. This was not simply a case of church versus lone scientist in an argument about the movement of the earth. It was a question of the nature and place of authority.

Galileo published his *Dialogue Concerning the Two Chief World Systems of the World*, in 1632.[42] He was subsequently accused of a number of heresies, including heliocentrism, and placed under house arrest from 1633 until his death nine years later. Here was the lone scientist, faithful to his experimental observations and mathematical calculations, confronting the full might, power and bigotry of the Roman Catholic Church and all its vested interests. Along with other works advocating heliocentrism by astronomers such as Johannes Kepler (1571–1630), Galileo's *Dialogue* was placed on the *Index Librorum Prohibitorum,* the index of books prohibited by the church as heretical.[43] The Galileo trial therefore becomes a clear example for the view that religion and science are in conflict. The church exercised institutional power based on superstition, in contrast to the new science which was based solely on observation and objective analysis. However, while Copernicus's *De Revolutionibus* had caused little controversy at the time of its publication in 1543 and was only briefly on the index of prohibited books in 1616, Galileo's work – which similarly argued for heliocentrism and was published less than a century later – brought down the full force of the Inquisition. What had changed between the mid-sixteenth and the mid-seventeenth centuries, and why so strong a reaction against a lone Italian astronomer whom the scientific establishment of the day regarded as a bit of a crank? Indeed, Galileo's ecclesiastical inquisitors were upholding the scientific consensus of the day while also being the most prolific sponsors of astronomical research. They were hardly against natural philosophy.

The case of Galileo has received considerable scholarly attention.[44] It is clear that the issues are complex; a critical historical approach reveals that it is not a matter simply of a bigoted religious establishment cracking down on a heroic lone scientist. What had emerged in the decades that separated Copernicus and Galileo was the power of the Reformation and a huge shift in the understanding of authority, particularly the authority of scripture and the authority of the church. By the mid-seventeenth century, the church was concerned about the power of an individual to decide unilaterally on an issue as theologically – and therefore politically – significant as whether the earth goes round the sun or the sun goes round the earth. By what authority could Galileo make such pronouncements and, crucially, by what mechanism could they be tested? The matter could not be decided by a simple appeal to the evidence because the interpretation of that evidence was contested. Galileo's own clearly stated aim was the honour of the church. Yet the implications of Galileo's observations and calculations concerning planetary movements for the interpretation of scripture were potentially considerable. How were scriptural texts that implied that the sun goes round the earth to be treated, now that an allegorical interpretation was less readily available to Reformed and Catholic interpreters alike? What were the theological implications of removing the earth from the stationary heart of the cosmos? These issues had to be confronted; the ecclesiastical and political stakes were high. The trial of Galileo was not simply about science verses theology or ecclesiastical power. It was about a rapidly changing religious and cultural environment in which the primary locus of authority had been shifted and remained insecure in such a way that the mechanisms for deciding on the veracity of Galileo's proposals were not at all clear. Today, we have procedures for the conduct of scientific debate and mechanisms for checking scientific claims and establishing those claims as facts: peer-reviewed journals, academic conferences, established practices of observation and interpretation, authorized and regulated communities of scientists in whom authority is vested by virtue of qualifications and institutional affiliation. No such mechanisms were available in seventeenth-century Italy: hence the danger of lone scientists making claims with significant implications but with no process for deciding on their trustworthiness or truth.

The trial of Galileo is not, therefore, a straightforward instance of a scientific approach to nature coming into conflict with a theological approach. The issues were far more complex. In fact, the wider history of the rise of early modern science indicates its very close relationship with theology, insofar as natural philosophers needed a purpose for their enquiries. As we will see, they found it in Christian piety.

The theological purpose of natural philosophy

In twenty-first-century culture, natural science enjoys enormous prestige. Scientists speak authoritatively on many matters, even theology. The power of the technological application of science in medicine, computing, manufacturing and the military is obvious. Scientific research attracts huge financial investment. It is therefore important to realize that the pioneers of modern science – the natural philosophers of the seventeenth and eighteenth centuries – enjoyed no such prestige. The purpose of the experimental investigation of nature was not at all clear. The case of one of the greatest scientists of the tradition, Isaac Newton, provides an important example.

In 1687, Newton, a Fellow of Trinity College, Cambridge, published his great *Principia Mathematica*, one of the most influential texts of modern natural philosophy. He sent copies to the heads of the Colleges of the University of Cambridge, but they did not understand its strange mathematical symbols. The mathematical calculus that Newton deployed seemed to be a mysterious coded language; specialist mathematicians were employed to tell the readers of the *Principia* what it meant.[45] Moreover, copies of the *Principia* were rare and expensive. This added to the sense that Newton was a harbinger of divine secrets and a prophet who was unlocking the mind of God. This was certainly how Newton perceived himself – a new Christ who was prophetically returning humanity to a once pristine knowledge of nature last enjoyed by Noah.[46] John Conduitt (1688–1737), Newton's biographer, wrote notes on 'Newton's suitability for canonization if not deification'. Conduitt, who married Newton's niece, regarded his subject as 'a Saint & his discoveries may well pass for miracles'.[47]

While it is now clear that Newton's physics is extremely powerful – we can use it to send a rocket to the moon – its purpose was far from clear in the last decades of the seventeenth century. In 1692, Richard Bentley (1662–1742), a young clergyman and classicist, who delivered the first series of Boyle Lectures defending religion from atheism, wrote to Newton to ask about the purpose of his *Principia*. Newton replied:

> When I wrote my treatise about our System I had an eye upon such principles as might work with considering men for the belief of a Deity and nothing can rejoice me more than to find it useful for that purpose.[48]

In other words, a central purpose of the *Principia*, a great work of natural philosophy that today we would call physics, was to support belief in God. By the time of the publication of the second edition in 1713, Newton had added an appendix known as a 'General Scholium'. Among other things, this outlined his theological views and the religious purpose of his treatise. Of God, Newton wrote:

> In him all things are contained and move, but he does not act on them nor they on him. God experiences nothing from the motions of bodies; the bodies feel no resistance from God's omnipresence. … We know him only by his properties and attributes and by the wisest and best construction of things in their final causes, and we admire him because of his perfections; but we venerate and worship him because of his dominion.[49]

Newton wrote far more about theology than he did about physics and nature. He left two million words on prophecy and temple history, including commentaries on portions of the second book of Kings, on Daniel and on Chronicles. Church history was also a major concern. He was particularly interested in the fourth-century debates on Christology and regarded Athanasius as the great corruptor of the Christian faith. His religious writings remained unpublished because they were eccentric and heretical and might have led to the loss of his Fellowship at Trinity College.[50] Newton famously rejected the divinity of Christ, whom he regarded as God's viceroy. This also entailed a rejection of the doctrine of the Trinity. Nevertheless, theological concerns were at the heart of the intellectual quest of one of England's great scientists.

Newton was a prominent figure in the founding of the 'Royal Society for Improving Natural Knowledge' and served as its twelfth president from 1703 to his death in 1727. The Royal Society, which flourishes today as one of the world's most prestigious scientific learned societies, was founded in 1660 and received its first royal charter from Charles II in 1662. The second charter, granted a year later, states that the studies of the Society were 'to be applied to further promoting by the authority of experiments the sciences of natural things and of useful arts, to the Glory of God the Creator, and the advantage of the human race'.[51] While the members of the Royal Society were keen to avoid dispute in matters pertaining to the particular religious doctrines and ecclesiastical politics that divided the church at the time, there is abundant evidence that they understood the principal goal of natural philosophy to be confirmation of the existence and power of God. As Gaukroger has argued in great detail, the religious motivations and goals of natural philosophy and experimental practice were fundamental to its legitimation in the seventeenth and eighteenth centuries.[52] This is reflected in the history of the Royal Society written in the late 1660s by one of its founders, Thomas Sprat (1635–1713), later bishop of Rochester. At a time when the Society was in dire financial straits and needed to justify its practices, he writes, 'I now proceed to the weightiest, and most solemn part of my undertaking; to make a defence of the Royal Society, and this new Experimental Learning, in respect of the Christian Faith.'[53] At this time, we also find an increasing tendency to see experimental philosophers as 'priests of nature' and revealers of the mysteries of God hidden within the natural order. Robert Boyle, the most remarkable of England's seventeenth-century experimenters, regarded natural philosophy as a way of resolving religious disputes by providing rational, empirical evidence. According to Boyle, experiments were best performed on Sundays as part of the wider church's pattern of worship.[54]

As part of the drive to support belief in Christianity, there were two particular religious motivations for the practice of experimental and mathematical natural philosophy. The first concerned the purpose and utility of creatures. For ancient and medieval Christianity, creatures were beneficial because they were signs of the creator. They resembled their divine cause and existed by participation in the life of God; they shimmered with the divine resemblance according to their own mode of being. Creatures had a pedagogical value in teaching about God's providence and how humanity should live. Their value to human beings rested in an intrinsic goodness derived from their resemblance to God. Once that symbolic world ebbed away and a more literal reading of creation prevailed, it seemed that the purpose or use of nature lay principally in meeting the material needs of human beings. In 1688, Robert Boyle wrote a treatise on the final causes of natural things, by which he meant their utility for human beings. He articulated the drive to understand the utility of nature.

> There are not many subjects in the whole compass of Natural Philosophy, that better deserve to be inquired into by Christian philosophers, than that which is discoursed of in the following Essay. For certainly it becomes such men to have curiosity enough to try at least, whether it can be discovered, that there are any knowable final causes, to be considered in the works of nature. Since, if we neglect this inquiry, we live in danger of being ungrateful, in overlooking the uses of things, that may give us just cause of admiring and thanking the author of them, and of losing the benefits, relating as well to philosophy as piety, that the knowledge of them may afford us.[55]

By experimental method, two things were to be discerned and admired: first, the power and intricate craftsmanship of God; secondly, the uses to which creatures could be put. While many uses for creatures could be identified, there were many that appeared to be harmful or of no value. Because such creatures no longer harboured any symbolic significance, a use had to be discerned. Most natural philosophers were content to let the benefits of certain creatures remain mysterious so that later generations could continue their investigations of nature, but others were bolder in their inferences. For example, the eighteenth-century priest, naturalist and author of *Spectacle de la Nature*, Noël-Antoine Pluche (1688–1761), surmised the purpose of woodworm to be the promotion of international trade.[56] Countries must trade timber and pitch in order to repair and protect the hulls of their ships that have been attacked by these creatures: 'Thus does this little Animal, which we so much complain of as being troublesome and injurious to us, become the very Cement which unites these distant Nations in one common Interest.'[57]

Harrison argues that the second motivation for experimental and mathematical investigation of nature concerned the effects of the Fall, on the condition of human rational and observational powers and the condition of wider nature.[58] For the patristic and medieval theologians, the narrative of the Garden of Eden in Genesis was a rich allegory. For example, human dominion over the animals was interpreted as the command to master the passions; tending the Garden was interpreted in terms the cultivation of the virtues.[59] As for Noah and the Flood, this was an allegory of the church tossed around on the seas of the world's corruption and sin. Once this symbolic and allegorical interpretation gave way to an exclusively literal reading of the text, the experience of paradise and the possession of knowledge unsullied by sin became a matter of history.[60] The seventeenth-century Puritan clergyman George Walker (c. 1581–1651) wrote 'In the state of innocency in the first creation, man had perfect naturall knowledge of all naturall things, arising and springing immediately from his naturall soule.'[61] The commands of Genesis were no longer about the spiritual and moral life of the human person; they were now literal commands to have dominion over the earth and subdue it. In the seventeenth century, the idea of returning to a time in history when humanity enjoyed the Edenic paradise became an intelligible aim. The practice of experimental and mathematical natural philosophy was one way in which the effects of the Fall – the expulsion from Eden, the Flood and the confusion of tongues – could be reversed. The first transgression of humanity in the form of Adam and Eve eating the fruit of the tree of knowledge had resulted in human reason and sense perception becoming compromised. Experimental practice – the repetition of the contrived observation of nature – was one way of assuaging these effects. The Flood caused a radical change in the topography and fertility of the earth such that the laborious cultivation of food was required. The confusion of languages arising from the fall of the tower of Babel was an event in history that resulted in the loss of an original, natural language and with it a replete knowledge of the created order. As Harrison states:

> Knowledge of creatures led to theological knowledge. But it served in addition to mitigate the consequences of the Fall and re-establish human dominion over nature. ... Knowledge, in other words, gives rise to improvement of the human lot, reversing the process of deterioration set in train by the Fall, and transforming the earth into a paradisal anticipation of the life to come. ... Natural philosophy was thus a potential panacea for the ills which came after the Fall.[62]

The discipline of discerning the workings and utility of creatures in order to provide support for belief in God became known as physico-theology, later referred to as natural theology.[63] As the term suggests, this was a combination of physics – the study of *physis* or 'nature' – and theology. In the seventeenth century, natural philosophers with no particular theological training believed that they were making significant theological contributions through their experimental observations and physico-mathematics. In contrast to the relation between theological learning and natural philosophy in the High Middle Ages, for example in the work of Aquinas, those who practised physico-theology did not regard metaphysics as mediating between natural philosophy and theology. It therefore claimed to be a more direct and literal application of the reading of nature onto the doctrine of God with little or no philosophical nuance. What kind of God emerged from this practice of physico-theology? What kind of creation emerged? These are the questions for the next section of this chapter.

Physico-theology, teleology and the designer God

It is very common to narrate the rise of the natural sciences in the sixteenth and seventeenth centuries in terms of the demise of a medieval teleological cosmos and its replacement by a purposeless mechanistic cosmos.[64] As we saw in the previous chapter, 'teleology' is the study of final causes or purposes within nature (pp. 63–4; 81–3). The natural philosophies of the Platonic and Aristotelian traditions and the Christian doctrine of creation as it evolved in the patristic and medieval periods were teleological: creatures were orientated to particular ends or goals and the cosmos as a whole exhibited a teleological structure. Acorns were ordered towards growth into an oak tree, the cygnet towards the swan and humanity towards knowledge and virtue. As Aquinas claimed, 'Every agent acts for an end.'[65] In early modern natural philosophy, however, final causes were regarded as unnecessary for the proper explanation of natural phenomena. Francis Bacon writes:

> It is right to lay down: 'to know truly is to know by causes.' It is also not bad to distinguish four causes: Material, Formal, Efficient and Final. But of these the Final is a long way from being useful; in fact it actually distorts the sciences except in the case of human actions.[66]

In acknowledging that final causes may be used in the explanation of human actions, Bacon is noting that human beings are intentional and deliberative; they can therefore choose between different goals or purposes and the means by which to achieve them. Teleology is therefore an acceptable mode of explanation with respect to human behaviour because such behaviour arises from minds that can set goals and decide on the means to achieve those goals. Wider nature, however, is to be explained not by *final* causes, but by *efficient* causes – those events and actions that immediately precede an effect in time and transmit their causal power via physical contact (see Chapter 3, pp. 80–1). If we want to know about the fall of heavy bodies, the orbit of the planets, the growth of a tree or the reproduction of animals, we refer to efficient causes, not final causes and purpose.

Mechanistic explanations, referring only to efficient causes, replaced Aristotelian accounts from the mid-seventeenth century. Mechanism was the idea that natural phenomena could be described with reference to a single level of the material universe known as micro-corpuscles. These tiny bodies were thought to act on one another to transmit a mechanical quantity of motion via physical contact. Collectively, the micro-corpuscles formed the macroscopic world that we experience. Explanation of macroscopic phenomena such as a plant flowering or an animal moving was via a reduction to the physics of micro-corpuscles. Just as one could explain the working of a printing press by reducing it to its moving parts and their action upon each other, so one could explain the working of an animal by reducing it to its micro-corpuscles and their action upon each other. Within a mechanistic cosmos, there are no purposes or goals as such; everything can be explained in terms of the mechanical actions of bodies upon one another. Those actions can be identified by the science of physics through mathematical explanation.[67]

Although the explanation of natural phenomena could be reduced to mechanical efficient causes for seventeenth-century natural philosophers, the need to explain the role of God in the creation and maintenance of a mechanical universe remained. The motif of the divine designer of the universe presented itself with particular force. Just as a designer was required for a mechanism such as a mechanical clock, so too there must be a designer of the cosmic mechanism. In his General Scholium to the *Principia Mathematica*, Isaac Newton writes: 'This most elegant system of the sun, planets, and comets could not have arisen without the design and dominion of an intelligent and powerful being.'[68] Despite receiving a sophisticated attack by David Hume (1711–1776) in his posthumously published *Dialogues Concerning Natural Religion* (1779), the notion of God as the designer of creation reached its apogee in 1802 with the publication of William Paley's (1743–1805) *Natural Theology, or Evidences of the Existence and Attributes of the Deity collected from the Appearances of Nature.*[69] Charles Darwin (1809–1882) published his *On the Origin of Species* in 1859 and apparently put an end to the notion of a divine designer. According to evolution, the order we witness in creation looks like design but is actually the result of a blind and directionless process of natural selection. Nevertheless, the idea that when we talk about creation we must be talking about God as the designer of the universe remains a common assumption. The design argument continues to receive considerable attention from philosophers, not least in the form of so-called intelligent design.[70]

As a number of historians have noted, early modern natural philosophy did not do away altogether with teleology, because the concept of a designed universe requires the deliberative intention of a supernatural designer.[71] The designer orientates his design towards a particular purpose. So Bacon's claim that final causes can be invoked with respect to human actions is extended to God: the creator and designer of the universe chooses the ends of his creatures and, through the creation of a cosmic mechanism, applies them to those ends. There are, therefore, divine purposes for the designed universe and, as we have seen in this chapter, it was the role of modern natural philosophy to discern those purposes. In so doing, the natural philosopher was discerning the will of God. Creatures were designed for the material benefit of humankind – that was their purpose and goal – and those material benefits were indications of the divine will.

This means that creation, although mechanical according to seventeenth-century natural philosophers, exhibited a teleological purpose that was given by God in the form of a design. To understand the nature of this teleology more clearly, let us consider a machine that will be familiar to us in the contemporary world: a photocopier. The goal or purpose of the machine is the production of copies of a given document. This teleological order is not, however, intrinsic to the materials from which the photocopier is built. Such order comes from the intentionality of the photocopier's designer and the photocopier's operator. The material nature of the photocopier – the metal, electronics and toner – has an order and orientation *imposed upon it* by the designer and operator. Such order and orientation does not emerge from the form of the photocopier's material parts, but has its origin in human design and manufacture, that is, in the structures and order first present in the designer's mind. The material stuff from which the machine is made is passive and indifferent to the form and order imposed upon it by the process of design and manufacture. Once the photocopier is manufactured and in operation, the designer and operator can withdraw and hope for no paper jams. This is how the teleological order of creation was imagined in early modern science: matter is passive and its teleological order is *external*.[72] Matter featured no *intrinsic* powers or orientation. Motion was explained not in terms of inherent powers towards particular ends, but in terms of forces that change a body's state of motion from the outside – pushes and pulls, if you like.

In the seventeenth century, a new concept arose which described the way in which an external teleology was applied to creation by the divine designer: laws of nature. The order of creation was imposed upon passive matter in the form of laws that can be expressed mathematically. Writing to the priest and mathematician Marin Mersenne (1588–1648) in 1630, Descartes declared:

> The mathematical truths which you call eternal have been laid down by God and depend on him entirely no less than the rest of his creatures. Indeed to say that these truths are independent of God is to talk of him as if he were Jupiter or Saturn and to subject him to the Styx and the Fates. Please do not hesitate to assert and proclaim everywhere that it is God who has laid down these laws in nature just as a king lays down laws in his kingdom.[73]

This view of teleological order differed very significantly from that proposed by Aristotle and Aquinas.[74] For Aristotle, nature is 'the distinctive form or quality of such things as have *within themselves* a principle of motion, such form or characteristic property not being separable from the things themselves, save conceptually'.[75] The goal or *telos* of something is given by its form – its defining essence, if you like – and this is intrinsic to the creature. For example, the form of the acorn – its acornness – is also its orientation to the goal of becoming an oak tree. The acorn contains within itself the potential to become an oak tree. Aristotle would say that the acorn possesses the form of oak tree potentially in a way that the acorn does not possess the form of, say, a buttercup or a horse chestnut. The form of oak tree possessed by the acorn in a potential fashion is actualized through the growth of the acorn in the ground. But that form is not distinguishable from the acorn; it is intrinsic to what the acorn is. For Aristotle, it is the form of something that bears also the *telos* of that creature – the oak tree.

In stipulating that the form is *intrinsic* to the creature, Aristotle is distinguishing natural things from artificial things that are created by human designers. Things that we make, such as beds, cars and photocopiers, have a form, and therefore a goal or purpose, that is not intrinsic to the matter from which they are made; it is extrinsic and derives from human intention. Because the form of the product is extrinsic, so too is the *telos* or purpose; the designer gives it and imposes it upon her material. Thus we arrive at an important Aristotelian teaching: art imitates nature. By 'art'

Aristotle means 'things that human beings make', whether they be portraits or photocopiers. When he claims that art imitates nature, he wants to say that when we make something like a bed or a car – things that are therefore *artificial* – and impose upon the material a form and purpose, we are imitating or relying upon an intrinsic purposiveness or teleology that is already present in natural things. Our purposiveness in making things imitates the purposes of the natural world. At its best, our artifice does not run against the grain of the intrinsic teleology of creatures, but works with it. For example, the master woodworker makes best use of the intrinsic qualities or form of the wood at his disposal to make something – a desk, say – to which the wood is particularly fitted.

Whereas the kind of teleology proposed by early modern natural science is extrinsic, the common reading of Aristotle is that there is a natural teleology that is intrinsic to creatures. For Aristotle, matter *always* possesses some kind of form. Matter is never just 'matter'; it is always 'a something' because its form defines it as a 'this' rather than a 'that' – a boy rather than an elephant, or an acorn rather than a sycamore seed. Aquinas, however, was able to avoid the dualism of 'internal' and 'external' teleology by invoking the doctrine of creation *ex nihilo*. In one sense, he argued that the purposes of God's creation are intrinsic to creatures themselves; they are not imposed from the outside, nor, crucially, is *matter passive*. Yet, while the forms of creatures – which define their purpose – are intrinsic to the material natures of those creatures, they exist only by participation in God who created them *ex nihilo* and sustains their existence at every moment. In fact, the forms of creatures reside in an exemplary way in what Aquinas calls (following a long Neoplatonic tradition) the divine ideas.[76] The achievement of Aquinas is to hold the intrinsic and extrinsic teleology of creatures together theologically. The forms of creatures, and therefore their goals and purposes, are in one sense intrinsic because they are possessed by creatures themselves. When creatures move towards their goal, that motion is really their own. But in another sense that purpose and goal is extrinsic, because it lies beyond the creature in the mind of God. So Aquinas achieves a blend of intrinsic and extrinsic teleology in which the former participates in the latter. The universe is neither purely natural (intrinsic teleology) nor artificial (extrinsic teleology); it is uniquely *created* by God out of nothing.

We are now in a position to examine the theological consequences of the divine design proposed by the physico-theology of the seventeenth and early eighteenth centuries. Because matter is passive and laws of nature given by God define its motions, the teleological order of nature does not belong to nature itself. Creation is therefore a work of divine artifice that is akin to a very big version of the artefacts made by people. No longer does art imitate nature as it had done for Aristotle and Aquinas: nature now imitates art. The natural world comes to look very much like a giant mechanism in which God imposes laws of nature, much as a king would impose laws to govern the populace of a country.

In effect, creation came to be understood as a 'thing' governed by God, who lay outside creation as its supreme and all-powerful ruler. This gives the notion that creation involves two *things* that stand alongside each other: God plus creation. The purpose of experimental natural philosophy was to discern the will of God and the utility of creatures in much the same way as one might try to discern the will of the human designer of an artefact and the uses to which that artefact might be put. Given the investigative methods and metaphysical presuppositions of the early modern scientist-theologians, it is not surprising that the God they discovered bore a striking resemblance to an extremely powerful human designer.

Perhaps most importantly, however, we see in the rise of modern science the failure to distinguish adequately between primary and secondary causation. In the previous chapter, we saw that God's primary causation is not of the same kind as the secondary causation of creatures. They are not univocal, but share an analogical relation. God is the primary cause in the sense that God sustains creation in existence and thereby applies secondary causes to their purposes. In any action within creation – for example, me pushing a mug across a table – we are not faced with the dilemma 'was it me or was it God?' It was both, but in utterly different ways. I am a real and potent secondary cause, but only through a participation in the utterly unique primary causation of God. The primary causation of God is the necessary basis for there being any real and potent secondary causes within creation. However, if matter features no intrinsic form, is passive and behaves according to laws of nature that are external to the created order and layered upon it, this suggests that there is no *genuine* creaturely causal agency within creation. God becomes the primary, all-powerful efficient cause who polices the behaviour of matter according to the laws of nature. To see why this is the case, think back to the photocopier. The designer manufactures the photocopier by drawing up plans and manipulating metal and plastic. The operator then applies the machine to action by introducing electricity and pressing the 'start' button. The machine runs, following the design and purpose given by the designer. At no point does the material of the photocopier *move itself*, because the explanation of its motion always lies elsewhere. Its principle of motion, as Aristotle would say, lies outside. It runs by virtue of the operator's causal action and the application of electricity according to the design imposed upon it. Similarly, in most conceptions of early modern natural philosophy, God becomes the 'designer' and 'operator' of creation via the laws of nature. Insofar as there are any secondary causes in this model, they are only instrumental. Creatures are not really creatures; they are amalgams of passive material stuff that become the *occasion* for God's action – hence the term 'occasionalism' which sometimes appears in this context. God does everything *to the exclusion* of any other kind of cause.

An alternative, which some commentators regard as Descartes's mature position, is that God governs creation, as its designer, through the laws of nature, but human minds – because they are, for Descartes, a non-material substance – may also act as causes.[77] In this model, however, God becomes merely another intelligent agent acting within creation alongside or in competition with human intelligent agents. God becomes a univocal cause among causes, rather than the 'wholly other' ontological basis for there being any created, secondary causes at all.

Examining the history of physico-theology as it arose in the seventeenth century, we can see that its understanding of God was very much a product of the way in which nature was conceived and investigated. In other words, a mechanistic cosmology in which matter is simply passive stuff, devoid of form and purpose, gave rise to a particular conception of God and his creative act. What emerged was a God conceived of as a supreme and all-powerful ruler standing alongside creation and acting within creation as one causal force among others. In the end, after the nascent natural science of the seventeenth century had been deemed legitimate through its association with Christian piety, it could receive a new purpose in the nineteenth century through its technological application. The ultimate theological consequence of such an approach to creation was that God could be jettisoned without fear of undermining the value of the experimental and mathematical exploration of nature. The laws of nature could be preserved without the need for a lawgiver. Phenomena could be explained entirely on their own terms with reference to efficient causes and, come the latter part of the nineteenth century, the evolution of species by natural selection. We can put the matter very simply with reference to the earlier example of me moving a mug across a table: if God's causal power is univocal with mine (i.e., of the same kind only infinitely more powerful), then it makes sense to ask, 'did God move the mug or did I move the mug?' Faced with that 'either/or' choice (a choice that would have been unintelligible to Aquinas), nineteenth-century natural science opted for natural causes; it accordingly had to abandon any hope of giving a plausible account of divine causation.

The legacy of physico-theology and the relation of science and theology

For a number of commentators, the God that emerged from seventeenth-century natural philosophy and natural theology – one that has remained in the common imagination ever since – is the God in whom the modern world does not believe; it is not the God of the traditional Christian doctrine of creation. [78] Notwithstanding its stunning success in increasing our knowledge of the universe and our ability to manipulate the natural world, the consequences of the rise of modern science for an adequate account of the doctrine of creation are therefore very significant. In this final section, we will examine the legacy for theology of the rise of modern natural science, beginning with its method.

At the heart of the success of seventeenth- and eighteenth-century natural philosophy lay a method of simplification. Isaac Newton wanted to understand motion more clearly and accurately, so rather than observing the complex motions of creatures within the natural order, he stripped away all context and extraneous factors in order to explore the physics of a single body in the vacuum of absolute space. This was a kind of 'idealized' motion – one that could not pertain in the real world but allowed a simple but accurate approximation to the real world. Using this method, Newton identified his three laws of motion. From this very simple model, extra factors such as an atmosphere or gravity could gradually be introduced. The model could thus be developed with increasing layers of complexity, until it reached something more proximate to the real world as we encounter it. This method of simplification, of dealing with very complex phenomena within nature by stripping away extraneous factors, is common in the natural sciences and is sometimes referred to as 'abstraction': processes and entities are reduced to their simplest and most basic parts. Laboratory science is a good example of this method: a process is isolated, removed from a complex context and observed within a laboratory. One might examine the human body in a similar way, by reducing it to its material parts through dissection or examining its chemical constituents. This allows us to isolate and treat certain parts of the body that are malfunctioning. Any simplified scientific model that is devised on the basis of a reduction to the component parts of a creature or organism is only an approximation to the complex entities in the real world.

The mechanistic physico-theology of the early modern period made such analysis an important part of the way that modern science conceives the world. This is for two reasons. First, as we have seen, the doctrine of creation that emerged from the seventeenth century conceived of creation as an artefact. In other words, it was understood as the product of divine manufacture. For Aristotle, human artistry was subsequent to, and reliant upon, nature and its intrinsic forms and purposes: art was understood to imitate nature. This was reversed in modern natural philosophy: nature now imitated art. This meant that, just as an artefact can be reduced to its component parts and is nothing more than the amalgamation of those parts, so too creatures were understood as nothing more than the amalgamation of their parts. Secondly, the materialism that came to dominate natural philosophy – the micro-corpuscles of the mechanistic ontology – meant that creatures were best analysed, not as wholes that were more than the sum of their parts, but in terms of the interaction of their components. Take the example of the unity and wholeness of a clock: it does not belong to the materials of the clock itself because they could not organize themselves into the form of a clock. Rather, that form and unity is due to the application of an external design by the clockmaker. Similarly, the structures of creatures came to be understood as lying outside their material natures in the designs of God. Once the modern 'designer God' had been confined to the realms of superstition and myth, all that was left were assemblages of material components that somehow – we know now how – assemble to form creatures. The idea that natural entities are understood by reducing them to their more fundamental component parts is known as 'reductionism'. It suggests, for example, that just as a clock can be disassembled to reveal its workings, so too a human body is best understood by reducing it to its essential components.

Perhaps the most striking aspect of the material reductionism of early modern natural philosophy was its failure to give an adequate account of *life*. For Aristotle and Aquinas, the natural was distinguished from the artificial in terms of a principle of motion. The natural – for example, a plant or a tree – had within itself its own principle of motion and rest. The artificial – for example, a bed or a clock – had its principle of motion externally, in the designer and manufacturer. Aristotle could also distinguish between the animate and the inanimate. The animate – that is, living things – were self-moving. Living organisms were a blended unity of matter and form; it was form that gathered the material into a living whole. By contrast, if there is nothing other than matter, matter is essentially passive and inanimate and the movements of matter are mechanical and due to efficient causation, there can be no genuine distinction between that which is moved and that which is self-moving. To put the issue another way: if a living organism is simply an amalgamation of chemical components that are not alive and this organism is best analysed by a reduction of the organism to those chemical components, it is difficult to identify what is particularly significant about the notion of 'life'. Living things are simply a particular combination of material parts and the 'dead' material parts are more fundamental, with no *intrinsic* orientation towards life.

The twentieth-century Jewish philosopher Hans Jonas (1903– 93) put this issue in a very arresting way. He points out that ancient Greek thought and the traditional theology of creation regarded matter and form as intrinsically orientated towards life. The inanimate was teleologically ordered towards the animate. Life was the purpose of the universe and, in that sense, it was more fundamental than the inanimate, even if the inanimate preceded it in time. With the rise of mechanistic cosmology and reductive methods in modern natural philosophy, it was the inanimate that had ontological as well as temporal priority. Life was a strange aberration in a tiny backwater of a fundamentally dead universe. In the end, even life was explained by a reduction to its lifeless components. Jonas writes:

> Accordingly, it is the existence of life within a mechanical universe which now calls for an explanation, and explanation has to be in terms of the lifeless. ... That there is life at all, and how such a thing is possible in a world of mere matter, is now the problem of thought. The very fact that we have nowadays to deal with the theoretical problem of life, instead of the problem of death, testifies to the status of death as the natural and intelligible condition.[79]

Historians of science have pointed out that the mechanistic understanding of nature began to collapse in the eighteenth century precisely because it could not account for phenomena such as life.[80] However, insofar as a materialist and mechanistic understanding of nature persists in certain quarters of science and in the popular imagination, a failure to give an account of the special and significant status of 'life' remains.

The scientific method of simplification or abstraction that we find in, for example, Newton's analysis of the motion of a body in a vacuum or reductivist tendencies of mechanical philosophy, has given rise to an important distinction in recent discussions of the relationship between science and theology, between 'methodological naturalism' and 'ontological naturalism'. 'Naturalism' is a complex label in contemporary philosophy, but is broadly the idea that the natural world is all there is. There is nothing beyond nature as we encounter it; there is no supernatural or transcendent realm. Very often this is allied to materialism – the view that every event in the universe, including emotions, thoughts, intention and causation, is a material event. 'Methodological naturalism' is the idea that science proceeds *as if* material nature is all there is. In other words, the scientific method of abstraction and reduction is simply that: a method. It brackets theology and the supernatural – lays them to one side – and examines material nature. It remains neutral concerning metaphysics and theology. Put simply, methodological naturalism makes no fundamental claims about what exists; it simply examines a particular part of reality composed of material nature using experimental observation and mathematical analysis. For some scientists, this is a way of preserving science's proper autonomy from metaphysics and theology. God can be put to one side, the natural world can be investigated and God can be reintroduced at a later stage if one wishes. 'Ontological naturalism', on the other hand, is more full bloodied: it is a claim about what there is. For the ontological naturalist, material nature exhausts reality. There is nothing more. Ontological naturalists are perforce atheists.

While many scientists, philosophers and theologians are not ontological naturalists, many are methodological naturalists. In claiming that naturalism is an appropriate method for science, methodological naturalism apparently allows science to get on with its business of examining the natural world, while metaphysics and theology get on with their own separate business. Within this approach is the claim that the reductive method of science – the reduction of natural processes and entities to their component parts and their investigation via experiment and mathematical analysis – is theologically and philosophically neutral. This leads to what Michael Hanby calls an 'extrinsicist' understanding of the relation between science, metaphysics and theology: these disciplines are 'extrinsic' to each other, having nothing to do with each other because of their differing methods and domains. Hanby argues, however, that methodological naturalism is very far from neutral: the method of science always masks an ontological naturalism. In other words, the *way* one investigates nature scientifically (method) already contains within itself a particular view of what nature *is* (ontology).[81] At a basic level – far more basic than Hanby's very sophisticated argument – this makes sense: when one investigates something, for example the nature of the human person, the *way* one investigates it will be moulded very much by what it *is* one thinks one is investigating. What one looks for will be determined by what one thinks is there to be seen. The way one investigates natural phenomena will very much determine what one sees and, crucially, *what one does not see*. Modern science claims to place before us the world as the world really is in itself and by its method renders nature transparent to our gaze: its method is neutral and simply presents the *literal* facts. To see why this claim might be brought into question, recall that the method of science as it emerged in the seventeenth century included a particular view concerning the nature of explanation. As we have seen with reference to Francis Bacon, proper scientific explanation of nature was understood to refer only to efficient causes and not to final causes or purposes. This is partly because final causes – purpose and intention – were deemed to belong exclusively to the human domain and, by extension, to God. What distinguished humans from wider nature, including animals, was purpose. Non-human nature was not *intrinsically* purposeful. But by adopting a method that refers only to efficient causation, the world that was observed by natural science was unsurprisingly found to be purposeless and mechanical. The decision to discount teleology, however, was arguably not one that arose from the empirical observation of the world; it arose from an ontological decision concerning what the world *is*: a mechanism composed of parts that interact by efficient causes. It is often claimed that science observes no purpose in nature because purpose is not there to be seen. Yet this jars with our basic intuitions and descriptions of the natural world. Biological accounts of this natural world have struggled for two hundred years to rid themselves of teleological descriptions of living organisms. In answer to the question 'why does the heart beat?' it proves immensely difficult to discount as untrue or trivial the statement 'in order to pump blood around the body'. Yet this is not a mechanical or efficient causal explanation. It is an explanation that refers to purpose: *in order to* pump blood around the body. Similarly, it is difficult to describe the immune system without referring to the purpose of restoring health. Some scientists will claim that there is a difference between explanation – which must always be in terms of efficient causes – and mere description. An efficient causal *explanation* of why the heart beats will refer to neurology and electrical impulses in the heart. We might *describe* the heart as beating in order to pump blood, but this is not a scientific explanation and is really metaphorical. This, however, generates a problematic division between the way we explain the world scientifically – and therefore what science permits us to see – and the way we perceive and describe the world at a more basic intuitive and common-sense level. The fact that the sciences, particularly the life sciences, have failed to purge themselves of teleological *descriptions* perhaps indicates that there is more to be seen of nature than the mechanical and efficient causal processes that are described in their *explanations*. In other words, it may be the very method of science, governed by *a priori* judgements concerning what the world is, that generates a failure to see purpose in nature.[82]

One further aspect of the relation between science and theology is particularly pertinent with respect to the doctrine of creation. This is that methodological naturalism, in bracketing God and the supernatural, cannot in fact make a neutral and indifferent decision concerning what counts as nature and how it relates to God. Hanby puts in this way:

> More simply, science is intrinsically related to theology because one cannot identify the object of scientific inquiry – namely, nature – without simultaneously distinguishing it from that which is not nature – namely, God – and without giving tacit specification to the character of this 'not'. ... Conceptions of nature determine in advance what sort of God is allowed to appear to thought and consequently, the range of meanings that can be intelligibly attached to 'creation'.[83]

The Thomist doctrine of creation that we examined in the previous chapter identified the world first and foremost as created, specified the nature of its relation to that which is uncreated and then proceeded to examine the world on that basis. In other words, the meaning of 'creation' and the world as created was specified at the beginning, as the *first thing* that must be said. In the rise of physico-theology in the seventeenth century – although at first glance it looks like theology and natural philosophy remain companions – the procedure is quite different. A particular conception of the world – one of mechanical causes and micro-corpuscles – was distinguished from an entirely separate supernatural realm, with no prior discussion of the meaning of 'creation' and no identification of the natural realm in terms of a relation to that which is *super*natural. Having established the nature of the world without recourse to theology, a God was introduced and placed alongside 'the world' on the only basis that offered hope of intelligibility *given the way that the world had already been understood*: as a designer akin to the human designer of an artefact. The implication is that, unless we say first and foremost that the world is created and understand what that claim means *and does not mean*, the God who emerges from science will be defined by the prior identification of the world as a self-standing object. Bringing theology and science back into intelligible and deep conversation is then much more difficult, demanding more than appeals to happy coincidences between science and theology and vague expressions of awe and wonder that betoken a creator. It is difficult, but by no means impossible. It requires, however, an examination of the metaphysical and theological decisions that underlie the undeniably staggering success of the modern natural sciences. There may be aspects of the world that we do not see because we do not first and foremost, before all else, identify the world as created.

Conclusion

The relationship between science and theology, particularly the doctrine of creation, is very complex. No longer can we assume a straightforward antagonism, but neither is a simple rapprochement appropriate. How the world is understood and what it is deemed to be affect very considerably the possibility of articulating an intelligible doctrine of creation. For premodern theologians, nature was a system of resemblances and symbols that could be read literally and allegorically alongside the book of scripture. This 'sacramental ontology', in which creatures participate in that which they signify, was of a piece with the Thomist doctrine of creation articulated in Chapter 3. Symbolic and allegorical relations could be understood as akin to analogical relations – a pattern of resemblances between creature and creator which fundamentally defined what a creature *is*.

When a literal reading of nature arose during the sixteenth and seventeenth centuries, creation became more akin to a self-standing artefact, which could be understood purely on its own terms. This gave rise to methods for investigating nature that did not refer to intrinsic purpose, but only to natural mechanical processes governed extrinsically by God through the laws of nature. Creation was understood to stand alongside God, obeying divine decrees that could be described mathematically.

The key suggestion of this chapter is that the relation of science to the theology of creation is more complex than is often thought. The seventeenth and eighteenth centuries mark a significant development of new methods for exploring nature; these were accompanied by significant changes in what nature is thought to be.

The legacy of that shift is felt very strongly today. If one grants that science makes metaphysical and theological claims in establishing its method for investigating nature, and those claims do not state that the most fundamental truth about the world is that it is created, then it becomes apparent that reintroducing an intelligible doctrine of creation at a later stage is very difficult. Why? Because the understanding of what it means to 'create' is already a function of the view that the world is simply a 'thing' or an artefact. The reintroduction of 'God' to such a scheme invariably leads to a 'God of the gaps', in which the divine simply fills the shrinking holes left by incomplete scientific explanations. If the debate between science and the theology of creation is to make any significant progress, attending to the theological and metaphysical roots of science will be very important. This is not for a moment to deny the stunning success of modern science in explaining and manipulating nature. It is only to suggest that such science might not be adequate to the full majesty of the subject of its study and the most fundamental truth of its being: the created world of God.

5

The Environment and the Gift of Creation: Beyond Nature and Culture

It is beyond reasonable doubt that humanity and the earth face an unprecedented crisis because of pollution, exploitation, population growth, global warming and climate change. This is the most pressing and intractable global ethical issue of our time, one that impacts on every human society and our relationship with the natural world. The principal greenhouse gas, carbon dioxide, is at its highest atmospheric levels in over 400,000 years. Its recent and relentless rise, which has accelerated dramatically in the last 60 years, is correlated very clearly with the use of fossil fuels. Nine of the ten warmest years on record have occurred since 2000, with (at the time of writing) 2015 the warmest on record. Global warming contributes to rising sea levels, which in turn damage coastal ecosystems, increase the risk of flooding and force populations inland, increasing population densities and putting pressure on agricultural land. Deforestation and shrinking biodiversity are having dramatic consequences on the global environment. Global warming contributes to climate change and the incidence of extreme weather events. Droughts and floods affect crop production and ecosystems.[1] It is widely accepted that the poorest communities of the world feel the effects of environmental abuse and climate change most immediately and with exponentially greater force. The environmental crisis will be with us for generations.

Although the natural, economic and cultural roots of climate change are debated, there is a general consensus that human activity related to technology, industrialization and the manipulation of nature is the main cause of the environmental crisis – it is anthropogenic. In a prescient article published in 1967, the medieval historian Lynn White Jr. famously attributed the abuse of the natural realm by technology and industry to Christianity. He wrote:

> Since both science and technology are blessed words in our contemporary vocabulary, some may be happy at the notions, first, that, viewed historically, modern science is an extrapolation of natural theology and, second, that modern technology is at least partly to be explained as an Occidental [Western], voluntarist realization of the Christian dogma of man's transcendence of, and rightful mastery over, nature. But, as we now recognize, somewhat over a century ago science and technology – hitherto quite separate activities – joined to give mankind powers which, to judge by many of the ecologic effects, are out of control. If so, Christianity bears a huge burden of guilt.[2]

White's argument centres on the replacement of pagan animism in antiquity with the idea that nature consists of indifferent objects that humanity can use at will. Christianity, he claimed, particularly in its Western form, is the most anthropocentric religion the world has ever seen.[3] This is exemplified in two key teachings found in the book of Genesis: that humanity is made in the image and likeness of God and the command that humanity has dominion over the earth and multiplies to fill it (Gen. 1.26-29).

This has clear resonance with many of the themes discussed in the previous chapter, although more recent historical research adds nuance. As we saw, Christian theology – more particularly, natural or physico-theology – played a significant role in the objectification of nature and the rise of modern natural science. To the extent that science and technology combined in the nineteenth century to exert power and dominion over nature, in a way that resonates with a literal reading of Gen. 1.26, the Christian tradition is implicated in the current environmental crisis. As well as Christian theology's historical entanglement in this crisis, there is also a sense that the doctrine of creation in particular should have resources to offer the debate concerning environmental ethics and our relationship with the natural world. It is also interesting that science and technology, as well as religion and theology, are seen as causes of the environmental crisis. In both cases – religion and science – blame has been accompanied by a demand for solutions.[4]

In this chapter, we will refer to a number of themes discussed earlier in the book in order to examine theologically the nature of the environmental crisis and to offer a possible theological response. The discussion will proceed in four distinct parts. Beginning with the rise of natural science in the seventeenth century and the associated change in the understanding of creation, the first section will examine the theological roots of the environmental crisis by revisiting some of the themes from the previous chapter.

The second section will examine the way that debates about the environment are often couched in terms of the modern separation of nature and culture. We will see that many responses to the environmental crisis assume this distinction. They propose either more human cultural intervention – for example, genetically engineered crops or the technological reduction of the effects of fossil fuels – or a retreat of human culture in order to leave behind a purer nature – for example, organic farming methods or a reduction in the use of fossil fuels. We will examine the way in which the overarching theological category of 'creation' helps to overcome the separation of human culture from wider nature.

Having identified more clearly the character and theological roots of the environmental crisis, the third section will return to a theme from Chapter 2 and the discussion of creation *ex nihilo*: gift. At the heart of the notion of creation out of nothing is the idea that creation is fundamentally a gift, but not only a gift: it is a gift that also instantiates its recipient. In turn, this provokes a creaturely response in the form of thanksgiving that is realized most truly in the celebration of the Eucharist.

The fourth section will reflect on the most fundamental gift of creation, one that is both natural and cultural: food. We will explore the meaning of the gift of food as the expression of reconciliation and communion in the story of Joseph and his brothers in Gen. 37– 50. This will lead to a study of food and sacrifice in the Levitical law and the way in which Christ, by means of his sacrifice, establishes again a reciprocal exchange between God and creation that restores our understanding of creation as gift and thanksgiving. We are drawn into the exchange of gifts between Father and Son by means of the food of the bread and wine of the Eucharist. This further elucidates the meaning of food in relation to God's reconciling gift of his life in Christ.

In concluding this chapter, we will see that a doctrine of creation as gift has powerful ethical implications that make a claim on humanity and place the dominant mode of relationship in the contemporary world – the free market and trade in commodities – into a deeper perspective. As we will see, the global free market – often regarded as the cause of the exploitation of nature – is parasitic upon a more fundamental ontology of gift.

The environmental crisis, the Reformation and natural science

In the previous chapter we examined a dramatic transition during the sixteenth century from the symbolic and allegorical reading of the book of nature and the book of scripture to a more literal reading. Nature ceased to be a symbolic realm that harboured references to the divine; it became a realm of objects whose value was no longer spiritual, but lay only in meeting the material needs of human beings. The physico-theologians of the seventeenth century set themselves the task of discovering the *uses* of creatures, not their *meaning*. As Peter Harrison puts it:

> The Christian doctrine of creation had always held that the natural world had a purpose, a purpose related to human welfare. However, up until the modern period, that purpose had encompassed both spiritual and material aspects of human existence. When the world could no longer be interpreted for its transcendental meanings, it was actively exploited solely for its material utility.[5]

The demise of the sacramental and symbolic reading of creation placed humanity in a unique position within the cosmic hierarchy in two important respects. First, it suggested that wider nature is provided by God to meet human material needs; physico-theology is the enterprise devoted to identifying the uses of creatures and, at the same time, discerning the power and craftsmanship of God. The meaning of non-human creation therefore becomes one-dimensional and literal: to be a natural resource for human beings. If nothing in creation has intrinsic significance, its value lies only in exchange, trade and consumption.

Secondly, the idea that humanity has power over nature to manipulate and improve it takes on a particular prominence. A more literal reading of Genesis suggests that the narrative of the Fall is to be understood primarily as historical rather than allegorical. This suggests that there was a time before humanity's first sin when nature was pristine and all was well in the garden of creation. Since then, creation has become an unkempt wasteland of weeds, thorns, disease and impending natural disaster. The idea that human beings can reverse the effects of the Fall by tending and even manipulating nature becomes very powerful in the seventeenth century. Moreover, natural philosophy was to be the means by which humanity restored a once perfect knowledge and dominion that required no labour. Of particular importance was Gen. 2.29 and Adam's naming of creatures. This was understood to refer to the dominion of humanity over the natural order. At the end of the second book of his *Novum Organum*, Francis Bacon (1561–1626) wrote:

> For by the Fall man declined from the state of innocence and from his kingdom over creatures. Both things can be repaired even in this life to some extent, the former by religion and faith, the latter by arts and sciences. For the Curse did not make the creation an utter and irrevocable outlaw. In virtue of the sentence 'In the sweat of thy face shalt thou eat bread' [Gen. 3.19], man, by manifold labours (and not by disputations, certainly, or by useless magical ceremonies), compels the creation, in time and in part, to provide him with bread, that is to serve the purposes of human life.[6]

For Bacon, knowledge and power become intertwined: knowing nature more or less means having power over nature. To know nature is to be able to predict and therefore manipulate its processes. As the philosopher Hans Jonas puts it, modern knowledge of nature is a 'know-how' and not a 'know-what'.[7] For Bacon, we do not examine what nature is, but how it works; in knowing how it works we can manipulate or improve its operations, much as we can with our own artefacts. This means that 'the task and purpose of human Power is to generate and superinduce on a given body a new nature or new natures'.[8] The manipulation of the natural becomes particularly powerful with the technological application of science in the nineteenth century. Its roots lie in the idea that human dominion as commanded in Genesis equates to the power to correct and improve nature, thus returning it to a pristine state that it once held at the beginning of history.[9] The combination of the material utility of creatures for human beings and the equation of knowledge and power in early modern science, all rooted in a literal interpretation of the books of scripture and nature, provides us with a sense of the deeper roots of our contemporary tendency to exploit and manipulate the natural world.

Another change in the understanding of the created natural order examined in the previous chapter is also relevant for interpreting the cultural and intellectual roots of the environmental crisis: the demise of teleology. In the seventeenth and eighteenth centuries, the notion of an intrinsic teleology in nature began to wane in the face of an increasing emphasis on efficient, mechanical causation. No longer did material nature have its own purposes and goals. Such purposes as material nature possessed had their origins externally, in the designs of God mediated through the imposition of natural laws onto passive matter. To the extent that the designs of God were compromised and faulty because of the Fall, humanity could correct and improve them via scientific and technological manipulation.

More importantly, however, a rejection of intrinsic natural purposiveness amounted to a devaluation of material nature itself. We often ascribe value and meaning to things by reference to their ends and goals. For ancient and medieval theologians, the value and meaning of creation lay not simply in the utility of creatures for human beings but in creation's manifestation of God's beauty and truth. That manifestation came through creaturely participation in God's life, according to particular natures or modes of being. It was intrinsic to the created order, yet had its origin extrinsically in God. By participation in the divine transcendent source of being, creation was understood to have an 'improper' share in a likeness of God and therefore the goal of sharing in that likeness through creation's own actualization.[10] Creation was understood as an end itself, an expression of divine gratuity and love. In the natural philosophy of the early modern period, however, the value assigned to material creation ceased to be intrinsic. Rather, it lay externally in its conformity to the laws of nature – that is, the designs of God – or its usefulness for humanity, which is as much as to say, its conformity to human designs. Material nature's value was now linked to external goals and purposes. The implication was that material nature had no value of its own, but only the value ascribed to it by a designer God to meet human needs and wants. The world simply became the occasion for the manifestation of divine power and, by association, human power. This reification of nature – turning the natural world into a 'thing' or 'object' – was one further manifestation of the imagination which makes possible the manipulation and exploitation of nature.[11]

The objectification of nature in the seventeenth century also established a fundamental division of the created order that many regard as characteristic of the modern period: the distinction between human culture and the domain of nature. Whereas ancient and medieval thinkers saw humanity as fundamentally embedded within nature as part of the all-encompassing category of creation, the modern imagination tends to think of human culture as something quite distinct from nature. Indeed, the division of nature and culture is inscribed into the structure of modern universities: the natural sciences deal with the realm of 'objects' and are therefore objective and indifferent. The humanities deal with the realm of 'subjects', otherwise known as subjective human culture. Nature therefore consists of everything non-human – the domain studied by physics, chemistry, biology, astronomy, natural history. The medical sciences treat human biology as an objective natural, not cultural, entity. This is the realm of 'laws of nature', of brute instinct and of necessity. Teleology (intrinsic purpose) and creaturely freedom are absent from this realm. By contrast, the humanities deal with human culture – politics, economics, law, business, literature, music, religion, history, art, sociology. This is the realm in which intention and purpose can be discerned because of the reign of self-conscious human freedom. We now turn to this separation of nature and culture as the basic framework in which environmental ethics is discussed.

Nature and culture

The ancient Christian hymn to creation, the Benedicite, places human beings in the heart of God's creation.[12] All creation praises the creator.

O ye Whales, and all that move in the Waters, bless ye the Lord:
praise him, and magnify him for ever.
O all ye Fowls of the Air, bless ye the Lord:
praise him, and magnify him for ever.
O all ye Beasts and Cattle, bless ye the Lord:
praise him, and magnify him for ever.
O ye Children of Men, bless ye the Lord:
praise him, and magnify him for ever.
O let Israel bless the Lord:
praise him, and magnify him for ever.

The book of Genesis recounts that Adam, although made in God's image and likeness, is nevertheless created from the dust of the earth. The medieval idea that humanity is a microcosm of creation, sharing in every aspect of created nature in being both material and intellectual (thus having something in common with everything from rocks to angels), ensured that humanity was at the heart of a unified creation, not separate from it.

In *We have Never Been Modern*, the French philosopher of science and social theorist Bruno Latour discusses 'the modern constitution' that challenges the place of humanity within the created order. This constitution consists of two practices. The first is the distinction of human culture from wider nature – what Latour calls 'purification'. According to Latour, it is characteristic of the modern mind to see human beings as constituting a separate realm of *cultural subjects* that stand over and against the realm of *natural objects*.[13] Nature is the realm of base instinct and necessity. Culture is the realm of human freedom and creativity.[14]

The second practice that constitutes Latour's 'modern constitution' is the reverse of the purification of nature and culture – the creation of hybrids of nature and culture in what Latour calls 'translation'. This practice of mixing natural and cultural entities 'creates mixtures between entirely new types of being, hybrids of nature and culture'.[15] This can link together 'the chemistry of the upper atmosphere, scientific and industrial strategies, the preoccupations of heads of state, the anxieties of ecologists'.[16] In other words, while the purification of nature and culture is very familiar because it structures even our education system, the two domains are impossible to separate and continually combine to generate hybrids of nature and culture. Is global warming, for example, a natural or cultural phenomenon? If it were straightforwardly natural, we could send the problem to scientists and ask for a solution. If it were obviously cultural, we could send it to the politicians, lawyers, philosophers or theologians and ask for a solution. But it is both natural and cultural – a hybrid. The negotiation of a solution to global warming therefore becomes complex, involving numerous disciplines and methodologies.[17]

An important event in the history of the relationship between science and the theology of creation demonstrates the importance of the distinction between nature and culture for modern man's self-understanding: the publication of *The Origin of Species* by Charles Darwin in 1859. We tend to look at the controversy surrounding Darwin's work through the lens of an alleged contradiction between the six-day creation in Genesis and the evolution of species over millions of years. However, the real controversy was arguably even deeper, concerning human self-understanding in relation to the natural world. One of the important implications of Darwin's work is that human beings are evolved from primates. This means a genetic continuity between humans and animals. Today, this is a very familiar idea. In the middle of the nineteenth century, it was a much more striking and potentially alarming idea. Why? When the subjection of nature by human culture was at the forefront of the common imagination, Darwin sewed the human race back into nature with the needle and thread of evolution and natural selection, challenging this bifurcation of nature and culture. Cartoons appeared in European periodicals depicting Darwin's head attached to of the body of a primate – a hybrid of nature and culture in black and white.[18] The idea that humanity is directly descended from apes seemed to have been an immediate source of controversy, as we see in the famous 'great debate' in Oxford in June 1860 between Thomas Huxley (1825–95), known as 'Darwin's bulldog', and the bishop of Oxford, Samuel Wilberforce (1805–73). A report written some thirty years after the debate claimed that Wilberforce asked whether 'it was through his grandfather or his grandmother that he claimed descent from a monkey?' Huxley supposedly replied, 'If then the question is put to me whether I would rather have a miserable ape for a grandfather or a man highly endowed by nature and possessed of great means of influence and yet employs these faculties and that influence for the mere purpose of introducing ridicule into a grave scientific discussion, I unhesitatingly affirm my preference for the ape.'[19] The irony is that, Darwin having placed humanity firmly back within the natural realm, the separation of nature and culture was then reasserted with extra force: human beings now understood the process of their own natural evolution and could reassert their cultural separation from, and dominance of, brute nature. In the fullness of time, this would include control of human genetics in order to achieve cultural ends. Though controversial, some biologists today claim that natural human evolution is over.[20] If evolution happens, it is *cultural* (via gene manipulation and selection) rather than *natural*.

For Latour, the separation of nature and culture has never worked because it is incoherent – hence his claim that we have never been 'modern'. The simultaneous purification and translation of the realms of nature and culture has always produced chaotic and confusing hybrids. The rampant creation of hybrids of nature and culture – phenomena that do not submit to our methods of classification and analysis according to these two categories – is out of control and the categories of nature and culture appear increasingly meaningless: 'The ozone hole is too social and narrated to be truly natural; the strategy of industrial firms and heads of state is too full of chemical reactions to be reduced to [the culture] of power and interests.'[21]

Nevertheless, debate concerning the environmental crisis still frequently assumes a clear distinction between nature and culture. On the one hand, there are those who demand more nature via a retreat of human culture. This means reverting to more 'natural' forms of, for example, agriculture, housing, transport, leisure and consumption. The term 'natural' is applied to anything from washing-up liquid to childbirth and it means little more than the absence of human activity and influence – a 'letting be'. This often reflects a romantic notion of a 'pure nature' – an idea that has plagued Christian theology for other reasons – that is devoid of cultural infection.[22] On the other hand, there are those who respond to the environmental crisis with a demand for more culture in the form of new economic policies, international protocols and strategic scientific interventions for the enhanced control of nature towards more desirable environmental goals. One strategy is to relinquish control over nature. The other strategy is to exert more control over nature. Either way, it is assumed that we inhabit a cultural realm that is distinct from nature.

Of course, nature has never existed in pure form outside the influence of human culture and activity. Before the invention of modern nature as a domain separate from human culture, all things, from rocks to angels, were contained within the more fundamental constitutive category of 'creation'. The question is, can the objectification of nature be overcome and nature's intrinsic value and worth asserted in a way that includes the human, without reducing nature to romantic ideas of beautiful meadows and untouched landscapes? Can a different approach to the environmental crisis be imagined, beyond appeals to a nature purified of human influence or the increasing dominion of culture? In the remainder of this chapter, I will propose one possible approach: creation understood as gift. The application of the concept of gift to the environmental crisis may move us beyond the commodification of nature. We will begin with the notion of creation *ex nihilo* as offering the most radical understanding of the gift before moving to the 'liturgy of the gift' in the form of sacrifice and the Eucharist. Returning to creation as gift, this will lead to the suggestion of an alternative economy based on symbolic gift exchange and a different valuation of creation beyond the modern categories of nature and culture.

Creation and gift

In recent years, the concept of 'gift' has been widely discussed within a range of disciplines, including theology, philosophy, anthropology and history.[23] The origins of this discussion lie in the work of the French sociologist Marcel Mauss and his publication of *The Gift* in 1923.[24] This is a comparative study in which Mauss uses research on gift-giving in societies in Polynesia, Melanesia and the American Northwest. He seeks to identify the common importance of gift-giving in the formation of societies that are otherwise extremely diverse. By gift, Mauss does not mean simply material presents of the sort that we exchange at Christmas. A gift can be a meal cooked for a family, attention given to a friend or a kiss given to a lover. Mauss's conclusions about the nature of gift-giving are various and complex, but perhaps his most important point is that gifts involve reciprocity. Mauss's conclusion is that there is never a pure one-way gift. To put the matter simply, true gifts are exchanged. This idea will be explored in more detail below.

Another conclusion proffered by Mauss concerns the meaning of gifts. A simple example will help to explain his view. At a marriage, the couple typically give and receive rings. These may or may not have a high monetary value. However, the significance of the rings is considerable: through symbol, they mediate a relationship between spouses. A wife looks at her wedding ring and is immediately reminded of the husband who gave it to her. This is also evocative of the constant round of gift exchange that constitutes a marriage – the giving of time, attention, care and love. For Mauss, the gift not only signals a relationship; it is also imbued with something of the giver's character or power. He writes that 'it follows that to make a gift of something to someone is to make a present of some part of oneself'.[25] This means the significance and meaning of a gift – whether it be a material gift or the gift of one's time, attention and skill – can bear almost no relation to its monetary value. We treasure gifts that are of no economic value at all, precisely because of the relationship they mediate and the value of the person from whom they were received. To put the matter in terms we encountered in Chapter 3, the gift is not merely a useful object – it bears meaning. This is most obviously the case with gifts that we make for each other, or gifts that are passed down generations and therefore accumulate significance and what we disparagingly call 'sentimental value'.

Mauss is clear that gift exchange is a more primitive and important social and economic foundation than barter. However, the reciprocity of gift giving is always under threat from the possibility that it will become merely market trade mediated by money. If I were to give you the gift of a birthday present, would you feel obliged to give me a birthday present in return? Would you not estimate the value of my 'gift' and buy a return 'gift' of roughly similar value? The category of gift could, therefore, be understood in terms of the market. The giving of a gift is always potentially as much about achieving a benefit for oneself as it is about conferring a good upon another. Even the charitable gift involves some kind of economic exchange: I give to Oxfam and, in return, receive a soothed conscience and the warm sense that I have benefitted another. So an important question emerges: can a true gift really ever be given, or are we always embroiled in trade? When I give to charity, am I 'buying' a soothed conscience and the sense that I have done all I can? More acutely for Christian theology, when I give the gift of myself in good deeds towards others, am I expecting some eschatological benefit in return?

These questions have led some philosophers, notably Jacques Derrida (1930–2004), to pursue the theoretical idea of a 'pure' gift.[26] Could there ever be a pure, utterly selfless donation? For this to be the case, such a gift would not feature reciprocity; it would be purely one-way. Because the action of giving any gift always leaves open the possibility that the giver is gratifying herself rather than being mindful of the other, Derrida concludes that the 'pure' gift must feature death. In other words, after the giving of the gift, the donor can only guarantee the gift's purity and one-way character by the annihilation of the self so that nothing can be received in return. Derrida's conclusion is that the true or pure gift marks 'the impossible'. All our gift giving is, in a sense, compromised in some way. It tends towards trade and self-gratification, at least as much as it tends towards altruism.

To some, this debate will seem like an extreme and cynical approach to the every-day practice and delight of the giving and receiving of gifts. Maybe gift giving works in practice but not in theory. So why is the gift of any theological significance? First, because, as the theologian John Milbank points out, 'gift' is an all-encompassing theological category.[27] As we will see in more detail below, creation is understood as a gift. Christ is God's gift of himself to creation. The Holy Spirit is known as the *donum* (the given) among patristic theologians (Isa. 11.2-3; Jn 20.22). Moreover, the church is the community of the gifted (Acts 2.1-13; 1 Cor. 12; Eph. 4.11) and grace is God's gratuitous gift for our salvation (Eph. 2.8). Secondly, this debate over the gift is important because certain forms of Christian ethics would seem to reflect Derrida's concern with the possibility of a pure gift. For example, does Jesus's injunction in Jn 15.13 – 'No one has greater love than this, to lay down one's life for one's friends' – exemplify the notion of a pure, one-way gift? If we assume that a fundamental disregard of self lies at the heart of the good life, then surely the genuine exchange of gifts cannot be intrinsic to the notion of gift; a reciprocal gift can only be an accidental and wholly unexpected, even undesired, response to an initial 'pure' gift. In order to be wholly selfless and altruistic, a gift must apparently be given without any expectation of a response. Therefore, should we abandon any notion of genuine reciprocity in our understanding of the gift, lest the purity of our gift-giving be compromised in such a way that our selflessness is tainted and we only *trade* with each other and God? Or is the notion of reciprocity intrinsic to the notion of gift itself? If so, how do we avoid trading ersatz gifts, whether between ourselves or with God? [28]

To address these issues, we must remember that theological reflection on the gift begins with the doctrine of creation. As we have seen in previous chapters, for Jewish, Christian and Islamic theology, God is understood to create *ex nihilo*, 'from nothing'. Creation is a free and totally unnecessary act of utter gratuity. It is unnecessary in the sense that God does not require creation in any sense, for God needs nothing. Creation is not self-standing and only ever exists through the continual gift of participation in the divine life. Every moment of creation's existence is sustained by God as an expression of the gratuity of the divine gift of created being.

Creation *ex nihilo* constitutes a radical asymmetry between God and creation. Whereas creatures enjoy a symmetrical relation – I distinguish myself from the desk at which I am sat by my material nature, and the desk distinguishes itself from me by its material nature – there is no such relation between God and creation. Creation does not establish itself as 'other' than God and only *then* become the recipient of God's gifts. To put the matter another way, creation's ability to receive the gifts of God *is itself a gift*. There is nothing that stands outside this economy of divine donation. God's graciousness in creation is not reliant on anything else, which is to say that God does not need there to be something beside himself so that he can then give his gifts. God creates the gift *and* the recipient of his gift: 'What do you have that you did not receive? And if you received it, why do you boast as if it were not a gift?' (1 Cor. 4.7). Creation is, as Milbank puts it, 'a gift of a gift to a gift'.[29] There is no 'pure nature' to which God subsequently donates the gifts of his love. Put another way, there is a paradox at the heart of the gift of creation: creation is autonomous because it is not God, but that is no autonomy at all because creation's 'otherness' is always received from God in his act of creation *ex nihilo*. God 'holds back' creation from himself in order that creation can be itself.

The utter dependence of creation on God suggests the impossibility of reciprocity (Rom. 11.34-35). While creation at every moment receives its very existence from God through participation, what could creatures possibly offer to God in return? In short, nothing.

Despite this apparent impossibility, the scriptures attest to God's gift of a reciprocal relationship with him through which we share in the divine life. This is expressed, for example, in contemporary Eucharistic liturgies at the offertory, when the following verses are recited, recalling the offering by King David on behalf of the people for the building of the Temple.

> Yours, O Lord, are the greatness, the power, the glory, the victory, and the majesty; for all that is in the heavens and on the earth is yours; yours is the kingdom, O Lord, and you are exalted as head above all. … *For all things come from you, and of your own have we given you.* (1 Chron. 29.11, 14)

To see the measure of the difficulty in establishing reciprocity even in creaturely relationships of profound asymmetry, consider a young child and her parents. A child has nothing of her own: shelter, food, education and clothing are all provided. The child has no economic power and is entirely dependent upon the daily gifts of her parents. At Christmas, the child's parents buy her a splendid present – a new bike. The child, however, has no means of buying her parents a gift; she has nothing that she has not already received. She receives the gift of her new bike with apparently no hope of reciprocating. Yet as she tears the paper from her new bike on Christmas morning, she turns to her parents, smiles and says, with joy and delight, 'thank you'. The smile and the 'thank you' are the reciprocal gift. In other words, for the child's bike to be truly a gift, it must be received and acknowledged as such, otherwise it becomes a mere object that is useful for getting to and from school. The exchange of gifts – the bike and the smile – cannot be reduced to trade because they are so utterly different in kind. Trade requires a degree of univocity – of sameness – in the goods traded, such that they can be subject to a *common currency* called money. The bike may have cost £150, but the value of the child's smile and 'thank you' cannot be subject to that kind of measure. One cannot trade smiles and bikes. While the child's exchange with her parents is not trade (and we cannot imagine reducing our most important relationships to trade), it is an example of reciprocal exchange within a highly asymmetric relationship of dependence, one that points to the need for gifts to be recognized *as gifts* through thanksgiving, lest they become merely useful objects.

Nevertheless, reciprocal gifts, even within the most asymmetrical relations between creatures, are not the same as exchange within the asymmetrical relation between God and creation. God does not give a gift to some *thing* that is already present. According to creation *ex nihilo*, God gives the recipient being whereby it can be the recipient of further gifts: a gift of a gift to a gift. This leads Milbank beyond the contrast between unilateral and reciprocal gifts to the paradox of 'unilateral exchange'.[30] There can only be reciprocity within God's Trinitarian life or between creatures, whereas the 'unilateral exchange' between God and creation is only ever a matter of God's influx, by which creation is given the power of receiving and returning to God. This has an important theological consequence: God's gifts to creation are never a matter of entitlement or right. Creation cannot make any claim on God because creation, in its entirety, is *always* in the mode of recipient. To be a creature is, first and foremost, before all else, to receive being. This is a unilateral gift from God to creation. But to receive being truthfully, *to be a creature*, is to acknowledge the gift in thankfulness. Creation returns to God the gift of praise and thanksgiving and, in that return, receives itself most fully as created. We are then back at the ancient hymn, the Benedicite, in which all creatures, including humanity and its culture, are fundamentally themselves in the praise of God: 'O ye Children of Men, bless ye the Lord: praise and magnify him for ever.'

How has this relationship of exchange between God and creation been expressed practically and liturgically? In the next section, we will examine the way in which sacrifice – the dedication of things to God as gifts – and return become the symbolic expression of the relation of creation to God. Human sin is the refusal of God's gifts: the rejection of our created nature in the prideful assertion of creaturely autonomy outside God's benevolence. Christ's self-offering restores the relationship of reciprocal exchange between creation and God. First, however, we will examine the meaning of food as God's fundamental gift in creation (Gen. 1.29) and its importance for communion and the restoration of relationships. Food is quintessentially natural *and* cultural – the fruit of the earth incorporated into human social interaction and enjoyment. How does food bear intrinsic meaning and value in addition to meeting our physical needs? We begin this discussion with the story of Joseph and his brothers in Gen. 37–42.

Gift, the Eucharist and the meaning of food

Joseph the dreamer was the favoured son of Jacob's old age. Joseph's eleven brothers, mired in jealousy, sold him into slavery in Egypt. He rose to prominence in Pharaoh's court because he was able to interpret Pharaoh's dreams. In these dreams God revealed that there would be seven years of plenty and seven years of famine. Pharaoh put Joseph in charge of agricultural and economic policy; reserves were accumulated during the seven years of plenty so that the lands could survive the seven years of famine. When the famine struck, people from far and wide were forced to travel to Egypt where Joseph sold them grain. Jacob and his remaining eleven sons were among those driven from Canaan to Egypt in search of food. They encountered their brother Joseph in the Egyptian court. He recognized them but they did not recognize him. Joseph's brothers were afraid that their plight was a direct consequence of what they had done to their brother and they fought among themselves while Joseph looked on. After many years, Joseph's brothers remained deeply guilty over what they had done to their brother; this affected all their relationships. Physical hunger drove Jacob's sons to seek food in Egypt, yet there is also an emotional, spiritual hunger lying at the heart of this story – a desire for reconciliation and peace.

Joseph shared food with his brothers – the grain that he had stored from the seven years of plenty. However, Joseph secretly gave back the money his brothers had brought to pay for the grain (Gen. 42.25). The food was therefore not traded: it was an unanticipated, secret gift from Joseph to his brothers. This becomes the *meaning* and the *use* of the food that Joseph had stored: a gift that eventually effected reconciliation with his brothers and the unity of what were to become the twelve tribes of Israel. Joseph's reconciling gift to his brothers was a result of his grateful and measured reception of the gifts of God's creation. The implication is that Joseph's gift bore something of himself to his brothers: his prudence and receptivity to God's will and providence, as well as his love for his brothers. Joseph's brothers returned with gifts (Gen. 43.11-15) and Joseph offered further gifts of food to his brothers (Gen. 43.16-25; 44.1). Reciprocity and communion were eventually restored in Jacob's blessing of his reconciled sons (Gen. 49.1-27).

In the story of Joseph, the meaning and value of food, the fruit of creation, was to be found in reconciliation and the celebration of communion.[31] The offering of gifts as expressions of thanksgiving and penance with the purpose of effecting reconciliation with God was the basis of the ancient practice of sacrifice. In the Temple in Jerusalem, the priestly families offered gifts to God on behalf of supplicants for the restoration of communion. These took the form of grain, oil or incense as well as animal sacrifice. Rather than these sacrifices being 'given up' or lost (which is the modern colloquial sense of 'sacrifice'), they were often returned to the people, sometimes in the form of food. This established a reciprocal economy of the gift within the elaborate system of Temple rituals. Such reciprocity established the worshippers' fellowship with God: the worshipper was invited by divine graciousness to offer gifts to God which were returned to form a relational bond. Ritually, this was expressed in the form of a meal shared in God's Temple using the gifts sacrificed on the altar. The return of sacrifices in the form of food, while certainly not an element of every Temple sacrifice, was nevertheless an important expression of fellowship with God and among God's people.

However, this reciprocity was broken by human sin, for sin is the refusal of God's gifts. Sacrifice was seemingly inadequate to renew humanity's intimate relationship with God. The author of the letter to the Hebrews puts it this way when writing of humanity's estrangement from the Holy of Holies, the inner sanctuary of God:

> This is a symbol of the present time, during which gifts and sacrifices are offered that cannot perfect the conscience of the worshipper, but deal only with food and drink and various baptisms, regulations for the body imposed until the time comes to set things right. (Heb. 9.9-10)

How can the relationship of reciprocal exchange with God be restored in the face of human sin? Because humanity has estranged itself from God, it is humanity which must offer sacrifice to God for the renewal of that reciprocal relation. However, any human action will be tainted by sin; it 'cannot perfect the conscience of the worshipper'. Only a divine action will be fully replete and perfect. Only a divine action can, once and for all, atone for human sin. The perfect once-and-for-all sacrifice can therefore only be offered by a divine humanity, namely the incarnation of God himself in the person of Jesus Christ. So it is Christ's sacrifice of himself on the cross, as both fully divine and fully human, which brings the salvation of humanity and the re-establishment of reciprocity with God.

The nature of Christ's sacrifice and atonement is, of course, a matter of considerable theological controversy. However, in contrast to later theories of the atonement that refer to civic legal practices of justice, punishment and recompense, the New Testament writers frequently refer to Christ's sacrifice with reference to the prevalent Jewish theology of sacrifice. For example, it has been argued that Christ's sacrifice is best understood through the narrative and practices of the Passover sacrifice of a lamb. I wish to discuss the suggestion that Christ's sacrifice is best understood in terms of the Jewish sin-offering. [32]

The ritual system of sin (or guilt) offerings is described particularly in Lev. 6.8–7.10. These sacrifices involve flour, grain, oil and animals. Some elements are 'wholly burned' (Lev. 6.8-23). However, there is an important element of reciprocity in these 'most holy' sacrifices. Whoever touches the flesh of the sacrificed animal in the ritual of the sin-offering is rendered holy and the animal is returned to the priests – but only to the priests – as food to be consumed in the holy place (Lev. 6.24-30). Similarly, every grain-offering baked in the oven is to be returned to the priest (Lev. 7.9). However, 'every other grain offering, mixed with oil or dry, shall belong to all the sons of Aaron equally' (Lev. 7.10). As sacrificial gifts are offered to God for atonement following the sin of the people, they are returned to the people for their nourishment. Typically, however, the reciprocity is enjoyed by the priests – they receive back the flesh of the animal of the sin-offering and guilt-offering, as well as the grain offering.

The letter to the Hebrews describes these sacrifices, which are offered year after year, as 'only a shadow of the good things to come' (Heb. 10.1). Christ's sacrifice is interpreted as the fulfilment of Levitical sacrifice. He is a priest according to the order of Melchizedek who, in being replete and without sin, offers himself not over and over again, but 'once for all' (Heb. 10.10). He is both priest and victim while also standing in our place. Christ represents all of humanity, yet is, at one and the same time, the sacrifice of God. But how is this sacrifice rendered reciprocal? In what sense is the sacrificial gift of Christ, offered to the Father, returned to the people? Is there any way in which, like the sin-offering, guilt-offering and grain offering described in Leviticus, the sacrifice of Christ is returned to the people as food? Is a relation of 'unilateral exchange' between creation and God restored? The sacrificial offering of Christ, who as sinless nevertheless represents every sinner, is returned to the people as food in the Eucharist in the form of the body and blood of the victim and priest (1 Cor. 10.16). Whereas the reciprocity of the sin-offering was enjoyed particularly by Levitical priests, now the church is 'a royal priesthood' (1 Pt. 2.9-10), so everyone partakes in the reciprocity of Christ's gift of himself: the people of God are a priestly people in receiving the gifts of Christ's once-and-for-all sacrifice in the Eucharist, this royal priesthood being made visible through the apostolic order of priests who preside at Christ's meal.

The Eucharist bears further meaning: it is also eschatological as an anticipation of the wedding feast of the Lamb. Meanwhile, the sacrificial offering of Christ on the cross is the manifestation of the eternal offering of the Son to the Father in the Holy Spirit. In other words, the sacrificial offering of Christ is not something that just happens to take place in first-century Palestine as a reaction to human sin; it belongs to the very Trinitarian life of God. Refracted through human sin and violence, Christ's obedient gift becomes bloody and violent. It is by means of the Eucharistic sacrificial gift that we are continually incorporated into the perfect sacrifice of Christ on the cross and the eschatological banquet of heaven, both of which are participations in the eternal reciprocity of the Trinity as the Son eternally offers himself to the Father in the Holy Spirit.

This understanding of the Eucharistic sacrifice does not involve the external mimicking of divine gratuity, as if we witness God's generosity at a distance and set about copying him. Rather, we are drawn *into* the infinitely merciful reciprocity of donation that is the divine life. This is the gracious sharing in the overflow of glory that the Father and the Son eternally exchange in the Spirit. By means of the return of Christ, the sacrificial victim and priest, as food in the Eucharist, we enter *into* the divine life – the divine economy of reciprocated gifts – to feast at the table of the Lord.

The Eucharist is therefore about the ultimate meaning and value of food. It is the providential gift of God for the sustenance of his creatures and the means of communion. Through a sacrificial meal, God restores his people to the divine economy of reciprocated gifts by the offering of his own life as our food: the body and blood of Christ. This points to the sacred nature of food as the fruit of God's creation and the means of communion. In this context, it is striking that one of the most damaging practices for our environment is the commodification and wastage of food which simultaneously renders large portions of the world's population without enough to eat. The food that found its meaning and value in reconciliation and communion in the story of Joseph and Christ's gift of the Eucharist is now a locus of separation and division in the contemporary world.

It is particularly striking that in many religious communities, food – which is both cultural and natural – is never treated as a mere commodity but is received thankfully as a gift.[33] Moreover, as we have seen, food bears *meaning* in liturgical practice and is not merely *useful* for the satiation of the body. The Eucharist, suffused with the imagery of the gift of Christ's body for the salvation of the world, is about the meaning of the food we receive as God's gift in creation. The meaning and purpose of food for the whole created order is communion and fellowship, including the restoration of reciprocal relationships of love that have been broken by sin. As the psalmist writes, 'The eyes of all look to you, and you give them their food in due season' (Ps. 145.15).

As we have seen throughout this book, God's gift of creation bears 'something of the giver to the recipient'. God does not offer in creation an object for our use, a commodity for our consumption or a domain for our exploitation. God does not offer in creation simply a manifestation of his own power that in turn invites a manifestation of human power. God offers in creation nothing less than his own gratuity. In other words, creation is the gift of a participation in the divine life. As John Milbank puts it, 'The Creature only *is*, as manifesting the divine glory, as acknowledging its own nullity and reflected brilliance. To be, it entirely honours God, which means it returns to him an unlimited, never paid-back debt.'[34] This is to say that what creatures receive from God – our very existence – could never be subject to a common measure with what creatures return to God. What creatures offer to God is honour and thankfulness *by being most fully themselves* as they have been gifted that nature by God. God grants to humanity, made in his image and likeness, the gift of entering his life by sharing in the eternal reciprocity of the Trinity through the offering of gifts, supremely the bread and wine of the Eucharist. In turn, this has implications for the meaning of the food given through the earth.

In contrast to this language of creation as gift, we live in a culture saturated in the language of the market and rights. In this context, a gift becomes merely an expression of the human will. Yet Christian theology does not sanction gifts simply as acts of the benevolent human will which copies a benevolent divine will. Instead, it has an *ontology* of gift grounded in the doctrine of creation. Existence itself is gift. What it is to be a creature is to receive the gift of existence *with thanksgiving*. God does not happen to be generous by an act of will; God *is* graciousness and creation is the expression of that eternal benevolence. As Nicholas Lash puts it:

> God's utterance lovingly gives life; gives all life, all unfailing freshness; gives only life, and peace, and love, and beauty, harmony and joy. And the life God gives is nothing other, nothing less, than God's own self. Life is God, given.[35]

Conclusion: Creation, gift and thanksgiving

The abuse and exploitation of nature through human culture characterizes our environmental crisis. What lies at the root of such exploitation is the idea that creation's value lies supremely in its utility for human beings. Lynn White Jr. was surely correct that a particular kind of anthropocentric approach to creation – the idea that the natural world is there for our use and subject to our dominion – is an important framework for exploitative and destructive practices. We saw earlier in this chapter how the commodification of nature as distinct from human culture – which is surely linked to the idea that creation is a 'thing' standing alongside God – also provides a framework for the abuse of the earth.

The free market further engenders the commodification of the natural world. It so dominates human relationships and our relationship with the environment that we treat it as an unassailable fact of life. Although markets are cultural constructs driven towards political ends, they are treated almost like natural organisms that have a stable metabolism of their own. If left to their own devices – that is, purified from cultural (political) intervention and external shock – markets will produce supremely efficient outcomes. This is *laissez-faire* (literally, 'leave do') economics. However, it is clear that markets do not convey to producers and consumers the full environmental costs of production and consumption. Those costs arise in the form of environmental damage and the exploitation of the poor. Amid the complexity of global modes of production and trade, it seems utterly futile and hubristic to presume to suggest an alternative. Yet one might realize that markets trading in a commodified nature are *always* parasitic on a more fundamental economy of gift. This makes a very considerable difference for a number of reasons. For example, market economics makes one foundational assumption: the world has scarce resources in the face of unlimited human desires. The question is: How do we distribute these scarce resources in the face of the unlimited human capacity for consumption? Economics deals with a fundamental problem of scarcity: there is not enough. At the heart of the doctrine of creation, however, is not lack but abundance. This can be seen in the Levitical command not to harvest to the very edge of the field.

> When you reap the harvest of your land, you shall not reap to the very edges of your field, or gather the gleanings of your harvest; you shall leave them for the poor and for the alien: I am the Lord your God. (Lev. 23.22)

Leaving a section of the field for the poor was a reminder that what we receive in creation is more than enough. In contemporary culture, we have no sense of what might be 'enough' because unlimited human desire is taken as an unassailable given. We reap to the edge of every field, and beyond. There will never be enough; there will always be a lack that creates anxiety and ever-greater production of commodities that, in turn, generate ever-more human wants. In fact, the problem is not scarcity but the utterly perverse distribution of creation's gifts by the free market that results in a large portion of the world's population battling hunger and pollution while the minority battle obesity and its associated diseases.

The economy of gift, however, is more fundamental than trade, for two reasons. First, reciprocal gift exchange is the mode of relationship that we most value and in which we find most meaning and fulfilment. We earn money by selling our labour in order to sustain a life in which the exchange of gifts – attention, care, love, creativity, talent, learning – can be maintained beyond the constraints of market trade. Of course, our work may also involve gift exchange and should never be reducible purely to a salary. There should be gains to work far beyond pay. This is a response to the reception of our own lives as gifts, as something purely contingent which elicits thankfulness – what the Christian tradition calls Eucharistic living.

The second reason why the economy of gift is more fundamental than the economy of trade is because gift is the basic mode of created existence as indicated by creation *ex nihilo*: a gift of a gift to a gift. Modes of production are parasitic on what is already given and received. In realizing that the created order is a gift, it immediately makes a claim on us because it 'bears something of the giver to the recipient' and invites our response in the form of a counter-gift. Crucially, however, what has been described in this book is a primordial mode of donation in which the giver (God) is utterly infused within the gift (creation) yet remains wholly other and infinitely transcendent. In Chapter 3, we described the distinction between divine and secondary in which God is not a cause among causes, but the basis of all creaturely causation – creaturely causation is a participation in God's primary causation. The primary cause infuses itself most deeply in any effect because, in the absence of the primary cause, there would be no causation at all (pp. 78–88). Similarly, God's gift of creation is not a gift among gifts. It is the fundamental basis of there being any exchange at all. In all human acts of donation, which is to say all human acts of *caritas*, there is an analogical participation in the most fundamental act of love which is God's gift of creation, renewed in the salvific gift of God in Jesus Christ. We are incorporated into that reciprocal exchange of redemption in the Eucharist which, in turn, interprets the meaning of the fruits of the earth that we call food. Without a Eucharistic response, the gift withers in stony ground, unrecognized for what it is because it has not been received, and becomes a mere artefact of God's design and power and thereby a commodity for our use. Reception of the gift requires one fundamental response above all else: thankfulness. Creation bears something of the divine giver to the recipient – a participation in God's life – and this places it beyond commodification.

Every generous act of giving, with every perfect gift, is from above, coming down from the Father of lights, with whom there is no variation or shadow due to change. In fulfilment of his own purpose he gave us birth by the word of truth, so that we would become a kind of first fruits of his creatures. (Jas 1.17-18)

Notes

Preface

1 St. Thomas Aquinas, *The 'Summa Theologica' of St. Thomas Aquinas.* Literally translated by Fathers of the English Dominican Province (London: Burns Oates and Washbourne, 2nd and rev. edn., 1920–2), 10 vols.

Chapter 1

1 Genesis is the first book of the Hebrew Bible, also known as the Tanakh or the Christian Old Testament. The Hebrew title of Genesis is 'Bereishit' meaning 'in the beginning'. It was translated from Hebrew into Greek in the late second century BC as part of the Greek translation of the Old Testament known as the Septuagint or 'LXX' (70, because there were 70 translators). In the late fourth century AD it was translated into Latin as part of St. Jerome's Vulgate version of the Bible. The title 'Genesis' is the Latinized version of the Septuagint's Greek title, meaning 'origin'.

2 The texts of *Atrahasis*, *Enuma Elish* (*The Epic of Creation*) and other ancient Near Eastern creation myths are available in Stephanie Dalley, *Myths from Mesopotamia: Creation, the Flood, Gilgamesh and others* (Oxford: Oxford University Press, rev. edn., 2000).

3 Bernard Batto, *In the Beginning: Essays on Creation Motifs in the Ancient Near East and the Bible* (Winona Lake, IN: Eisenbrauns, 2013), p. 28 and Joseph Blenkinsopp, *Creation, Un-Creation, Re-Creation: A Discursive Commentary on Genesis 1-11* (London: T&T Clark, 2011), p. 13. See also W. G. Lambert, 'Mesopotamian Creation Stories', in Markham J. Geller, and Mineke Schipper (eds), *Imagining Creation* (Leiden: Brill, 2007), pp. 15–59.

4 See John Day, *From Creation to Babel: Studies in Genesis 1-11* (London: Bloomsbury Academic, 2013), ch. 6.

5 Translation from Lambert, 'Mesopotamian Creation Stories', p. 18.

6   Batto, *In the Beginning*, p. 36.

7   For a study of the continuity of Genesis with creation myths of the ancient Near East, particularly with respect to temple building, see Jon D. Levenson, *Creation and the Persistence of Evil: The Jewish Drama of Divine Omnipotence* (Princeton, NJ: Princeton University Press, 1988). See also R. W. L. Moberly, *The Theology of the Book of Genesis* (Cambridge: Cambridge University Press, 2009), chs. 3 and 4.

8   The dates of texts in the Old Testament tend to revolve around the destruction of the Temple in Jerusalem at the end of the sixth century BC and the ensuing exile in Babylon, hence they are labelled 'pre-exilic', 'exilic' or 'post-exilic'. It is worth remembering that certain sections of Genesis are much older than others. For example, given its linguistic structure the oldest section is probably ch. 49, which is Jacob's poetic blessing of his sons who were to represent the twelve tribes of Israel.

9   For an account of debates concerning the dating of Genesis, see Thomas Brodie, *Genesis as Dialogue: A Literary, Historical, and Theological Commentary* (Oxford: Oxford University Press, 2001), ch. 10.

10 Blenkinsopp, *Creation, Un-Creation, Re-Creation*, p. 7.

11 This pattern of creation in Genesis 1 is discussed in many contemporary works and has been a focus of modern commentary since at least the eighteenth century. See, for example, John Day, *From Creation to Babel*, p. 1 and Ronald Hendel, *The Book of Genesis: A Biography* (Princeton: Princeton University Press, 2013), p. 33.

12 Augustine, 'The Literal Meaning of Genesis', IV.24 in Saint Augustine, *On Genesis*, trans. Edmund Hill, O.P. (New York: New City Press, 2002), p. 254.

13 See Philo, *Special Laws*, I.66–67 in *The Works of Philo: Complete and Unabridged*, trans. C. D. Yonge (Peabody, Massachusetts: Hendrickson Publishers, 2002), p. 540: 'We ought to look upon the universal world as the highest and truest temple of God.'

14 See Margaret Barker, *Creation: A Biblical Vision for the Environment* (London: T&T Clark, 2010), ch.1. Barker expounds in detail the links between the order of creation and the order of Temple worship. See also James C. VanderKam, *The Book of Jubilees* (Sheffield: Sheffield Academic Press, 2001).

15 Jubilees 1.28.

16 Jubilees 2.1. All translations are from James H. Charlesworth (ed.), *The Old Testament Pseudepigrapha* vol. 2 (London: Darton, Longman & Todd, 1985).

17 See Barker, *Creation*, pp. 38ff and ch.2, Joseph Blenkinsopp, 'Structure of P', *Catholic Biblical Quarterly* 38 (1976), pp. 275–92 and Peter J. Kearney, 'Creation Liturgy: The P Redaction of Exodus 25-40', *Zeitschrift für die alttestameutliche Wissenschaft* 89 (1977), pp. 375–87.

18 To cite just one of many examples, note the seven-day inauguration of Solomon's Temple as described in 1 Kgs. 8.65 and 2 Chron. 7.8-9, mirroring the seven-day creation of the cosmic temple.

19 For example, the creation epic described in *Enuma Elish* concludes with the construction of the temple to the victorious god Marduk and his subsequent enthronement (*Enuma Elish* VI.51–65, cited in Blenkinsopp, *Creation, Un-Creation, Re-Creation*, p. 36). See John H. Walton, *The Lost World of Genesis One: Ancient Cosmology and the Origins Debate* (Downers Grove, IL: Intervarsity Press, 2009), propositions 8 and 9.

20 Day, *From Creation to Babel*, p. 21.

21 Thomas Aquinas, *Summa Theologiae*, III.60.2.*responsio*: 'Signs are given to men, to whom it is proper to discover the unknown by means of the known. Consequently a sacrament properly so-called is that which is the sign of some sacred thing pertaining to man; so that properly speaking a sacrament, as considered by us now, is defined as being the "sign of a holy thing so far as it makes men holy".'

22 Peter Harrison, *The Bible, Protestantism and the Rise of Natural Science* (Cambridge: Cambridge University Press, 1998), ch. 4.

23 See Augustine, 'The Literal Meaning of Genesis', IV.30 (p. 258) and R.R. Reno, *Genesis* (London: SCM Press, 2010), pp. 60–2.

24 Augustine, 'The Literal Meaning of Genesis', IV.32 (p. 259): 'And because nothing else remained to be fashioned there was made morning [on the seventh day] after that evening [the sixth day] in such a way that it would not be the starting point for fashioning another creature, but the start of quiet rest for the universal creation in the quiet rest of the creator.' See also Augustine, 'The Literal Meaning of Genesis', IV.36–37 (pp. 261–2).

25 See Reno, *Genesis*, p. 61.

26 'Fiat' is a Latin term meaning 'let it be'. It is a decree that sanctions something. Mary submits to the will of God when she says to the angel, 'Let it be with me according to your word.' (in the Latin vulgate translation of the Bible: *fiat mihi secundum verbum tuum*) (Lk. 1.37).

27 Reno, *Genesis*, p. 61.

28   As John Day notes, in Gen. 2.4b–3.24 the text in fact refers to
     'Yahweh Elohim'. In the remainder of Genesis and throughout the
     Pentateuch (except Exod. 9.30), the reference is simply to 'Yahweh'.
     Day's explanation of the combination of 'Yahweh' and 'Elohim' in
     Gen. 2 and 3 seems natural: in a polytheistic environment a later
     redactor added 'Elohim' to 'Yahweh' to make crystal clear that the
     God of Gen. 1–2.4a and Gen. 2.4b–3 is one and the same deity.
     See John Day, *From Creation to Babel*, p. 25. See also Blenkinsopp,
     Creation, Un-Creation, Re-Creation, p. 55.

29   Only later tradition names the man 'Adam'. This is derived from the
     Hebrew *ādām* meaning 'the man' or 'human being'.

30   By contrast, Blenkinsopp seems to assume a similarity between
     human labour for the gods in *Attrahasis* and the man's labour in
     Eden. See Blenkinsopp, *Creation, Un-Creation, Re-Creation*, p. 61.

31   On the view that the *imago dei* also subsists in the human
     community, see Gregory of Nyssa, *On the Making of Man*, trans.
     H.A. Wilson, in Philip Schaff and Henry Wace (eds), *The Nicene and
     Post-Nicene Fathers*, Second Series, vol. 5 (Edinburgh: T&T Clark,
     1994), XVI.17–18, p. 406.

32   The text does not name the fruit. Only later Western Christian
     tradition, after the publication of the Vulgate translation of the Bible
     in the fifth century, claims that the fruit is an apple. This is probably
     because of a wordplay on the Latin for apple (*malum*) and apple tree
     (*malus*) and the Latin adjective for evil (*malus*).

33   For a brief account of the different views of good and evil among
     modern biblical scholars, see John Day, *From Creation to Babel*,
     pp. 42–4.

34   Irenaeus, *Against the Heresies*, IV.38.1 in Alexander Roberts
     and James Donaldson (eds), *Ante-Nicene Fathers vol. 1: The
     Apostolic Fathers, Justin Martyr, Irenaeus* (Peabody, Massachusetts:
     Hendrickson Publishers, 1994), p. 521.

35   Augustine, 'The Literal Meaning of Genesis', IX.6, pp. 431–2.

36   Augustine, *Confessions*, trans. F. J. Sheed (Indianapolis: Hackett
     Publishing Company, 2006), III.7, p. 44; *Enchiridion on Faith,
     Hope, and Charity*, paragraph 11 in Saint Augustine, *On Christian
     Belief*, ed. Boniface Ramsey (Hyde Park, New York: New City Press,
     2005), p. 278.

37   For a time Augustine espoused the idea that creation consists of two
     conflicting principles, good and evil, both with positive ontological
     status. This was the teaching of the third-century Persian thinker

Mani and his followers, the Manichees. In contemporary culture, the best example of a Manichean cosmology can be found in the Star Wars movies. On Augustine's mature view, evil does not have a positive existence; it is the absence of existence.

38 Augustine, *The City of God against the Pagans*, trans. R. W. Dyson (Cambridge: Cambridge University Press, 1998), XIV.10, pp. 602–3.

39 Augustine provides a reflection on the unintelligibility of foolishness, the kind of foolishness exhibited in eating the fruit of the tree of knowledge: 'So if one is unable to see darkness despite one's eyes being open and clear, it is not absurd to say that it is impossible to understand foolishness, which is a darkness of the mind.' See Augustine, *On Order (De Ordine)*, trans. Silvano Borruso (South Bend, Indiana: St. Augustine's Press, 2007), Book 2, First Debate, 3.10, p. 63.

40 Origen, *The Song of songs: Commentary and Homilies*, trans. R.P. Lawson (Westminster, Maryland: Newman Press, 1957), Book III, p. 223.

41 Later theologians, notably Augustine, were to nuance the notion of the literal sense of scripture. The literal sense referred to what the author wanted to convey. As such, the author may have desired to convey a symbolic or figurative teaching. For a helpful discussion, see William M. Wright IV, 'The Literal Sense of Scripture According to Henri de Lubac: Insights from Patristic Exegesis of the Transfiguration' in *Modern Theology* 28 (2), 2012, pp. 252–77. See also Rowan Williams, 'The Discipline of Scripture' in Williams, *On Christian Theology* (Oxford: Blackwell, 2000), pp. 44–59.

42 Later known as the tropological sense of scripture.

43 Origen, *On First Principles (De principiis)*, trans. G.W. Butterworth (Notre Dame, IN: Ave Maria Press, 2013), IV.3.1, pp. 383–4.

44 Augustine, 'The Literal Meaning of Genesis', I.39, pp. 186–7.

45 Peter Harrison, *The Bible, Protestantism and the Rise of Natural Science*, p. 127.

46 Creationists are usually regarded as theologically conservative. However, because creationism accepts the terms of the debate established by Darwinism – non-theological premises that regard natural history and empiricism as the only truthful account of nature and creation – they are engaged in an enterprise more reminiscent of modern *liberal* theology.

47 Plato, *Republic*, trans. Desmond Lee (London: Penguin, 1987), 607b5-6, p. 376.

Chapter 2

1   Plato, *Timaeus*, trans. R.G. Bury (Cambridge, Massachusetts: Harvard University Press, 1999).

2   Aristotle, *Physics (Books V-VIII)*, trans. P.H. Wicksteed and F. M. Cornford (Cambridge, Massachusetts: Harvard University Press, 1995), VIII.1, pp. 277–9.

3   On the interwoven doctrines of creation in the Jewish, Christian and Islamic traditions, see David B. Burrell, *Freedom and Creation in Three Traditions* (Notre Dame, Indiana: University of Notre Dame Press, 1993).

4   See Steven Shapin and Simon Schaffer, *Leviathan and the Air-pump: Hobbes, Boyle and the Experimental Life* (Princeton: Princeton University Press, 1985) for a fascinating account of the political significance of the vacuum in Boyle's air-pump investigations of the seventeenth century.

5   Plotinus, *Enneads V*, trans. A. H. Armstrong (Cambridge, Massachusetts: Harvard University Press, 1984), V.2.1, pp. 59–61.

6   We may think that there must been some connection or similarity between God and creation. The relation between God and creation will be discussed in more detail later in this chapter and in Chapter 3.

7   When we describe God as like a creature in a univocal way (literally 'with one voice'), we are suggesting that we can speak of God and his creative act *in the same way* (with the same voice) as we can speak of creaturely creativity so that we might think of God's creativity as a very grand or supremely powerful version of human creativity. The thrust of this chapter is that God's act of creation *ex nihilo* is utterly unique and not univocal with our creativity, although our creativity is related by analogy to God's creativity. All our acts of 'creativity' assume God's primordial and unique act of creation *ex nihilo*. The analogical relation of our creativity with God's act of creation will be discussed in the next chapter.

8   A fine exposition of creation *ex nihilo* is available in Ian A. McFarland, *From Nothing: A Theology of Creation* (Louisville, Kentucky: Westminster John Knox Press, 2014), especially ch.4. See also the articles in a special edition of the journal *Modern Theology*: Janet Soskice (ed.), *Modern Theology*: Special issue: 'Creation "Ex Nihilo" and Modern Theology', 29(2), 2013, pp. 1–192. For critiques of creation *ex nihilo* arising from feminist concerns and process theology, see Thomas Jay Oord, ed., *Theologies of Creation:*

Creatio Ex Nihilo *and its New Rivals* (London: Routledge, 2015) and Catherine Keller, *Face of the Deep: A Theology of Becoming* (New York: Routledge, 2003).

9 Notable exceptions are Justin Martyr (c. AD 100–c. AD 165) and Clement of Alexandria (c. AD 150–c. AD 215).

10 The text is therefore usually known as the Masoretic text. It is the authoritative Hebrew text of the Tanakh (the Hebrew Bible) for Rabbinic Judaism.

11 For a thorough survey of the different interpretations of Genesis 1, arguing for creation *ex nihilo*'s scriptural basis, see Paul Coplan and William Lane Craig, *Creation out of Nothing: A Biblical, Philosophical, and Scientific Exploration* (Grand Rapids, Michigan: Baker Academic 2004), pp. 36–60. See also Gordon J. Wenham, *World Biblical Commentary: Genesis 1-15* (Nashville, Tennessee: Thomas Nelson, 1987), pp. 11–14. Wenham argues that verse 1 of Genesis constitutes a main clause describing the first act of creation (*the* beginning in an absolute rather than temporal sense) while vv. 2 and 3 describe God's subsequent creative act. Wenham translates the Hebrew of Genesis 1.1 very similarly to the Septuagint, as: 'In the beginning God created the heaven and the earth.'

12 For example, the New International Version and the New American Bible.

13 Ἐν ἀρχῇ ἐποίησεν ὁ θεὸς τὸν οὐρανὸν καὶ τὴν γῆν.

14 A much more detailed account of this interpretation of Gen. 1.1 is available in R.R. Reno's excellent theological commentary, *Genesis* (London: SCM Press, 2010). For a helpful discussion of this understanding of 'beginning' in Ambrose of Milan's Hexameron sermons of AD 387, see N. Joseph Torchia, O.P., *Creatio ex Nihilo and the Theology of St. Augustine: The Anti-Manichaean Polemic and Beyond* (New York: Peter Lang, 1999), p. 20.

15 The wisdom literature is generally thought to include Job, Proverbs, Ecclesiastes, and the deuterocanonical books Sirach (Ecclesiasticus) and Wisdom. For God as the creator and source of all things, see Prov. 8.22-30 and Job 38.4–39.30.

16 Gerhard May, *Creatio Ex Nihilo: The Doctrine of 'Creation out of Nothing' in Early Christian Thought*, trans. A.S. Worrall (London: T&T Clark, 2004), p. 21.

17 See Janet M. Soskice, '*Creatio ex nihilo*: its Jewish and Christian foundations', in David Burrell et al. (eds), *Creation and the God of Abraham* (Cambridge: Cambridge University Press, 2010), pp. 24–39, especially pp. 33–5.

18 See *The Shepherd of Hermas*, Book 1, ch. 1: 'God, who dwells in the heavens, and made out of nothing the things that exist.' The text is available in Bart D. Ehrman (trans.), *The Apostolic Fathers vol. 2* (Cambridge, Massachusetts: Harvard University Press, 2003).

19 Tatian, 'Address of Tatian to the Greeks' in *Ante-Nicene Fathers* vol. 2, trans. J. E. Ryland, ed. Alexander Roberts and James Donaldson (Peabody, Massachusetts: Hendrickson Publishers, 1995), ch. 5, p. 67. See also ch. 12.

20 Theophilus of Antioch, 'To Autolycus', I.4 in *Ante-Nicene Fathers* vol. 2, trans. J.E. Ryland et al., p. 90.

21 May, *Creatio Ex Nihilo*, xi.

22 Ernan McMullin, 'Creation *ex nihilo*: early history', in Burrell et al. (eds), *Creation and the God of Abraham*, pp. 17–18. See also May, *Creatio Ex Nihilo*, pp. 24–5. For May, Judaism does not establish a clear doctrine of creation *ex nihilo* until the Middle Ages in the context of a dispute with Arabic Neoplatonism and Aristotelianism.

23 Janet M. Soskice, '*Creatio ex nihilo*: its Jewish and Christian foundations', p. 25 (emphasis original). Note that Soskice's phrase is a deliberate rejoinder to Gerhard May's claim that creation *ex nihilo* is not compelled by the biblical text.

24 Augustine, *The City of God against the Pagans*, trans. R. W. Dyson (Cambridge: Cambridge University Press, 1998), XI.10, p. 462.

25 Augustine, *The City of God against the Pagans*, XI.10, p. 462.

26 Aquinas, *Summa Theologiae*, 1a.4.3. For those unfamiliar with Aquinas's theology, an obvious question may come to mind: On what basis does he make these claims about God? How does he know all this? As a theologian, Aquinas has a clear method: the exposition of sacred scripture in concert with the 'holy teaching' (*sacra doctrina*) of the church. When considering the doctrines of God and creation, Aquinas sees himself as expositing what is taught in scripture through the church by using the tools of philosophical learning in order to bring clarity and detail. What Aquinas wants to say here is that theologians are concerned with distinguishing between speech about God and speech about creatures. If we speak of God in terms appropriate to creatures without reflection or qualification, we are speaking only of a mythological figure. To avoid such idolatrous speech, he uses three guiding principles (*triplex via* or 'threefold way'), drawn largely from the sixth-century Christian Neoplatonist Dionysius the Pseudo-Areopagite (c. AD 500). First, in speaking about God we are necessarily speaking about the creator or 'first cause' of all things, who must therefore be distinguished from his

effects. We therefore speak of God by 'the way of causality' (*via causalitatis*). Secondly, we must remove from our speech about God all categories and modes of reason that belong properly to the created realm, such as time or change. This is known as 'the way of remotion' (*via remotionis*) because we must *remove* creaturely categories from our speech about God. This is essentially the method of negative theology whereby we are better to say what God is *not* rather than what God *is*. So: God is not temporal or subject to change because these are categories which belong to creation. Thirdly, Aquinas uses 'the way of eminence' (*via eminentiae*) or what we might call the logic of perfection: if we are to speak of God at all, we must ascribe to God the greatest perfection, or 'eminence'. In this context, this means ascribing to God the greatest unity and aseity. Throughout, Aquinas's basic principle is this: we must be very careful what we say of almighty God and it is the theologian's job to ensure that we are speaking of God rather than a creature of myth. On Aquinas's threefold method, see *Summa Theologiae* 1a.12.12; *Summa Contra* I.14; Rudi te Velde, *Aquinas on God: The 'Divine Science' of the Summa Theologiae* (Aldershot: Ashgate, 2006), p. 76 and Fran O'Rourke, *Pseudo-Dionysius and the Metaphysics of Aquinas* (Notre Dame, Indiana: University of Notre Dame Press, 2005), pp. 31–41.

27 Aquinas, *Summa Theologiae*, 1a.3.6.

28 It is important not to confuse the philosophical category of substance with the modern English term 'substance'. When speaking of substance today, we are usually referring to some kind of material stuff ('this white substance is sugar'). When ancient and medieval philosophers and theologians use the term substance, they are *not* pointing to something's material nature. They are pointing to what something is, essentially, in itself. For Aquinas, as well as material substances such as human beings there are non-material substances such as angels. According to Aristotle in book 12 of his *Metaphysics*, there are five kinds of substance, the highest being God who is an eternal and immutable substance.

29 Note the potentially confusing terminology. An accidental change is *not* a change that happens by accident. It is a change to the incidental qualities – the so-called 'accidents' – of something.

30 Note that a substantial change may not involve any material change. The material nature of a tree is wood and the material nature of a desk is wood but they have different 'forms' which means that, according to Aristotle and Aquinas, their substantial natures – what they *are* – are different.

31 Aquinas, *Summa Theologiae*, 1a.3.5. ad 1; 1a.3.6. ad 2.

32 Aquinas, *Summa Theologiae*, 1a.3.4. *sed contra*.

33 Aquinas, *Summa Theologiae*, 1a.4.2. *responsio*.

34 Aquinas, *Summa Contra Gentiles Book Two: Creation*, trans. James F. Anderson (Notre Dame, Indiana: University of Notre Dame Press, 1975), II.6.1.

35 Aquinas, *Summa Theologiae*, 1a.3.4.*responsio*; *Summa Theologiae*, 1a.4.3.ad 3. The rediscovery of the importance of the metaphysics of participation in Aquinas's theology is one of the most important recent developments in Thomist scholarship. See Rudi te Velde, *Aquinas and God*, pp. 139–46; Jan Aertsen, *Nature and Creature: Thomas Aquinas's Way of Thought* (Leiden: Brill, 1988), pp. 123–7; John Wippel, *The Metaphysical Thought of Thomas Aquinas: From Finite Being to Uncreated Being* (Washington, DC: The Catholic University Press of America, 2000), ch.4.

36 Aquinas, *Summa Contra Gentiles*, I.22.9 (my translation and emphases).

37 Aquinas, *Summa Theologiae*, 1a.13.7. *responsio*: 'Since therefore God is outside the whole order of creation, and all creatures are ordered to Him, and not conversely, it is manifest that creatures are really related to God Himself; whereas in God there is no real relation to creatures, but a relation only in idea, inasmuch as creatures are referred to Him.' See also *Summa Theologiae*, 1a.45.3.ad 1. For a critique of Aquinas's view, see William Lane Craig, 'Timelessness, Creation, and God's Real Relation to the World', *Laval théologique et philosophique* 56 (1), 2000, pp. 93–112. For a defence of Aquinas's view in response to Craig, see Matthew R. McWhorter, 'Aquinas on God's Relation to the World', *New Blackfriars* 94 (1049), January 2013, pp. 3–19.

38 Aquinas, *Summa Theologiae* 1a.28.1 and *Quaestiones disputatae de potentia*, question 7, article 11, available in Thomas Aquinas, *The Power of God*, trans. Richard J. Regan (Oxford: Oxford University Press, 2012), p. 225.

39 Aquinas, *The Power of God*, question 7, article 11 (p. 225): 'The intellect sometimes considers two things as beings, only one or neither of which is such, as when the intellect considers two future things, or one present and the other future, and understands one with a relation to the other, asserting that one is prior to the other. And so these relations are only conceptual, as resulting from the way of understanding.'

40 Aquinas *Summa Theologiae* 1a.45.3.ad 1; *The Power of God*, question 3 article 3, pp. 41–3.

41 The intricacies of the Trinitarian doctrine of God lie beyond the immediate scope of this book. One question will occur to some readers, however: Having established the importance of the simplicity of God, does the doctrine of the Trinity introduce plurality or complexity into God? To answer this question, it is important to be clear at the outset that the doctrine of the Trinity does not mean that there are three individuals or people in the Godhead. Neither does it mean that there is complexity. Rather, God does not *have* relations; God is pure relationality of love in such a way that the threefold persons of the Trinity are also a perfect and eternal unity. It may be helpful to note that the doctrines of divine simplicity and the Trinity, rather than being mutually exclusive, are mutually interpretative because each tells us what the other does *not* mean. On the one hand, the doctrine of the Trinity, in pointing to the relation of love in God, makes it clear that, whatever we mean by divine simplicity, we do *not* mean that God is a kind of monad, a 'thing' or something like a lone individual. God is love and love is a relationship; God is the perfect and eternal relationship of love in Father, Son and Holy Spirit. Similarly, the doctrine of divine simplicity makes it clear that whatever we mean by the Trinity we do *not* mean that God has a structure such that God is composed of three persons. We *have* relations whereas God *is* pure relation. Neither does the Trinity mean that God *possesses* love because God *is* love. This kind of eternal relation in God is not inimical to simple unity, but constitutive of that unity. Finally, we should note that, while Aquinas speaks of 'difference' in God (the difference of the persons), he is clear that in God there is no diversity, division or inequality (which would certainly compromise simplicity). See *The Power of God*, question 9, article 8, p. 266.

42 Aquinas, *Summa Theologiae*, 1a.28.1.*responsio*: 'But when something proceeds from a principle of the same nature, then both the one proceeding and the source of procession, agree in the same order; and then they have real relations to each other. Therefore as the divine processions are in the identity of the same nature, as above explained (1a.27, articles 2 and 4), these relations, according to the divine processions, are necessarily real relations.'

43 Aquinas, *Summa Theologiae*, 1a.45.7.

44 Aquinas titles his question on God's creative act as *de modo emanationis rerum a primo principio* – 'on the emanation of things from the first principle' (*Summa Theologiae*, 1a.45.1). While a *necessary* emanation or a stretching of divine being such as one finds in Neoplatonism is precluded in Christian theology, creation is described by Aquinas as a freely willed emanation from God.

45 Aquinas, *Summa Theologiae*, 1a.45.6.*responsio*. See also Aquinas,
   The Power of God, question 10, article 2, counter-objection 2, p. 285:
   'The processions of creatures are imitations of the processions of
   the divine Persons.' The work of Gilles Emery provides the finest
   recent exposition of Aquinas's teaching on the Trinity and creation.
   For a succinct review of this research, see Gilles Emery, 'Trinity and
   Creation', in Rik van Nieuwenhove and Joseph Wawrykow (eds),
   The Theology of Thomas Aquinas (Notre Dame, Indiana: University
   of Press, 2005), pp. 58–75. Emery cites in particular a number of
   texts from Aquinas's commentary on the Sentences of Peter Lombard
   (*Scriptum super libros sententiarum magistri Petri Lombardi
   Episocopi Parisiensis*), for example book 1, distinction 14, question
   1, article 1: 'The eternal procession of the persons are the cause and
   reason of the production of creatures' (p. 59).

46 Aristotle, *Metaphysics (Books I-IX)*, trans. Hugh Tredennick
   (Cambridge, Massachusetts: Harvard University Press, 1996), VII.7,
   pp. 338–9; *Physics (Books I-IV)*, trans. P.H. Wicksteed and F.M.
   Cornford (Cambridge, Massachusetts, 1996), II.7, p. 165; Aquinas,
   Summa Theologiae, 1a.45.7.*responsio*: 'Every effect in some degree
   represents its cause, but diversely. For some effects represent only the
   causality of the cause, but not its form; as smoke represents fire. Such
   a representation is called a "trace": for a trace shows that someone
   has passed by but not who it is.'

47 Aquinas, *Summa Theologiae*, 1a.45.2. ad 2; *Summa Contra Gentiles*
   II.19; *The Power of God*, question 3, article 2, pp. 39–41.

48 See Aquinas, *Summa Theologiae*, 1a.46.1. ad 7.

49 Anselm of Canterbury, *The Major Works*, ed. Brian Davies and
   G.R. Evans (Oxford: Oxford University Press, 1998), 'Monologion',
   ch.8, pp. 20–2.

50 Aquinas, *Summa Theologiae*, 1a.46.1.*responsio*.

51 Aquinas, *Scriptum super Libros Sententiarum Petri Lombardi*
   (Writings of the 'Sentences' of Peter Lombard), book 2, distinction
   1, question 1, article 2, *responsio*. The translated text is available in
   Steven E. Baldner and William E. Carroll (eds and trans.), *Aquinas
   on Creation: Writings on the 'Sentences' of Peter Lombard 2.1.1*
   (Toronto: Pontifical Institute of Mediaeval Studies, 1997).

52 Ibid.

53 Aquinas, *The Power of God*, question 5, article 1, p. 134.

54 Baldner and Carroll, *Aquinas on Creation: Writings on the
   'Sentences' of Peter Lombard 2.1.1*, book 2, distinction 1, question 1,
   article 2, *responsio*, p. 75.

55 Aquinas, *Summa Theologiae*, 1a.46.3.ad 1.

56 A good example of an abject failure to understand the *nihil* in creation *ex nihilo* is Lawrence M. Krauss, *A Universe from Nothing: Why There is Something Rather than Nothing?* (London: Simon and Schuster, 2012).

57 For a fine, succinct account of creation *ex nihilo* in relation to contemporary quantum cosmology, see William R. Stoeger, 'The Big Bang, quantum cosmology and *creatio ex nihilo*', in Burrell et al. (eds), *Creation and the God of Abraham*, pp. 152–75.

58 John Webster, '"Love is also a Lover of Life": *Creatio Ex Nihilo* and Creaturely Goodness', *Modern Theology* 29 (2), 2013, pp. 156–71 (quotation appearing on p. 156).

59 See Keller, *Face of the Deep: A Theology of Becoming*. For a defence of Augustine's doctrine of creation against criticisms from process and feminist theology, see Rowan Williams, '"Good for Nothing"? Augustine on Creation' in Williams, *On Augustine* (London: Bloomsbury, 2016), ch.4.

60 Webster, 'Love is Also a Lover of Life', p. 168.

Chapter 3

1 See pp. 46–7.

2 Although 'teleology' is now a common term in philosophy and theology, *teleologia* is not conclusively attested until 1728 when, in his *Philosophia Rationalis, Sive Logica*, the German philosopher Christian Wolff refers to a branch of natural philosophy that deals with the ends of things.

3 Aquinas, *Summa Theologiae* 1a.13.1.

4 Aquinas, *Summa Theologiae*, 1a.4.3; 1a.13.2; 1a.45.7.

5 Aquinas, *Truth (De Veritate)* vol. 3, trans. Robert W. Schmidt (Indianapolis: Hackett Publishing Company, 1994), 22.2 ad 1, p. 42.

6 Aquinas, *Summa Theologiae*, 1a.13.1 *responsio*. For an explanation of the terms 'excellence' and 'remotion', see Chapter 2 footnote 26, p. 166.

7 Aquinas, *Summa Theologiae*, 1a.13.5.*responsio*.

8 Ibid.

9 Ibid.

10 Aquinas, *Summa Theologiae*, 1a.13.6.*responsio*.

11 Aquinas, *Summa Theologiae*, 1a.13.

12 Aquinas, *Summa Theologiae*, 1a.13.6.*responsio*: 'Hence as regards what the name signifies [*rem significatam*], these names are applied primarily to God rather than to creatures, because these perfections flow from God to creatures; but as regards the imposition of the names, they are primarily applied by us to creatures which we know first. Hence they have a mode of signification [*modum significandi*] which belongs to creatures, as said above (article 3).'

13 Aquinas, *Summa Theologiae*, 1a.4.3.*responsio*.

14 The claim that there are metaphysical implications to Aquinas's teaching on analogy has proved controversial in recent years. Nevertheless, he discusses the analogical nature of being in numerous places, notably *De principiis naturae* [On the Principles of Nature], VI.33-34 (available in Joseph Bobik, trans., *Aquinas on Matter and Form and the Elements* (Notre Dame, Indiana: University of Notre Dame Press, 1998)) and Aquinas, *Commentary on Aristotle's Metaphysics*, trans. John P. Rowan (Notre Dame, Indiana: Dumb Ox Books, 1995), Book IV, paragraph 535.

15 For Aquinas, participation refers to the taking part in something. More particularly, 'when something receives in a particular way that which belongs to another in a universal way, it is said "to participate" in that, as human being is said to participate in animal because it does not possess the intelligible structure of animal according to its total commonality.' Thomas Aquinas, *An Exposition of the 'On Hebdomads' of Boetius* (*Expositio libri De hebdomamdibus*), trans. Janice L. Schultz and Edward A. Synan (Washington, DC: Catholic University of America Press, 2001), II.70–80, p. 19.

16 There is a debate in Thomist scholarship concerning the meaning of *ens* (or *esse*) *commune*. This is discussed by Rudi te Velde in *Participation and Substantiality in Thomas Aquinas* (Leiden: Brill, 1995), pp. 188–94. I wholly concur with te Velde that *esse commune* for Aquinas refers to created being and does not encapsulate God.

17 The concept of the *analogia entis* was given its most sophisticated modern articulation by the twentieth-century German–Polish Catholic philosopher Erich Przywara (1889–1972). See his *Analogia Entis: Metaphysics: Original Structure and Universal Rhythm*, trans. John R. Betz and David Bentley Hart (Grand Rapids, Michigan: Eerdmans, 2014). In addition to an outstanding translation, Betz and Hart provide a superb introduction to Pryzwara's complex thought. Karl Barth famously referred to the *analogia entis* as the invention

of the anti-Christ and the only good reason not to become a Roman Catholic. For an assessment of Barth's (mistaken) view, see Keith Johnson, *Karl Barth and the* Analogia Entis (London: Bloomsbury, 2010) and Thomas Joseph White, O.P. (ed.), *The Analogy of Being: Invention of the Anti-Christ or Wisdom of God?* (Grand Rapids, Michigan: Eerdmans, 2011).

18 See Rudi te Velde, *Aquinas on God*, p. 145 n.47 on being's contraction *to* an essence rather than the essence receiving being. Te Velde avoids the notion that the essence of a creature, although really distinct from its existence, is a thing prior to the reception of existence. As te Velde puts it, 'The nature results from the contraction [of being] instead of explaining it.' The metaphysical issues lying behind this issue, which are very detailed and complex, lie beyond the purview of the current book. One of the best recent discussions can be found in David C. Schindler, 'What's the Difference? On the Metaphysics of Participation in a Christian Context', *The St. Anselm Journal* 3(1) (2005), pp. 1–27 available with respondent papers at: http://www.anselm.edu/Institutes-Centers-and-the-Arts/Institute-for-Saint-Anselm-Studies/Saint-Anselm-Journal/Archives/Vol-3-No-1-fall-2005.htm (accessed June 2016).

19 There are countless examples in scripture, particularly in the psalms and wisdom literature. To cite only three: Ps. 103.19; Mat. 6.26 and Rom. 8.28.

20 Aquinas, *Summa Contra Gentiles*, III.1.69; *Summa Theologiae,* 1a.105.5.*responsio*: 'Some have understood God to work in every agent in such a way that no created power has any effect in things, but that God alone is the ultimate cause of everything wrought; for instance, that it is not fire that gives heat, but God in the fire, and so forth.'

21 The distinction between primary and secondary causes is preserved in many Christian traditions, notably in the Westminster Confession of Faith of 1643, a highly influential expression of Protestant Reformed theology: 'God from all eternity, did, by the most wise and holy counsel of His own will, freely, and unchangeably ordain whatsoever comes to pass; yet so, as thereby neither is God the author of sin, nor is violence offered to the will of the creatures; nor is the liberty or contingency of second causes taken away, but rather established' (III.1).

22 Aquinas, *The Power of God (De potential dei)*, trans. Richard J. Regan (Oxford: Oxford University Press, 2012), question 3, article 7, p. 58 (emphasis mine).

23 Aquinas, *Commentary on the Book of Causes*, trans. Vincent A. Guagliardo, O.P. (Washington, DC: The Catholic University Press of America, 1996), proposition 1, p. 5. As the translator notes, the phrase rendered 'infuses' (*plus est influens super causatum suum*) can be literally translated 'pours forth more abundantly on its effect'.

24 Aquinas, *The Power of God*, question 3, article 7, p. 58. Strictly speaking, in referring to 'a heavenly body' Aquinas means the celestial bodies generally. Chief among these, however, is the sun.

25 Aquinas, *Summa Theologiae*, 1a.8.1.

26 Aquinas, *Summa Theologiae*, 1a.22.3; 1a.105.5.

27 Aquinas, *Summa Theologiae*, 1a.22.3.*responsio*.

28 Aquinas, *Summa Theologiae*, 1a.105.7. *responsio*.

29 Aquinas, *Summa Contra Gentiles*, III(2).100–102; *Summa Theologiae*, 1a.105.6. ad 1.

30 Aristotle's texts came via Islamic theologians and philosophers such as the Persian scholar Ibn Sīnā (known in the Latin West as Avicenna, 980–1037) and the Andalusian scholar Ibn Rušd (known in the Latin West as Averroes, 1126–1198).

31 Aristotle, *Physics (Books I-IV)*, trans. P. H. Wicksteed and F. M. Cornford (Cambridge, Massachusetts, 1996), II.3.194 b 25–195, b 30, pp. 129–39; *Metaphysics (Books I-IX)*, trans. Hugh Tredennick (Cambridge, Massachusetts: Harvard University Press, 1996) I.3.983 a 25–b 7, pp. 18–19. A very clear exposition of Aristotle's view of causation is available in Jonathan Lear, *Aristotle: The Desire to Understand* (Cambridge: Cambridge University Press, 1988), especially pp. 28–42.

32 Note that an important implication of creation *ex nihilo* is that there is no material cause in creation.

33 So, for example, the Alexandrian theologian John Philoponus (c. 490–c. 570) writes, 'He sums up in brief form what has been said, [saying] that the types of the enumerated causes are four: the material cause, the formal, the efficient, the final.' Philoponus, *On Aristotle's Physics* 2, trans. A. R. Lacey (London: Duckworth, 1993), 245.25 (p. 59).

34 Aquinas, *Summa Theologiae*, 1a.22.2; 1a.44.4; *Summa Contra Gentiles*, III(1).2.

35 Aquinas, *Summa Theologiae*, 1a.44.4. ad. 3.

36 Aquinas, *Summa Contra Gentiles*, III(1).19.5.

37 Aquinas, *Summa Contra Gentiles*, III(1).20 on 'how things imitate divine goodness'.

38 See, for example, Justin P. McBrayer and Daniel Howard-Snyder (eds), *The Blackwell Companion to the Problem of Evil* (Oxford: Wiley-Blackwell, 2013); Marilyn McCord Adams, *Horrendous Evils and the Goodness of God* (Ithaca: Cornell University Press, 2000); Peter van Inwagen, *The Problem of Evil* (Oxford: Oxford University Press, 2008); Eleonore Stump, *Wandering in Darkness: Narrative And The Problem Of Suffering* (Oxford: Oxford University Press, 2012).

39 Augustine, 'Enchiridion on Faith, Hope and Charity', paragraphs 11–14 in Boniface Ramsey (ed.), *On Christian Belief* (New York: New City Press, 2005), pp. 278–80. Aquinas, *Summa Contra Gentiles*, III(1).7 and 11.

40 There is sometimes confusion about what is meant by 'giving reasons for something'. Certain kinds of explanation refer broadly to what we called above 'efficient causes'. We could give reasons for cancer in terms of the efficient causes of the cancer – for example, a genetic mutation that makes someone predisposed to develop the disease, or smoking that leads to the cancerous mutation of cells. This is one kind of 'reason' and is the mode of explanation we might expect from medical science. Another kind of reason would refer to final causes. What is the purpose of cancer in relation to the good ends of human beings? It is this kind of reason or explanation – a *justification* – that is lacking when evil is understood as the privation of the good.

41 Richard Swinburne, *The Existence of God*, 2nd edn. (Oxford: Oxford University Press, 2004), ch. 11. Swinburne argues that certain 'higher order goods' (e.g., extreme courage or generosity) require certain kinds of evil as an occasion to manifest themselves. In making good parasitic on evil in this way, his theodicy is precisely the reverse of the *privatio boni* tradition.

42 John Milbank, *Being Reconciled: Ontology and Pardon* (London: Routledge, 2004), ch.1.

43 Aquinas, *Summa Contra Gentiles*, III(1).20.7.

44 David Bentley Hart, 'Providence and Causality: On Divine Innocence', in Francesca Aran Murphy and Philip G. Ziegler (eds), *The Providence of God: Deus Habet Concilium* (London: Bloomsbury, 2009), pp. 34–56 and *The Doors of the Sea: Where Was God in the Tsunami?* (Grand Rapids, Michigan: Eedrmans Publishing Company, 2005), pp. 82–104. See also John Webster, 'On the Theology of Providence', in Murphy and Ziegler (eds), pp. 158–78.

45 Aquinas, *Summa Theologiae*, 1a.105.5.*responsio*: 'And since the form of a thing is within the thing, and all the more, as it approaches

nearer to the First and Universal Cause; and because in all things God Himself is properly the cause of universal being which is innermost in all things; it follows that in all things God works intimately.'

46 Aquinas, *Summa Theologiae*, 1a.105.5.*responsio* (my emphasis).

47 Aquinas, *Summa Theologiae*, 1a.22.3.*responsio*.

48 David Bentley Hart, *The Doors of the Sea*, p. 85.

Chapter 4

1 John William Draper, *History of the Conflict between Religion and Science* (1875) (Cambridge: Cambridge University Press, 2009); Andrew Dickson White, *A History of the Warfare of Science with Theology in Christendom* (1896), 2 vols (Cambridge: Cambridge University Press, 2009). The canonical works of the New Atheism are Richard Dawkins, *The God Delusion* (London: Penguin, 2006), Daniel C. Dennett, *Breaking the Spell: Religion as a Natural Phenomenon* (London: Penguin, 2007) and Sam Harris, *The End of Faith: Religion, Terror, and the Future of Reason* (London: Simon and Schuster, 2004). Responses to New Atheism are numerous. The most sophisticated is David Bentley Hart, *Atheist Delusions: The Christian Revolution and Its Fashionable Enemies* (New Haven: Yale University Press, 2009).

2 Stephen Jay Gould, *Rocks of Ages: Science and Religion in the Fullness of Life* (New York: Ballantine Books, 2002). Even among those who accept Gould's view of non-overlapping magisterial authority (inevitably reduced to the acronym 'NOMA'), there is disagreement about where the boundaries of those magisteria lie. In effect, Gould's NOMA is a repetition of the fact-value distinction: science allegedly deals with facts, religion with values.

3 The literature in the field of 'science and religion' is now very extensive. For general introductions and historical treatments, see John Hedley Brooke, *Science and Religion: Some Historical Perspectives* (Cambridge: Cambridge University Press, 1991); Thomas Dixon, *Science and Religion: A Very Short Introduction* (Oxford: Oxford University Press, 2008); Thomas Dixon, Geoffrey Cantor and Stephen Pumfrey (eds), *Science and Religion: New Historical Perspectives* (Cambridge: Cambridge University Press, 2011); Peter Harrison (ed.), *The Cambridge Companion to Science and Religion* (Cambridge: Cambridge University Press, 2010);

Peter Harrison, *The Territories of Science and Religion* (Chicago: University of Chicago Press, 2015); Tom McCleish, *Faith and Wisdom in Science* (Oxford: Oxford University Press, 2014). The most important but demanding theological treatments of Darwinism are Conor Cunningham, *Darwin's Pious Idea: Why the Ultra-Darwinists and Creationists Both Get it Wrong* (Grand Rapids, Michigan: Eerdmans, 2010) and Michael Hanby, *No God, No Science? Theology, Cosmology, Biology* (Oxford: Wiley-Blackwell, 2013).

4   This approach to natural philosophy was famously described by Francis Bacon (1561–1626) in his work *Novum Organum* ('New Method', deliberately titled to supplant Aristotle's treatises on philosophical method, collectively entitled *Organon*). The Baconian method was a sophisticated application of inductive reasoning, namely, the drawing of general conclusions based on specific and limited observations of nature. See Francis Bacon, *The New Organon*, ed. Lisa Jardine and Michael Silverthorne (Cambridge: Cambridge University Press, 2000). On the production of scientific matters of fact and the culture of experimental science in the seventeenth and eighteenth centuries, see Steven Shapin, *Never Pure: Historical Studies of Science as if It Was Produced by People with Bodies, Situated in Time, Space, Culture, and Society, and Struggling for Credibility and Authority* (Baltimore, Maryland: John Hopkins University Press, 2010), Steven Shapin and Simon Schaffer, *Leviathan and the Air-pump: Hobbes, Boyle and the Experimental Life* (Princeton: Princeton University Press, 1985) and Stephen Gaukroger, *The Emergence of a Scientific Culture: Science and the Shaping of Modernity 1210-1685* (Oxford: Oxford University Press, 2008), chs. 10 and 11.

5   The distinction is too simple for a number of reasons. Descartes, for example, was very well aware of the importance of experiment in natural philosophy, although such experiments were confirmatory of laws of nature that could, in principle, be known by reason *a priori* because they are necessary truths.

6   Plato, *Timaeus*, trans. R. G. Bury (Cambridge, MA: Harvard University Press, 1999).

7   R. Martens, 'A commentary on Genesis, Plato"s Timaeus and Kepler"s Astronomy', in G. Reydams-Schils (ed.), *Plato's Timaeus as Cultural Icon* (Notre Dame, IN: University of Notre Dame Press, 2003), pp. 251–66. See also the essay by Michael J.B. Allen, 'The Ficinian Timaeus and Renaissance Studies' in the same volume, pp. 238–50.

8   Mid-twentieth-century historians of science, notably Alexander Koyré, tended to see a discontinuity between medieval natural

philosophy and early modern science due to a renewed Platonism during the sixteenth century, particularly the new interest in mathematics. See Alexander Koyré, 'Galileo and Plato', *Journal of the History of Ideas* 4 (1943), pp. 401–28. Stephen Gaukroger is an example of a contemporary historian of science who contests such readings, although his breathtaking study of the emergence of scientific culture fails, I think, to do justice to medieval deployments of mathematics, particularly in the field of optics. See Gaukroger, *The Emergence of a Scientific Culture*, especially pp. 169–95 and 246–9.

9 Edward Grant, *The Foundations of Modern Science in the Middle Ages: Their Religion, Institutional and Intellectual Contexts* (Cambridge: Cambridge University Press, 1996), p. 149.

10 Newton was involved in an extensive debate with the German philosopher and mathematician Gottfried Wilhelm Leibniz (1646–1716) concerning who first invented the calculus. A standard study of this controversy is A. Rupert Hall, *Philosophers at War: The Quarrel between Newton and Leibniz* (Cambridge: Cambridge University Press, rev. ed., 1998).

11 Nicholas of Cusa, *De docta ignorantia*, 2.12 available in Nicholas of Cusa, *On Learned Ignorance: A Translation and an Appraisal of De Docta Ignorantia*, trans. Jasper Hopkins (Minneapolis, MN: The Arthur J. Banning Press, 2nd ed., 1985).

12 In the multilayered hermeneutics of patristic and medieval exegesis, passages of scripture that did not fit with straightforward observations of the natural world could be dealt with by reference to symbolism and allegory. For example, when the chronicler writes, 'The world is firmly established; it shall never be moved' (1 Chron. 16.30), this can be taken figuratively to mean that the earth will not decay under God's providence. Taken purely literally, the text presents more of a challenge in the face of Copernicus's observations.

13 Islamic natural philosophy was dominant in the Early and High Middle Ages, being far more advanced than any Christian enterprise. An account of Islam and natural philosophy is beyond the scope of this book. For a recent study, see John Freely, *Light from the East: How the Science of Medieval Islam Helped to Shape the Western World* (New York: I.B. Tauris, 2015).

14 Isaac Newton, *The Principia: Mathematical Principles of Natural Philosophy* (3rd ed., 1726), trans. I. Bernard Cohen and Anne Whitman (Berkeley, California: University of California Press, 1999).

15 On the nature of the scientific revolution, see, for example, David Wootton, *The Invention of Science: A New History of the Scientific Revolution* (London: Penguin, 2016) and Margaret J. Osler (ed.),

Rethinking the Scientific Revolution (Cambridge: Cambridge University Press, 2008). One of the most influential works in this field is Thomas S. Kuhn, *The Structure of Scientific Revolutions* (Chicago: University of Chicago Press, 3rd ed., 1996).

16 Some of the key works are Peter Harrison, *The Bible, Protestantism and the Rise of Natural Science* (Cambridge: Cambridge University Press, 1998); Peter Harrison, *The Fall of Man and the Foundations of Science* (Cambridge: Cambridge University Press, 2007); Stephen Gaukroger, *The Emergence of a Scientific Culture* and John Hedley Brooke, *Science and Religion: Some Historical Perspectives*.

17 Peter Harrison, *The Bible, Protestantism and the Rise of Natural Science* and idem., *The Fall of Man and the Foundations of Science*. See also Scott Mandelbrote and Jitse Meer (eds), *Nature and Scripture in the Abrahamic Religions: Up to 1700* (2 vols) (Leiden: Brill, 2008).

18 Many scholars locate the origins of the theological shifts discussed in this chapter much earlier than the Reformation, notably in the work of John Duns Scotus (c. 1266–c. 1308) and William of Ockham (c. 1287–c. 1347). It is beyond the immediate purview of this book to enter into this complex philosophical and historical debate, but see Brad S. Gregory, *The Unintended Reformation: How a Religious Revolution Secularized Society* (Cambridge, Massachusetts: Harvard University Press, 2012), ch. 1; Amos Funkenstein, *Theology and the Scientific Imagination: From the Middle Ages to the Seventeenth Century* (Princeton: Princeton University Press, 1986); John Milbank, *Theology and Social Theory: Beyond Secular Reason*, 2nd ed. (Oxford: Wiley-Blackwell, 2006), pp. 302–6; Louis Dupré, *The Passage to Modernity: An Essay in the Hermeneutics of Nature and Culture* (New Haven: Yale University Press, 1993), pp. 170 ff.

19 Origen, *On First Principles* (*De principiis*), trans. G.W. Butterworth (Notre Dame, Indiana: Ave Maria Press, 2013), IV.2.4. Henri de Lubac *Medieval Exegesis: the Four Senses of Scripture*, 3 vols., trans. Marc Sebanc and E. M. Macierowski (Grand Rapids, MI: Eerdmans, 1998–2009) and Peter Harrison, *The Bible, Protestantism and the Rise of Natural Science*, pp. 15–33.

20 As noted in Chapter 1 (see n. 40), the meaning of the *sensus literalis*, the 'literal' or 'plain' sense, is far from plain in patristic and medieval theology. For an important medieval explanation, see Thomas Aquinas, *Summa Theologiae*, 1a.1.10.

21 See Denys Turner, 'Allegory in Christian late antiquity' in Rita Copeland and Peter T. Struck, *The Cambridge Companion to Allegory* (Cambridge: Cambridge University Press, 2010), pp. 71–82

and Denys Turner, *Eros and Allegory, Medieval Exegesis of the Song of Songs* (Kalamazoo: Cistercian Publications, 1995).

22 Harrison, *The Bible, Protestantism and the Rise of Natural Science*, p. 20.

23 Augustine, *Confessions*, trans. F. J. Sheed (Indianapolis: Hackett Publishing Co., 2006), XIII.21.30, p. 307.

24 Michael J. Curley (trans.), *Physiologus: A Medieval Book of Nature Lore* (Chicago: University of Chicago Press, 1979). See also M.-D. Chenu, O.P., *Nature, Man and Society in the Twelfth Century*, trans. Jerome Taylor and Lester K. Little (Toronto: University of Toronto Press, 1997), pp. 104–5.

25 Harrison, *The Bible, Protestantism and the Rise of Natural Science*, p. 23.

26 One should bear in mind the standard distinction between symbol and allegory. In the symbolic world, one thing stands for or points to another. Indeed, a symbol may point to many different things. Allegory, by contrast, has a narrative structure in which its symbolic elements have fixed reference throughout. For example, John Bunyan's *Pilgrim's Progress* is a sustained narrative *allegory* of the Christian journey, in which the characters' *symbolic* reference is sustained throughout. Similarly, the narratives of Noah and the flood (Gen. 6.9–9.17) or the parable of the Good Samaritan (Lk. 10.25-37) can be interpreted allegorically with reference to their symbolic patterns. In this chapter, I use the terms 'sign' and 'symbol' interchangeably. In some semiotic theories there is a subtle difference. Signs point beyond themselves to a different order in such a way that there is a more arbitrary connection between the sign and the thing signified. Particularly in modern thought, the sign and the thing signified have no necessary or intrinsic connection. By contrast, the etymology of 'symbol' (the Greek *syn-bole*) implies a throwing together of two orders. The symbol introduces us into an order to which it itself belongs. The sign, on the other hand, throws us away from one order and into another. See Louis-Marie Chauvet, *Symbol and Sacrament*, trans. Patrick Madigan, S.J. and Madeleine Beaumont (Collegeville, Minnesota: The Liturgical Press, 1995), pp. 112–13.

27 Did it matter that no definitive observations of the pelican feeding her young in this way were available? Not really. These symbols, while derived in some way from nature and the conflation of observations, carried spiritual rather than literal significance. See Harrison, *The Bible, Protestantism and the Rise of Natural Science*, p. 31 on Augustine's view of the pelican in the *Physiologus*.

28 Aquinas, *Summa Theologiae*, 1a.1.10.*responsio*: 'The multiplicity of these senses [of scripture] does not produce equivocation or any other kind of multiplicity, seeing that these senses are not multiplied because one word signifies several things, but because the things signified by the words can be themselves types of other things.' See Amos Funkenstein, *Theology and the Scientific Imagination*, pp. 55–6.

29 John Cassian, *Conferences*, 14.8 and Nicholas of Lyra, First Prologue to the *Postillae litterales*, translated and quoted in Denys Turner, 'Allegory in Christian late antiquity', pp. 71–2. See also Philip D. W. Krey and Lesley Smith (eds), *Nicholas of Lyra: The Senses of Scripture* (Leiden: Brill, 2000).

30 Augustine, *On Christian Teaching*, trans. R.P.H. Green (Oxford: Oxford University Press, 1997), III.7, p. 74: 'If, then, it is a carnal form of slavery to follow a sign divinely instituted for a useful purpose instead of the thing that it was instituted to represent, is it not far worse to accept as things the humanly instituted signs of useless things?' For an exacting reading of Augustine on the sign that makes clear why Augustine does not regard the sign as merely of instrumental value or use, see Rowan Williams, *On Augustine* (London: Bloomsbury, 2016), ch.3: 'To "use" the love of neighbour or the love we have for our own bodies (a favourite example of Augustine's) is simply to allow the capacity for gratuitous or self-forgetful *dilectio* opened up in these and other such loves to be opened still further. The language of *uti* (use) is designed to warn against an attitude towards any finite person or object that terminates their meaning in their capacity to satisfy my desire, and treats them as the end of desire, conceiving my meaning in terms of them and theirs in terms of me.' (p. 44). See also Matthew Levering, *The Theology of Augustine: An Introductory Guide to His Most Important Works* (Grand Rapids, Michigan: Baker Academic, 2013), ch.1.

31 Aquinas, *Summa Theologiae*, 2a2ae.180.4.*responsio* quoting Augustine, *True Religion (De Vera Religione)*, 29, available in St Augustine, *On Christian Belief*, ed. Boniface Ramsey, trans. Edmund Hill, O.P. (Hyde Park, New York: New City Press, 2005), p. 64.

32 For an example of the interpretation of the books of scripture and nature, see Robert Grosseteste's *Hexaemeron* (a commentary on the six days of creation), written in the first half of the thirteenth century: *On the Six Days of Creation: A Translation of the Hexaemeron*, trans. C.F.J. Martin (Oxford: Oxford University Press, 1996), I.12.1-4 (pp. 66–7) and IX.7.1-2 (pp. 280–2).

33 Harrison, *The Bible, Protestantism and the Rise of Natural Science*, p. 45.

34 Harrison, *The Bible, Protestantism and the Rise of Natural Science*, pp. 109–10; Chenu, *Nature, Man and Society in the Twelfth Century*, p. 117; Roger French and Andrew Cunningham, *Before Science: The Invention of the Friars' Natural Philosophy* (Aldershot: Scolar Press, 1996), pp. 76–9.

35 Aquinas, *Summa Theologiae*, 1a.1.10.*responsio*.

36 Harrison, *The Bible, Protestantism and the Rise of Natural Science*, pp. 92–107.

37 Gregory, *The Unintended Reformation*, pp. 88–9.

38 Martin Luther, "Concerning the Letter and the Spirit" from *Answer to the Hyperchristian, Hyperspiritual, and Hyperlearned Book by Goat Emser in Leipzig*, in *Martin Luther's Basic Theological Writings*, ed. Timothy F. Lull (Minneapolis: Fortress Press, 1989), p. 77.

39 The origins and effects of iconoclasm in the Reformation – the destruction of material symbolic order in favour of the primacy of the word and abstract idea – is well documented and its immediate effects are clearly visible in the empty plinths and plain interiors of Britain's medieval churches and cathedrals. See Eamon Duffy, *The Stripping of the Altars: Traditional Religion in England, 1400-1580* (New Haven: Yale University Press, 2nd ed., 2005) and Gregory, *The Unintended Reformation*.

40 Harrison, *The Bible, Protestantism and the Rise of Natural Science*, p. 114. See also Gaukroger, *The Emergence of Scientific Culture*, ch.4.

41 Francis, *De Augmentis Scientiarum*, Book 3, ch. 2, in John M. Robertson (ed.), *The Philosophical Works of Francis Bacon* (London: G. Routledge & Sons, 1905), p. 456.

42 Galileo Galilei, *Dialogue Concerning Two Chief World Systems*, trans. Stillman Drake (Berkeley, Los Angeles: University of California Press, 2nd edn., 1967).

43 Copernicus's *De Revolutionibus* had been placed on the index in 1616, although a 'corrected' version that removed the heliocentrism was prepared and approved four years later because it was useful for calculating the calendar.

44 For a detailed recent study, see Annibale Fantoli, *The Case of Galileo: A Closed Question?*, trans. George V. Coyne (Notre Dame: University of Notre Dame Press, 2012). A particularly interesting view of the Galileo affair can be found in Paul Feyerabend, 'Galileo and the

Tyranny of Truth', in *Farewell to Reason* (London: Verso, 1987), pp. 247–64.

45 Stephen Snobelen, 'On Reading Isaac Newton's *Principia* in the Eighteenth Century', *Endeavour* 22(4) (1998), pp. 159–63 and Snobelen, 'Isaac Newton, heretic: the strategies of a Nicodemite', *British Journal for the History of Science* 32 (1999), pp. 381–419.

46 Frank Manuel, *The Religion of Isaac Newton* (Oxford: Oxford University Press, 1974), p. 19: 'That Newton was conscious of his special bond to God and that he conceived of himself as the man destined to unveil the ultimate truth about God's creation does not appear in so many words in anything he wrote. But peculiar traces of his inner conviction crop up in unexpected ways. More than once Newton uses *Jeova sanctus unus* as an anagram for *Isaacus Neeuutonus*. ... The downgrading of Christ in Newton's theology ... makes room for himself as a substitute.' See also B.J.T. Dobbs, *The Janus Face of Genius: The role of alchemy in Newton's thought* (Cambridge: Cambridge University Press, 1991), pp. 150ff. On Newton's Arian and anti-Trinitarian theology, see Rob Iliffe, *Priest of Nature: The Religious Worlds of Isaac Newton* (Oxford: Oxford University Press, 2017).

47 John Conduitt, 'Notes on Newton''s suitability for canonization if not deification' (c. 1727–8), Keynes Ms. 130.14, King's College, Cambridge, UK. Available at: http://www.newtonproject.sussex.ac.uk/view/texts/normalized/THEM00176 (accessed September 2016).

48 H.W. Turnbull (ed.), *The Correspondence of Isaac Newton*, vol. 3 (Cambridge: Cambridge University Press, 1961), p. 233.

49 Newton, *The Principia*, trans. I. Bernard Cohen and Anne Whitman, 'General Scholium', pp. 941–2.

50 The Newton Project based at the University of Sussex, UK, has made available all Newton's writings including his theological and alchemical works. Many of the manuscripts are in archives in the National Library of Israel (mainly theological, bought by the Jewish scholar Abraham Yahuda following Sotheby's sale of Newton's personal papers – the Portsmouth Papers – in 1936) and King's College, Cambridge (mainly alchemical, bought by John Maynard Keynes following the same sale). See http://www.newtonproject.sussex.ac.uk (accessed September 2016).

51 The Charters of the Royal Society are available at: https://royalsociety.org/about-us/governance/charters/ (accessed September 2016).

52 Gaukroger, *The Emergence of Scientific Culture*, ch. 1.

53 Thomas Sprat, *History of the Royal Society of London for the Improving of Natural Knowledge* (London, 1667), Section XIV, p. 345. Of course, one must ask whether Sprat's *History of the Royal Society* is representative of the wider views and informing ideologies of the Society's members. For a sustained analysis that demonstrates that Sprat's priorities as expressed in this quote were shared by the Society's key figures, see Peter Harrison, 'Religion, the Royal Society, and the Rise of Science', *Theology and Science* 6 (2008), pp. 255–71.

54 Shapin and Schaffer, *Leviathan and the Air-Pump*, p. 319.

55 Robert Boyle, *A Disquisition about the Final Causes of Natural Things* (London, 1688), p. A2.

56 Harrison, *The Bible, Protestantism and the Rise of Natural Science*, p. 175.

57 Noël-Antoine Pluche, *Spectacle de la Nature: or Nature Display'd*, 5th edn. revised and corrected, vol. 3 (London, 1770), p. 318, quoted in Harrison, *The Bible, Protestantism and the Rise of Natural Science*, p. 175.

58 For a comprehensive account of the role of the Fall narrative on the rise of natural science, see Peter Harrison, *The Fall of Man and the Foundations of Science*.

59 See, for example, Gregory of Nyssa, *Homilies on the Song of Songs*, trans. Richard A. Norris (Atlanta, Georgia: Society of Biblical Literature, 2012).

60 On Genesis as history, see Harrison, *The Bible, Protestantism and the Rise of Natural Science*, pp. 121–9.

61 George Walker, *The History of Creation* (London, 1651), p. 193, quoted in Harrison, *The Bible, Protestantism and the Rise of Natural Science*, p. 211.

62 Harrison, *The Bible, Protestantism and the Rise of Natural Science*, pp. 230–1.

63 Physico-theology flourished at the turn of the eighteenth century. Prominent works include John Ray, *Three Physico-Theological Discourses* (London, 1693) and William Whiston, *A New Theory of the Earth, from its Original to the Consummation of all Things* (London, 1696).

64 For example, Ian G. Barbour, *Issues in Science and Religion* (New York: HarperCollins, 1971).

65 Aquinas, *Summa Theologiae*, 1a2ae.1.2.*responsio*. See also, for example, *Summa Theologiae*, 1a.5.4; 1a.19.4.*responsio*.

66 Francis Bacon, *The New Organon*, Book II, aphorism 2, p. 102.

67 Stephen Gaukroger, *The Collapse of Mechanism and the Rise of Sensibility* (Oxford: Oxford University Press, 2010), pp. 58–64. See also Walter Ott, *Causation and the Laws of Nature in Early Modern Philosophy* (Oxford: Oxford University Press, 2009), ch. 7.

68 Isaac Newton, *Principia Mathematica*, p. 940.

69 William Paley, *Natural Theology, or Evidences of the Existence and Attributes of the Deity collected from the Appearances of Nature*, eds. Matthew D. Eddy and David Knight (Oxford: Oxford University Press, 2006).

70 On intelligent design, see Stephen C. Meyer, *Darwin's Doubt: The Explosive Origin of Animal Life and the Case for Intelligent Design* (New York: HarperCollins, 2014) and William A. Dembski and James M. Kushiner (eds), *Signs of Intelligence: Understanding Intelligent Design* (Grand Rapids, Michigan: Brazos Press, 2001).

71 Margaret Osler, 'From Immanent Natures to Nature as Artifice: The Reinterpretation of Final Causes in Seventeenth Century Natural Philosophy', *The Monist* 79 (1996), pp. 388–407.

72 On the theological implications of the passivity of matter, see Gary B. Deason, 'Reformation Theology and the Mechanistic Conception of Nature' in David C. Lindberg and Ronald L. Numbers, *God and Nature: Historical Essays on the Encounter between Christianity and Science* (Berkeley: University of California Press, 1986), pp. 167–91.

73 René Descartes, *The Philosophical Writings of Descartes: Volume 3, The Correspondence*, trans. John Cottingham, Robert Stoothoff, Dugald Murdoch, and Anthony Kenny (Cambridge: Cambridge University Press, 1991), p. 23. In fact, just as a king can change the laws of his kingdom according to his will, so too God could change the laws of nature according to his will. This is one of the rationales for the continual repetition of scientific experiments in the seventeenth and eighteenth centuries: to make sure that God had not changed his mind.

74 For a more detailed discussion, see Simon Oliver, 'Aquinas and Aristotle's Teleology', *Nova et Vetera* 11 (3), 2013, pp. 849–70.

75 Aristotle, *Physics (Books I-IV)*, trans. P.H. Wicksteed and F.M. Cornford (Cambridge, Massachusetts: Harvard University Press, 1996), II.1.193b1-b5, p. 115. My italics.

76 Aquinas, *Summa Theologiae*, 1a.15.

77 Walter Ott, *Causation and the Laws of Nature in Early Modern Philosophy*, ch. 9.

78 Michael Buckley, *At the Origins of Modern Atheism* (New Haven: Yale University Press, 1987); Louis Dupré, *The Passage to Modernity: An Essay in the Hermeneutics of Nature and Culture* (New Haven: Yale University Press, 1993).

79 Hans Jonas, *The Phenomenon of Life: Toward a Philosophical Biology* (Evanston, Illinois: Northwestern University Press, 2001), p. 10.

80 Stephen Gaukroger, *The Collapse of Mechanism and the Rise of Sensibility*, pp. 355–83: 'A mechanics that was unable to account for physical phenomena such as electricity and chemistry was hardly going to be able to provide a basis for understanding animate bodies. … Electricity and chemistry had encouraged an understanding of matter as something active, an understanding wholly antithetical to the mechanist programme, but they were unable to offer any account of what this activity was in general terms, and to what extent it characterized matter beyond the local phenomena that these disciplines studied' (pp. 355–6).

81 Hanby, *No God, No Science?*, p. 34: 'Method and abstraction thus understood are not preontological. Rather they are themselves the expression of an *a priori* mechanistic ontology which is "predicated upon the possibility of the exhaustive intelligibility of things" achieved through analysis, even if the advent of statistical dynamics and quantum physics and the demise of Laplacean determinism have placed this ideal permanently beyond reach.' Quoting David L. Schindler, Ordering Love: Liberal Societies and the Memory of God (Grand Rapids, Michigan: Eerdmans, 2011), p. 395.

82 An important aspect of Hanby's argument is that the scientific world is so distant from our basic intuitions and perceptions that it threatens to become unrecognizable and unintelligible. In other words, science has lost its proper object of study – the natural world – because of an inadequate metaphysical account of what the world is, and an inadequate doctrine of creation that can describe how and why there is a world in the first place. He writes that 'the universe, historically and theoretically, is an irreducibly metaphysical and theological idea. … Creation is what the world *is*, and the doctrine of creation is essential to an understanding of the universe that is both comprehensive and nonreductive; and that the scientific and Darwinian revolutions, for all their stunning success in increasing our knowledge of the universe, have left us with a universe so reduced and fractured that it threatens to undermine the rationality and intelligibility of their own achievement.' Hanby, *No God, No Science?*, p. 36.

83 Hanby, *No God, No Science?*, p. 19.

Chapter 5

1   A full set of data on global climate change is available at http://
    climate.nasa.gov and http://www.eea.europa.eu/themes/climate
    (accessed 5 September 2016).

2   Lynn White Jr., 'The Historical Roots of our Ecological Crisis',
    Science 155 (1967), pp. 1203–7 (quotation appearing on p. 1206).

3   White, 'The Historical Roots of our Ecological Crisis', p. 1205.

4   Many argue that the real culprit is the unassailable religion of
    today – liberal free-market capitalism. A detailed discussion of this
    fundamental root of the environmental crisis is beyond the purview
    of this chapter, although the appeal to 'gift' is implicitly an appeal
    to a different and more fundamental economic order beyond that
    of free-market trade. See the extensive and influential work Michael
    S. Northcott: *The Environment and Christian Ethics* (Cambridge:
    Cambridge University Press, 2008); idem., *A Moral Climate: The
    Ethics of Global Warming* (London: DLT, 2007); idem., *A Political
    Theology of Climate Change* (London: SPCK, 2014). For a more
    wide-ranging theological critique of capitalist liberalism with clear
    implications for environmental ethics, see John Milbank and Adrian
    Pabst, *The Politics of Virtue: Post-Liberalism and the Human Future*
    (Lanham, Maryland: Rowman and Littlefield International, 2016).
    For an excellent and detailed theological ethics of the environment,
    see Willis Jenkins, *Ecologies of Grace: Environmental Ethics and
    Christian Theology* (Oxford: Oxford University Press, 2008).

5   Peter Harrison, *The Bible, Protestantism and the Rise of Natural
    Science* (Cambridge: Cambridge University Press, 1998), p. 206.

6   Francis Bacon, *The New Organon* (*Novum Organum*), Lisa Jardine
    and Michael Silverthorne, eds (Cambridge: Cambridge University
    Press, 2000), Book II, paragraph 52, p. 221.

7   Hans Jonas, *The Phenomenon of Life: Toward a Philosophy of
    Biology* (Evanston: Northwestern University Press, 2001), p. 204,
    cited in Michael Hanby, *No God, No Science? Theology, Cosmology,
    Biology* (Oxford: Wiley-Blackwell, 2013), p. 132.

8   Bacon, *The New Organon*, Book II, aphorism 1, p. 102.

9   Hanby, *No God, No Science?*, p. 132: 'It is rather that scientific
    knowledge is knowledge *by means of control* and that the *truth*, and
    thus for all intents and purposes the *being* – of *things* – becomes
    precisely identical with *our* various capacities for measurement and
    control of them in the form of predictive success, the replication

of experimental results, or their successful manipulation to fit our purposes.'

10 Creation's participation in God is 'improper' in the sense that it is not proper to creation – that is, something creation has simply by virtue of itself. Creation's participation in God is always a matter of divine gift.

11 For a more detailed exploration of the intrinsic value of material creation in the thought of Augustine, see Simon Oliver, 'Augustine on Creation, Providence and Motion', *International Journal of Systematic Theology* 18(4), 2016, pp. 379–98.

12 See Rachel Muers, 'Creatures', in Michael S. Northcott and Peter M. Scott (eds), *Systematic Theology and Climate Change: Ecumenical Perspectives* (London: Routledge, 2014), pp. 90–107.

13 Bruno Latour, *We Have Never Been Modern*, trans. Catherine Porter (London: Harvester Wheatsheaf, 1991).

14 In a fascinating study, Stephen Gaukroger argues that the period from the mid-eighteenth to the mid-nineteenth centuries saw that naturalization of the human. This involved a shift from metaphysical and theological understandings of the human to an empirically based, scientific understanding. This naturalized study of humanity is principally distinguished from metaphysics rather than culture. Nevertheless, Gaukroger's work indicates the ambiguity of human culture's relation to nature in the modern period. The naturalization of the human through the early nineteenth century is arguably complimented by the rising prominence of human culture over nature in the later nineteenth century. See Stephen Gaukroger, *The Natural and the Human: Science and the Shaping of Modernity 1739-1841* (Oxford: Oxford University Press, 2016).

15 Latour, *We Have Never Been Modern*, p. 10.

16 Latour, *We Have Never Been Modern*, p. 11.

17 Latour's discussion is extremely sophisticated and a full examination is beyond the purview of this chapter. An important aspect of his argument is that nature and culture are separated so that natural categories can later be imported to justify certain cultural practices. For example, the domain of human familial relations is cultural. However, observations of the dominance of males in primate communities has been imported into discussions of human social practices in order to demonstrate that male dominance is 'natural' and therefore a non-negotiable given. For an argument along these lines, see Donna Haraway, *Simians, Cyborgs and Women: The Reinvention of Nature* (London: Free Association Books, 1991), p. 11: 'Despite the claims of anthropology to be able to understand human beings solely with the concept of culture, and of sociology to

need nothing but the idea of the human social group, animal societies have been extensively employed in rationaliztion and naturalization of the oppressive orders of domination in the human body politic.' For a more detailed discussion of Latour's understanding of the modern constitution, see Simon Oliver, 'The Eucharist before Nature and Culture', *Modern Theology* 15(3), 1999, p. 331–53.

18 For example, 'A venerable Orang-outang: a contribution to unnatural history' published in *The Hornet*, 22 March 1871.

19 See J. R. Lucas, 'Wilberforce and Huxley: A Legendary Encounter', *The Historical Journal* 22(2) (1979), pp. 313–30.

20 https://www.theguardian.com/science/2002/feb/03/genetics.research (accessed September 2016).

21 Latour, *We Have Never Been Modern*, p. 6.

22 See Louis Dupré, *Passage to Modernity: An Essay in the Hermeneutics of Nature and Culture* (New Haven: Yale University Press, 1993) and Richard L. Fern, *Nature, God and Humanity: Envisioning an Ethics of Nature* (Cambridge: Cambridge University Press, 2002), ch. 5.

23 For a wide range of approaches, see Wendy Davies and Paul Fouracre (eds), *The Languages of Gift in the Early Middle Ages* (Cambridge: Cambridge University Press, 2010), Mark Osteen (ed.), *The Question of the Gift: Essays Across Disciplines* (London: Routledge, 2002); Allan D. Schrift (ed.), *The Logic of the Gift: Toward an Ethic of Generosity* (New York: Routledge, 1997); Kathryn Tanner, *Economy of Grace* (Minneapolis: Augsburg Fortress, 2005); Antonio Lopez, *Gift and the Unity of Being* (Cambridge: James Clarke & Co, 2014); John Milbank, *Being Reconciled: Ontology and Pardon* (London: Routledge, 2003) and 'The Gift of Ruling: Secularization and Political Authority', *New Blackfriars* 85 (March 2004), pp. 212–38. The discussion that follows – and, indeed, this book – is very much indebted to John Milbank's work and our conversations over many years. Errors and oversimplifications of a highly complex debate are entirely my own.

24 Marcel Mauss, *The Gift: The Form and Reason for Exchange in Archaic Societies*, trans. W.D. Halls (London: Routledge, 2007).

25 Mauss, *The Gift*, p. 16.

26 Jacques Derrida, *Given Time: I. Counterfeit Money*, trans. Peggy Kamul (Chicago: University of Chicago Press, 1994) and idem., *The Gift of Death*, trans. David Wills (Chicago: University of Chicago Press, 1996).

27 Milbank, *Being Reconciled*, p. ix. Milbank's extensive publications on the gift have been extremely influential over recent years. See also, for example, John Milbank, 'Can a Gift be Given? Prolegomena to

a Future Trinitarian Metaphysic', *Modern Theology* 11(1), 1995, pp. 119–61; idem., 'The Soul of Reciprocity Part One: Reciprocity Refused', *Modern Theology* 17(3), 2001, pp. 335–91; idem., 'The Soul of Reciprocity Part Two: Reciprocity Granted', *Modern Theology* 17(4), 2001, pp. 485–507. Milbank is frequently in critical conversation with the Catholic philosopher Jean-Luc Marion whose mature philosophy of the gift can be found in *Being Given: Toward a Phenomenology of Givenness*, trans. Jeffrey Kosky (Stanford: Stanford University Press, 2002).

28 In a helpful discussion of the gift in postmodern thought, which includes consideration of Jean-Luc Marion and John Milbank, Kevin Hart compares this debate concerning the purity of the gift to the Donatist schism in the fourth and fifth centuries. See Kevin Hart, *Postmodernism: A Beginner's Guide* (Oxford: Oneworld Publications, 2004), ch.7. A further very informative and succinct analysis of Milbank and the American theologian Kathryn Tanner can be found in Sarah Coakley, 'Why Gift? Gift, gender and Trinitarian relations in Milbank and Tanner', *Scottish Journal of Theology* 61(2), 2008, pp. 224–35.

29 John Milbank, *The Suspended Middle: Henri de Lubac and the Debate concerning the Supernatural* (Grand Rapids, Michigan: Eerdmans, 2nd ed., 2014), p. 96.

30 Milbank, *The Suspended Middle*, p. 108.

31 This is reminiscent of the meal following the return of the prodigal son in Lk. 15.11-32. The son had squandered the gifts of his father by treating them as mere consumable resources. Upon his return, a new gift is offered in the form of a meal to effect and express the reconciliation of father and son.

32 See, for example, 2 Cor. 5.21 or Heb. 9.28 or Exod. 29.14.

33 Angel F. Mendez-Montoya, *The Theology of Food: Eating and the Eucharist* (Oxford: Wiley-Blackwell, 2012); Norman Wirzba, *Food and Faith: A Theology of Eating* (Cambridge: Cambridge University Press, 2011), especially ch. 6; David Grumett and Rachel Muers (eds), *Theology on the Menu: Asceticism, Meat and Christian Diet* (London: Routledge, 2010).

34 Milbank, 'Can a Gift be Given? Prolegomena to a Future Trinitarian Metaphysic', p. 135.

35 Nicholas Lash, *Believing Three Ways in One God* (Notre Dame, IN: University of Notre Dame Press, 1992), p. 104 quoted in Wirzba, *Food and Faith*, p. 181.

Bibliography

Adams, Marilyn McCord. *Horrendous Evils and the Goodness of God*. Ithaca: Cornell University Press, 2000.

Aertsen, Jan. *Nature and Creature: Thomas Aquinas's Way of Thought*. Leiden: Brill, 1988.

Allen, Michael J. B. 'The Ficinian Timaeus and Renaissance Studies'. In *Plato's Timaeus as Cultural Icon*, edited by G. Reydams-Schil, 238–50. Notre Dame, IN: University of Notre Dame Press, 2003.

Aristotle. *Physics (Books V-VIII)*. Translated by P. H. Wicksteed and F. M. Cornford. Cambridge, MA: Harvard University Press, 1995.

Aristotle, *Physics (Books I-IV)*. Revised edition. Translated by P. H. Wicksteed and F. M. Cornford. Cambridge, MA, 1996.

Aristotle, *Metaphysics (Books I-IX)*. Translated by Hugh Tredennick. Cambridge, MA: Harvard University Press, 1996.

Aristotle, *Metaphysics (Books X-XIV)*. *Oeconomica, Magna Moralia*. Translated by H. Tredennick and G. Cyril Armstrong. Cambridge, MA: Harvard University Press, 1997.

Anselm of Canterbury. *The Major Works*. Edited by B. Davies and G. R. Evans. Oxford: Oxford University Press, 1998.

Augustine. *On Christian Teaching*. Translated by R. P. H. Green. Oxford: Oxford University Press, 1997.

Augustine. *The City of God against the Pagans*. Translated and edited by R. W. Dyson. Cambridge: Cambridge University Press, 1998.

Augustine. *On Genesis*. Translated by Edmund Hill, O.P. and edited by John E. Rotelle, O. S. A. Hyde Park, New York: New City Press, 2002.

Augustine. *On Christian Belief*. Edited by Boniface Ramsey, translated by Edmund Hill, O.P. et al. Hyde Park, New York: New City Press, 2005.

Augustine. *Confessions*. Translated by F. J. Sheed. Indianapolis: Hackett Publishing Company, 2006.

Augustine, *On Order (De Ordine)*. Translated by Silvano Borruso. South Bend, IN: St. Augustine's Press, 2007.

Bacon, Francis. *The New Organon*, 1620. Edited by Lisa Jardine and Michael Silverthorne. Cambridge: Cambridge University Press, 2000.

Baldner, Steven E., and William E. Carroll, eds and trans. *Aquinas on Creation: Writings on the 'Sentences' of Peter Lombard 2.1.1.* Toronto: Pontifical Institute of Mediaeval Studies, 1997.

Barbour, Ian G. *Issues in Science and Religion.* New York: HarperCollins, 1971.

Barker, Margaret. *Creation: A Biblical Vision for the Environment.* London: T&T Clark, 2010.

Batto, Bernard. *In the Beginning: Essays on Creation Motifs in the Ancient Near East and the Bible.* Winona Lake, IN: Eisenbrauns, 2013.

Blenkinsopp, Joseph. 'Structure of P'. *Catholic Biblical Quarterly* 38 (1976): 275–92.

Blenkinsopp, Joseph. *Creation, Un-creation, Re-creation: A Discursive Commentary on Genesis 1–11.* London: T&T Clark, 2011.

Boyle, Robert. *A Disquisition about the Final Causes of Natural Things.* London, 1688.

Brodie, Thomas L. *Genesis as Dialogue: A Literary, Historical, and Theological Commentary.* Oxford: Oxford University Press, 2001.

Brooke, John Hedley. *Science and Religion: Some Historical Perspectives.* Cambridge: Cambridge University Press, 1991.

Buckley, Michael. *At the Origins of Modern Atheism.* New Haven: Yale University Press, 1987.

Burrell, David B. *Freedom and Creation in Three Traditions.* Notre Dame, IN: University of Notre Dame Press, 1993.

Burrell, David B., Carlo Cogliati, Janet M. Soskice and William M. Stoeger, eds. *Creation and the God of Abraham.* Cambridge: Cambridge University Press, 2010.

Charlesworth, James H., ed. *The Old Testament Pseudepigrapha*, vol. 2. London: Darton, Longman & Todd, 1985.

Chauvet, Louis-Marie. *Symbol and Sacrament.* Translated by Patrick Madigan, S.J. and Madeleine Beaumont. Collegeville, MN: The Liturgical Press, 1995.

Chenu, Marie-Dominique O.P., *Nature, Man and Society in the Twelfth Century.* Translated by Jerome Taylor, Lester K. Little. Toronto: University of Toronto Press, 1997.

Coakley, Sarah. 'Why Gift? Gift, gender and Trinitarian relations in Milbank and Tanner'. *Scottish Journal of Theology* 61, no. 2 (2008): 224–35.

Coplan, Paul, and William Lane Craig. *Creation out of Nothing: A Biblical, Philosophical, and Scientific Exploration.* Grand Rapids, MI: Baker Academic 2004.

Craig, William Lane. 'Timelessness, Creation, and God's Real Relation to the World', *Laval théologique et philosophique* 56, no. 1 (2000): 93–112

Cunningham, Conor. *Darwin's Pious Idea: Why the Ultra-Darwinists and Creationists Both Get it Wrong.* Grand Rapids, MI: Eerdmans, 2010.

Curley, Michael J., trans. *Physiologus: A Medieval Book of Nature Lore.* Chicago: University of Chicago Press, 1979.

Dalley, Stephen. *Myths from Mesopotamia: Creation, the Flood, Gilgamesh and Others.* Oxford: Oxford University Press, 2000.

Davies, Wendy, and Paul Fouracre, eds. *The Languages of Gift in the Early Middle Ages.* Cambridge: Cambridge University Press, 2010.

Dawkins, Richard. *The God Delusion.* London: Penguin, 2006.

Day, John. *From Creation to Babel: studies in Genesis 1-11.* London: Bloomsbury, 2013.

Deason, Gary B. 'Reformation Theology and the Mechanistic Conception of Nature'. In *God and Nature: Historical Essays on the Encounter between Christianity and Science,* edited by David C. Lindberg and Ronald L. Numbers, 167–91. Berkeley, Los Angeles: University of California Press, 1986.

Dembski, William A., and James M. Kushiner, eds. *Signs of Intelligence: Understanding Intelligent Design.* Grand Rapids, MI: Brazos Press, 2001.

Dennett, Daniel C. *Breaking the Spell: Religion as a Natural Phenomenon.* London: Penguin, 2007.

Derrida, Jacques. *Given Time: I. Counterfeit Money.* Translated by Peggy Kamul. Chicago: University of Chicago Press, 1994.

Derrida, Jacques. *The Gift of Death.* Translated by David Wills. Chicago: University of Chicago Press, 1996.

Descartes, René. *The Philosophical Writings of Descartes: Volume 3, The Correspondence.* Translated by John Cottingham, Robert Stoothoff, Dugald Murdoch, and Anthony Kenny. Cambridge: Cambridge University Press, 1991.

Dixon, Thomas. *Science and Religion: A Very Short Introduction.* Oxford: Oxford University Press, 2008.

Dixon, Thomas, Geoffrey Cantor, and Stephen Pumfrey, eds. *Science and Religion: New Historical Perspectives.* Cambridge: Cambridge University Press, 2011.

Dobbs, B. J. T. *The Janus Face of Genius: The Role of Alchemy in Newton's Thought.* Cambridge: Cambridge University Press, 1991.

Draper, John William. *History of the Conflict between Religion and Science.* 1875. Cambridge: Cambridge University Press, 2009.

Duffy, Eamon. *The Stripping of the Altars: Traditional Religion in England, 1400–1580.* 2nd edn. New Haven: Yale University Press, 2005.

Dupré, Louis. *The Passage to Modernity: An Essay in the Hermeneutics of Nature and Culture*. New Haven: Yale University Press, 1993.

Ehrman Bart D., trans. *The Apostolic Fathers*, vol. 2. Cambridge, MA: Harvard University Press, 2003.

Emery, Giles. 'Trinity and Creation'. In *The Theology of Thomas Aquinas*, edited by Rik van Nieuwenhove and Joseph Wawrykow, 58–75. Notre Dame, IN: University of Notre Dame Press, 2005.

Fantoli, Annibale. *The Case of Galileo: A Closed Question?* Translated by George V. Coyne. Notre Dame: University of Notre Dame Press, 2012.

Fern, Richard L. *Nature, God and Humanity: Envisioning an Ethics of Nature*. Cambridge: Cambridge University Press, 2002.

Fergusson, David. *Cosmos and the Creator: An Introduction to the Theology of Creation*. London: SPCK, 1998.

Fergusson, David. *Creation: Guides to Theology*. Grand Rapids, MI: Eerdmans, 2014.

Feyerabend, Paul. *Farewell to Reason*. London: Verso, 1987.

Freely, John. *Light from the East: How the Science of Medieval Islam Helped to Shape the Western World*. New York: I. B. Tauris, 2015.

French, Roger, and Andrew Cunningham. *Before Science: The Invention of the Friars' Natural Philosophy*. Aldershot: Scolar Press, 1996.

Funkenstein, Amos. *Theology and the Scientific Imagination: From the Middle Ages to the Seventeenth Century*. Princeton: Princeton University Press, 1986.

Galileo, Galilei, *Dialogue Concerning Two Chief World Systems*. 1632. Translated by Stillman Drake. Berkeley, Los Angeles: University of California Press, 1967.

Gaukroger, Stephen. *The Emergence of a Scientific Culture: Science and the Shaping of Modernity 1210–1685*. Oxford: Oxford University Press, 2008.

Gaukroger, Stephen. *The Collapse of Mechanism and the Rise of Sensibility*. Oxford: Oxford University Press, 2010.

Gaukroger, Stephen. *The Natural and the Human: Science and the Shaping of Modernity 1739–1841*. Oxford: Oxford University Press, 2016.

Gould, Stephen Jay. *Rocks of Ages: Science and Religion in the Fullness of Life*. New York: Ballantine Books, 2002.

Grant, Edward. *The Foundations of Modern Science in the Middle Ages: Their Religious, Institutional and Intellectual Contexts*. Cambridge: Cambridge University Press, 1996.

Gregory, Brad S. *The Unintended Reformation: How a Religious Revolution Secularized Society*. Cambridge, MA: Harvard University Press, 2012.

Gregory of Nyssa, *Homilies on the Song of Songs*. Translated by Richard A. Norris. Atlanta, GA: Society of Biblical Literature, 2012.

Gregory of Nyssa, 'On the Making of Man'. In *The Nicene and Post-Nicene Fathers*, Second Series, vol. 5, translated by H.A. Wilson, edited by Philip Schaff and Henry Wace. Edinburgh: T&T Clark, 1994.

Grosseteste, Robert. *On the Six Days of Creation: A Translation of the Hexaemeron*. Translated by C. F. J. Martin. Oxford: Oxford University Press, 1996.

Grumett, David, and Rachel Muers, eds. *Theology on the Menu: Asceticism, Meat and Christian Diet*. London: Routledge, 2010.

Hall, A. Rupert. *Philosophers at War: The Quarrel between Newton and Leibniz*. Revised edition. Cambridge: Cambridge University Press, 1998.

Hanby, Michael. *No God, No Science? Theology, Cosmology, Biology*. Oxford: Wiley-Blackwell, 2013.

Haraway, Donna. *Simians, Cyborgs and Women: The Reinvention of Nature*. London: Free Association Books, 1991.

Harris, Sam. *The End of Faith: Religion, Terror, and the Future of Reason*. London: Simon and Schuster, 2004.

Harrison, Peter. *The Bible, Protestantism and the Rise of Natural Science*. Cambridge: Cambridge University Press, 1998.

Harrison, Peter. *The Fall of Man and the Foundations of Science*. Cambridge: Cambridge University Press, 2007

Harrison, Peter. 'Religion, the Royal Society and the Rise of Science',*Theology and Science* 6 (2008): 255–71.

Harrison, Peter, ed. *The Cambridge Companion to Science and Religion*. Cambridge: Cambridge University Press, 2010.

Harrison, Peter. *The Territories of Science and Religion*. Chicago: University of Chicago Press, 2015.

Hart, David Bentley. *The Doors of the Sea: Where Was God in the Tsunami?* Grand Rapids, MI: Eedrmans Publishing Company, 2005.

Hart, David Bentley. *Atheist Delusions: The Christian Revolution and Its Fashionable Enemies*. New Haven: Yale University Press, 2009.

Hart, David Bentley. 'Providence and Causality: On Divine Innocence'. In *Providence of God: Deus Habet Concilium*, edited by Francesca Aran Murphy and Philip G. Ziegler, 34–56. London: Bloomsbury, 2009.

Hart, Kevin. *Postmodernism: A Beginner's Guide*. Oxford: Oneworld Publications, 2004.

Hendel, Ronald. *The Book of Genesis: A Biography*. Princeton: Princeton University Press, 2013.

Iliffe, Rob. *Priest of Nature: The Religious Worlds of Isaac Newton*. Oxford: Oxford University Press, 2017.

Inwagen, Peter van. *The Problem of Evil*. Oxford: Oxford University Press, 2008.

Irenaeus. 'Against the Heresies'. In *Nicene Fathers vol. 1: The Apostolic Fathers, Justin Martyr*, edited by Alexander Roberts, and James Donaldson. Peabody, MA: Hendrickson Publishers, 1994.

Jenkins, Willis. *Ecologies of Grace: Environmental Ethics and Christian Theology*. Oxford: Oxford University Press, 2008.

Johnson, Keith. *Karl Barth and the* Analogia Entis. London: Bloomsbury, 2010.

Jonas, Hans. *The Phenomenon of Life: Toward a Philosophical Biology*. Evanston, IL: Northwestern University Press, 2001.

Kearney, Peter J. 'Creation Liturgy: The P Redaction of Exodus 25-40'. *Zeitschrift für die alttestameutliche Wissenschaft* 89 (1977): 375–87.

Keller, Catherine. *Face of the Deep: A Theology of Becoming*. New York: Routledge, 2003.

Koyré, Alexander. 'Galileo and Plato'. *Journal of the History of Ideas* 4 (1943): 401–28.

Krauss, Lawrence M. *A Universe from Nothing: Why There is Something Rather than Nothing?* London: Simon and Schuster, 2012.

Krey, Philip D. W., and Lesley Smith, eds. *Nicholas of Lyra: The Senses of Scripture*. Leiden: Brill, 2000.

Kuhn, Thomas S. *The Structure of Scientific Revolutions*. 3rd edn. Chicago: University of Chicago Press, 1996.

Lambert, G. 'Mesopotamian Creation Stories'. In *Imagining Creation*, IJS Studies in Judaica, edited by Markham J. Geller and Mineke Schipper, 15–59, vol. 5. Leiden: Brill, 2007.

Lash, Nicholas. *Believing Three Ways in One God*. Notre Dame, IN: University of Notre Dame Press, 1992.

Latour, Bruno. *We Have Never Been Modern*. Translated by Catherine Porter. London: Harvester Wheatsheaf, 1991.

Lear, Jonathan. *Aristotle: The Desire to Understand*. Cambridge: Cambridge University Press, 1988.

Levenson, Jon D. *Creation and the Persistence of Evil: The Jewish Drama of Divine Omnipotence*. Princeton: Princeton University Press, 1988.

Levering, Matthew. *The Theology of Augustine: An Introductory Guide to His Most Important Works*. Grand Rapids, MI: Baker Academic, 2013.

Lopez, Antonio. *Gift and the Unity of Being*. Cambridge: James Clarke & Co, 2014.

Lubac, Henri de. *Medieval Exegesis: The Four Senses of Scripture*. 3 vols. Translated by Marc Sebanc, and E. M. Macierowski. Grand Rapids, MI: Eerdmans, 1998–2009.

Lucas, J. R. 'Wilberforce and Huxley: a legendary encounter'. *The Historical Journal* 22, no. 2 (1979): 313–30.

Lull, Timothy F., ed. *Martin Luther's Basic Theological Writings.* Minneapolis: Fortress Press, 1989.

McBrayer, Justin P., and Daniel Howard-Snyder, eds. *The Blackwell Companion to the Problem of Evil.* Oxford: Wiley-Blackwell, 2013.

McCleish, Tom. *Faith and Wisdom in Science.* Oxford: Oxford University Press, 2014.

MacDonald, N., M. W. Eilliott and G. Macaskill, eds. *Genesis and Christian Theology,* Grand Rapids, MI: Eerdmans, 2012.

McFarland, Ian A. *From Nothing: A Theology of Creation.* Louisville, KY: Westminster John Knox Press, 2014.

McWhorter, Matthew R. 'Aquinas on God's Relation to the World'. *New Blackfriars* 94, no. 1049 (January 2013): 3–19.

Mandelbrote, Scott, and Jitse Meer, eds. *Nature and Scripture in the Abrahamic Religions: Up to 1700.* 2 vols. Leiden: Brill, 2008.

Manuel, Frank. *The Religion of Isaac Newton.* Oxford: Oxford University Press, 1974.

Marion, Jean-Luc. *Being Given: Toward a Phenomenology of Givenness.* Translated by Jeffrey Kosky. Stanford: Stanford University Press, 2002.

Martens, R. 'A commentary on Genesis, Plato's Timaeus and Kepler's Astronomy'. In *Plato's Timaeus as Cultural Icon,* edited by G. Reydams-Schils, 251–66. Notre Dame, IN: University of Notre Dame Press, 2003.

Mauss, Marcel. *The Gift: The Form and Reason for Exchange in Archaic Societies.* 1923. Translated by W. D. Halls. London: Routledge, 2007.

May, Gerhard. *Creatio Ex Nihilo: The Doctrine of 'Creation out of Nothing' in Early Christian Thought.* Translated by A. S. Worrall. London: T&T Clark, 2004.

Mendez-Montoya, Angel F. *The Theology of Food: Eating and the Eucharist.* Oxford: Wiley-Blackwell, 2012.

Meyer, Stephen C. *Darwin's Doubt: The Explosive Origin of Animal Life and the Case for Intelligent Design.* New York: HarperCollins, 2014.

Milbank, John. 'Can a Gift be Given? Prolegomena to a Future Trinitarian Metaphysic'. *Modern Theology* 11, no. 1 (1995): 119–61.

Milbank, John. 'The Soul of Reciprocity Part One: Reciprocity Refused'. *Modern Theology* 17, no. 3 (2001): 335–91.

Milbank, John. 'The Soul of Reciprocity Part Two: Reciprocity Granted'. *Modern Theology* 17, no. 4 (2001): 485–507.

Milbank, John. *Being Reconciled: Ontology and Pardon.* London: Routledge, 2004.

Milbank, John. 'The Gift of Ruling: Secularization and Political Authority'. *New Blackfriars* 85 (March 2004): 212–38.

Milbank, John. *Theology and Social Theory: Beyond Secular Reason.* 2nd edn. Oxford: Wiley-Blackwell, 2006.

Milbank, John. *The Suspended Middle: Henri de Lubac and the Debate concerning the Supernatural.* 2nd edn. Grand Rapids, MI: Eerdmans, 2014.

Milbank, John, and Adrian Pabst. *The Politics of Virtue: Post-Liberalism and the Human Future.* Lanham, MD: Rowman and Littlefield International, 2016.

Moberly, R. W. L. *The Theology of the Book of Genesis.* Cambridge: Cambridge University Press, 2009.

Newton, Isaac. *The Principia: Mathematical Principles of Natural Philosophy.* 2nd edn, 1727. Translated by I. Bernard Cohen, and Anne Whitman. Berkeley, CA: University of California Press, 1999.

Nicholas of Cusa, *On Learned Ignorance: A Translation and an Appraisal of De Docta Ignorantia.* Translated by Jasper Hopkins. Minneapolis, MN: The Arthur J. Banning Press, 2nd ed., 1985.

Northcott, Michael S. *A Moral Climate: The Ethics of Global Warming.* London: DLT, 2007.

Northcott, Michael S. *The Environment and Christian Ethics.* Cambridge: Cambridge University Press, 2008.

Northcott, Michael S. *A Political Theology of Climate Change.* London: SPCK, 2014.

Northcott, Michael S., and Peter M. Scott, eds. *Systematic Theology and Climate Change: Ecumenical Perspectives.* London: Routledge, 2014.

Oliver, Simon. 'The Eucharist before Nature and Culture'. *Modern Theology* 15, no. 3 (1999): 331–53.

Oliver, Simon. *Philosophy, God and Motion.* London: Routledge, 2005.

Oliver, Simon. 'Aquinas and Aristotle's Teleology'. *Nova et Vetera* 11, no. 3 (2013): 849–70.

Oliver, Simon. 'Augustine on Creation, Providence and Motion'. *International Journal of Systematic Theology* 18, no. 4 (2016): 379–98.

Oord, Thomas Jay, ed. *Theologies of Creation: Creatio Ex Nihilo and its New Rivals.* London: Routledge, 2015.

Origen. *The Song of Songs: Commentary and Homilies.* Translated by R. P. Lawson. Westminster, MD: Newman Press, 1957.

Origen. *On First Principles (De principiis).* Translated by G. W. Butterworth. Notre Dame, Notre Dame , IN: Ave Maria Press, 2013.

O'Rourke, Fran. *Pseudo-Dionysius and the Metaphysics of Aquinas.* Notre Dame, IN: University of Notre Dame Press, 2005.

Osler, Margaret. 'From Immanent Natures to Nature as Artifice: The Reinterpretation of Final Causes in Seventeenth Century Natural Philosophy'. *The Monist* 79 (1996): 388–407.

Osler, Margaret J., ed. *Rethinking the Scientific Revolution.* Cambridge: Cambridge University Press, 2008.

Osteen, Mark, ed. *The Question of the Gift: Essays Across Disciplines.* London: Routledge, 2002.

Ott, Walter. *Causation and the Laws of Nature in Early Modern Philosophy.* Oxford: Oxford University Press, 2009.

Paley, William. *Natural Theology, or Evidences of the Existence and Attributes of the Deity Collected from the Appearances of Nature.* 1802. Edited by Matthew D. Eddy and David Knight. Oxford: Oxford University Press, 2006.

Philo. *The Works of Philo: Complete and Unabridged.* Translated by C. D. Yonge. Peabody, MA: Hendrickson Publishers, 2002.

Philoponus, John. *On Aristotle's Physics* 2. Translated by A. R. Lacey. London: Duckworth, 1993.

Plato. *Republic.* Translated by Desmond Lee. London: Penguin, 1987.

Plato. *Timaeus,* Translated by R. G. Bury. Cambridge, MA: Harvard University Press, 1999.

Plotinus. *Enneads V.* Translated by A. H. Armstrong. Cambridge, MA: Harvard University Press, 1984.

Pluche, Noël-Antoine. *Spectacle de la Nature: or Nature Display'd.* 5th edn revised and corrected, vol. 3. London, 1770.

Przywara, Erich. *Analogia Entis: Metaphysics: Original Structure and Universal Rhythm.* Translated by John R. Betz and David Bentley Hart. Grand Rapids, MI: Eerdmans, 2014.

Ray, John. *Three Physico-Theological Discourses.* London, 1693.

Reno, R.R. *Genesis.* London: SCM Press, 2010.

Robertson, John M., ed. *The Philosophical Works of Francis Bacon.* London: G. Routledge & Sons, 1905.

Schindler, David C. 'What's the Difference? On the Metaphysics of Participation in a Christian Context'. *The St. Anselm Journal* 3, no.1 (2005): 1–27.

Schrift, Allan D., ed. *The Logic of the Gift: Toward an Ethic of Generosity.* New York: Routledge, 1997.

Shapin, Steven, and Simon Schaffer. *Leviathan and the Air-pump: Hobbes, Boyle and the Experimental Life.* Princeton: Princeton University Press, 1985.

Shapin, Steven. *Never Pure: Historical Studies of Science as if It Was Produced by People with Bodies, Situated in Time, Space, Culture, and Society, and Struggling for Credibility and Authority.* Baltimore, MD: John Hopkins University Press, 2010.

Snobelen, Stephen. 'On Reading Isaac Newton's *Principia* in the Eighteenth Century'. *Endeavour* 22, no. 4 (1998): 159–63.

Snobelen, Stephen. 'Isaac Newton, heretic: The Strategies of a Nicodemite', *British Journal for the History of Science* 32 (1999): 381–419.

Soskice, Janet, ed. Special issue: 'Creation "Ex Nihilo" and Modern Theology', *Modern Theology* 29, no. 2 (2013): 1–192.

Sprat, Thomas. *History of the Royal Society of London for the Improving of Natural Knowledge.* London, 1667.

Stump, Eleonore. *Wandering in Darkness: Narrative And The Problem Of Suffering.* Oxford: Oxford University Press, 2012.

Swinburne, Richard. *The Existence of God.* 2nd edn. Oxford: Oxford University Press, 2004.

Tanner, Kathryn. *Economy of Grace.* Minneapolis: Augsburg Fortress, 2005.

Tanner, Kathryn. *God and Creation in Christian Theology: Tyranny or Empowerment?* Minneapolis: Augsburg Fortress, 2005.

Tatian. 'Address of Tatian to the Greeks'. In *Ante-Nicene Fathers vol.2,* translated by J. E. Ryland, edited by Alexander Roberts and James Donaldson, 59–83. Peabody, MA: Hendrickson Publishers, 1995.

Theophilus of Antioch. 'To Autolycus'. In *Ante-Nicene Fathers vol.2,* translated by Marcus Dods, edited by Alexander Roberts and James Donaldson, 85–121. Peabody, MA: Hendrickson Publishers, 1995.

Thomas Aquinas, *The 'Summa Theologica' of St. Thomas Aquinas.* Literally translated by Fathers of the English Dominican Province. 2nd and revised edition. 10 volumes. London: Burns Oates and Washbourne, 1920–1922.

Thomas Aquinas. *Summa Contra Gentiles Book One: God.* Translated by Anton C. Pegis. Notre Dame, IN: University of Notre Dame Press, 1975.

Thomas Aquinas. *Summa Contra Gentiles Book Two: Creation.* Translated by James F. Anderson. Notre Dame, IN: University of Notre Dame Press, 1975.

Thomas Aquinas. *Summa Contra Gentiles Book Three Part I: Providence.* Translated by Vernon J. Bourke. Notre Dame, IN: University of Notre Dame Press, 1975.

Thomas Aquinas. *Summa Contra Gentiles Book Three Part II: Providence.* Translated by Vernon J. Bourke. Notre Dame, IN: University of Notre Dame Press, 1975.

Thomas Aquinas. *Summa Contra Gentiles Book Four: Salvation.* Translated by Charles J. O'Neil. Notre Dame, IN: University of Notre Dame Press, 1975.

Thomas Aquinas. *Truth (De Veritate),* 3 vols, trans. Robert W. Schmidt, S.J. Indianapolis: Hackett Publishing Company, 1994.

Thomas Aquinas. *Commentary on Aristotle's Metaphysics.* Translated by John P. Rowan. Notre Dame, IN: Dumb Ox Books, 1995.

Thomas Aquinas. *Commentary on the Book of Causes.* Translated by Vincent A. Guagliardo, O.P. Washington, DC: The Catholic University Press of America, 1996.

Thomas Aquinas. 'On the Principles of Nature' (De principiis naturae). In Aquinas on Matter and Form and the Elements, translated by Joseph Bobik. Notre Dame, IN: University of Notre Dame Press, 1998.

Thomas Aquinas. An Exposition of the 'On Hebdomads' of Boetius (Expositio libri De hebdomamdibus). Translated by Janice L. Schultz and Edward A. Synan. Washington, DC: Catholic University of America Press, 2001.

Thomas Aquinas. The Power of God. Translated by Richard J. Regan. Oxford: Oxford University Press, 2012.

Torchia, N. Joseph, O.P. Creatio ex Nihilo and the Theology of St. Augustine: The Anti-Manichaean Polemic and Beyond. New York: Peter Lang, 1999.

Turnbull, H. W., ed. The Correspondence of Isaac Newton, vol. 3. Cambridge: Cambridge University Press, 1961.

Turner, Denys. Eros and Allegory, Medieval Exegesis of the Song of Songs. Kalamazoo: Cistercian Publications, 1995.

Turner, Denys. 'Allegory in Christian late antiquity'. In The Cambridge Companion to Allegory, edited by Rita Copeland, and Peter T. Struck, 71–82. Cambridge: Cambridge University Press, 2010.

VanderKam, James C. The Book of Jubilees. Sheffield: Sheffield Academic Press, 2001.

Velde, Rudi A. te. Participation and Substantiality in Thomas Aquinas. Leiden: Brill, 1995.

Velde, Rudi A. te. Aquinas on God: The 'Divine Science' of the Summa Theologiae. Aldershot: Ashgate, 2006.

Walker, George. The History of Creation. London, 1651.

Walton, John H. The Lost World of Genesis One: Ancient Cosmology and the Origins Debate. Downers Grove, IL: Intervarsity Press, 2009.

Webster, John. 'On the Theology of Providence'. In Providence of God: Deus Habet Concilium, edited by Francesca Aran Murphy and Philip G. Ziegler, 158–78. London: Bloomsbury, 2009.

Webster, John. 'Trinity and Creation'. International Journal of Systematic Theology 12, no. 1 (2010): 4–19.

Webster, John. 'Love is also a Lover of Life': Creatio Ex Nihilo and Creaturely Goodness'. Modern Theology 29, no. 2 (2013): 156–71.

Wenham, Gordan J. World Biblical Commentary: Genesis 1-15. Nashville, Tennessee: Thomas Nelson, 1987.

William Whiston. A New Theory of the Earth, from its Original to the Consummation of all Things. London, 1696.

White, Andrew Dickson. A History of the Warfare of Science with Theology in Christendom. 2 vols. 1896. Cambridge: Cambridge University Press, 2009.

White Jr., Lynn. 'The Historical Roots of our Ecological Crisis'. *Science* 155 (1967): 1203–7.

White, Thomas Joseph O.P., ed. *The Analogy of Being: Invention of the Anti-Christ or Wisdom of God?* Grand Rapids, MI: Eerdmans, 2011.

Williams, Rowan. 'The Discipline of Scripture', in *On Christian Theology*, edited by Rowan Williams, 44–59. Oxford: Blackwell, 2000.

Williams, Rowan. *On Augustine*. London: Bloomsbury, 2016.

Wippel, John. *The Metaphysical Thought of Thomas Aquinas: From Finite Being to Uncreated Being*. Washington, DC: The Catholic University Press of America, 2000.

Wirzba, Norman. *Food and Faith: A Theology of Eating*. Cambridge: Cambridge University Press, 2011.

Wootton, David. *The Invention of Science: A New History of the Scientific Revolution*. London: Penguin, 2016.

Wright, William M. IV. 'The Literal Sense of Scripture According to Henri de Lubac: Insights from Patristic Exegesis of the Transfiguration'. *Modern Theology* 28, no. 2 (2012): 252–77.

Internet sources

European Environment Agency. 'Climate Change'. Accessed 5 September 2016. http://www.eea.europa.eu/themes/climate

NASA. 'Global Climate Change'. Accessed 5 September 2016. http://climate.nasa.gov

The Newton Project. Accessed 1 September 2016. http://www.newtonproject.sussex.ac.uk

The Royal Society. 'The Charters of the Royal Society'. Accessed 1 September 2016. https://royalsociety.org/about-us/governance/charters/

St. Anselm College. *St. Anselm Journal*, vol. 3, no. 1 (fall 2005). Accessed 8 June 2016. http://www.anselm.edu/Institutes-Centers-and-the-Arts/Institute-for-Saint-Anselm-Studies/Saint-Anselm-Journal/Archives/Vol-3-No-1-fall-2005.htm

Appendix: Reading Aquinas

Aquinas lived for only fifty years, but his theological works are staggering in their extent and sophistication. They range from so-called 'disputed questions' on particular topics – for example, the power of God, truth or the nature of virtue – to philosophical works and commentaries on Aristotle and Neoplatonic writers. He also wrote a number of biblical commentaries. Aquinas's major works are usually identified as the *Summa Theologiae* ('Summary of Theology', begun in the mid-1260s and remaining unfinished at his death in 1274), the *Summa Contra Gentiles* ('Summary Against the Non-Believers' – a title given to this work by later editors) and the *Commentary on the 'Sentences' of Peter Lombard*, the fruit of his first period of teaching in Paris from 1252 to 1256. Many of Aquinas's works are structured in a question-and-answer format, reflecting the pattern of discussion between master and students in seminars in medieval universities. The *Summa Theologiae*, the most frequently cited of Aquinas's works, is structured in just this way.

The *Summa Theologiae* is divided into three parts, with the second part in turn being divided into two:

- *Prima Pars* (first part, abbreviated to '1a'): 119 questions concerning God and creation;
- *Prima secundae* (part 2(a) or 'the first part of the second part', abbreviated to '1a2ae'): 114 questions concerning humanity, ethics and law;
- *Secunda secundae* (part 2(b) or 'the second part of the second part', abbreviated to '2a2ae'): 189 questions concerning theological virtues (faith, hope and charity) and the practice of religion;
- *Tertia Pars* (third part, abbreviated to '3a'): 90 questions concerning the incarnation, salvation and the sacraments.

Each **part** is divided into **questions** that deal with a particular theological issue (e.g., the Trinity). In turn, each question is divided in **articles**, each article dealing with a specific aspect of the question. For example, in **question 93** of the **Prima Pars**, Aquinas is concerned with 'man in God's image'. He divides this **question** into nine **articles**, each dealing with a specific issue, for example 'whether there is an image of God in man' (article 1) or 'what is the difference between "image" and "likeness"?' (article 9).

Each **article** begins with a set of possible answers to the question posed by the article. In the seminar setting, these were usually provided by students. The master (Aquinas) then offers a brief alternative view known as the *sed contra* ('on the contrary') taken from scripture or the Church Fathers followed by his considered *responsio* (*respondeo dicendum* – 'I reply, saying', or simply *responsio* – 'the reply'). The reply is the main part of the text and generally contains Aquinas's own view of the matter. Following the reply, Aquinas returns to his original set of possible answers to the article's question. One by one, he rebuts or nuances the original set of answers.

A reference to the *Summa Theologiae* will include

- **Part** (1a (*Prima Pars*), 1a2ae (*Prima Secundae*), 2a2ae (*Secunda Secundae*) or 3a (*Tertia Pars*))
- **Question**
- **Article**

Take the following reference: *Summa Theologiae*, **1a.93.7**. This refers to:

- Part: *prima pars*, 1a
- Question: 93
- Article: 7

If reference is made to Aquinas's reply in an article, the term '*responsio*' is added at the end of the reference: 1a.93.7.*responsio*. Occasionally you will see the reply abbreviated as 'co.' for *corpus* (the reply being the main body of the text).

The appearance of '*sed contra*' ('on the other hand') at the end of a reference refers to Aquinas's brief, usually single-sentence, answer to an article's question that appears immediately before his detailed reply. For example: 1a.93.7.*sed contra* or simple 's.c.'

The abbreviation 'ad' (*adversus*) refers to one of the numbered alternative answers to the question at the very end of an article. For example: 1a.93.7.ad 2.

INDEX